Spon's
Asia Pacific
Construction
Costs
Handbook

Spon's Asia Pacific Construction Costs Handbook

Edited by
DAVIS LANGDON & SEAH INTERNATIONAL

First edition

E & FN SPON
An Imprint of Chapman & Hall

London · Glasgow · New York · Tokyo · Melbourne · Madras

Published by E & FN Spon, an imprint of Chapman & Hall, 2–6 Boundary Row, London SE1 8HN, UK

Chapman & Hall, 2–6 Boundary Row, London SE1 8HN, UK

Blackie Academic & Professional, Wester Cleddens Road, Bishopbriggs, Glasgow G64 2NZ, UK

Chapman & Hall Inc., One Penn Plaza, 41st Floor, New York NY 10119, USA

Chapman & Hall Japan, Thomson Publishing Japan, Hirakawacho Nemoto Building, 6F, 1-7-11 Hirakawa-cho, Chiyoda-ku, Tokyo 102, Japan

Chapman & Hall Australia, Thomas Nelson Australia, 102 Dodds Street, South Melbourne, Victoria 3205, Australia

Chapman & Hall India, R. Seshadri, 32 Second Main Road, CIT East, Madras 600 035, India

First edition 1994
© 1994 E & F N Spon

Printed in England by
Clays Ltd, St Ives plc, Bungay, Suffolk

ISBN 0 419 17570 9

A catalogue record for this book is available from the British Library

Contents

		page
Preface		vii
Acknowledgements		viii
How to use this book		x
Abbreviations		xi
Conversion factors		xii
Davis Langdon & Seah International		xv

PART ONE: REGIONAL OVERVIEW — 1

1	The construction industry in the Asia Pacific region	3

PART TWO: INDIVIDUAL COUNTRIES — 11

2	Introductory notes to country sections	13
	Introduction	13
	Key data	13
	The construction industry	13
	Construction cost data	13
	Exchange rates and inflation	15
	Useful addresses	17
	Statistical notes	17
3	Individual countries	19
	Australia	21
	Brunei	37
	Canada	49
	People's Republic of China	67
	Hong Kong	91
	Indonesia	109
	Japan	127
	Malaysia	145
	New Zealand	163
	Philippines	177
	Singapore	191
	South Korea	209
	Thailand	225
	United Kingdom	237
	United States of America	259

  page

4   Amplified descriptions of construction items   275

PART THREE: COMPARATIVE DATA   283

5   Introductory notes   285

6   Key national indicators   286
     Population   286
     The economy   287
     Geography   288

7   Construction output indicators   289
     Construction output   289
     Construction output per capita   290

8   Construction cost data   291
     Mason/bricklayer and unskilled labour costs   291
     Site manager and qualified architect labour rates   292
     Materials costs - cement and concrete aggregates   293
     Materials costs - ready mixed concrete and reinforcing steel   294
     Materials costs - common bricks and hollow concrete blocks   295
     Materials costs - softwood for joinery and quilt insulation   296
     Materials costs - sheet glass and plasterboard   297
     Materials costs - emulsion paint and vinyl floor tiles 298
     Approximate estimating - factories and warehouses   299
     Approximate estimating - offices   300
     Approximate estimating - housing   301
     Approximate estimating - hospitals and schools   302
     Approximate estimating - theatres and sports halls   303
     Approximate estimating - hotels   304

     Index   305

Preface

In 1988 the Editors compiled the first *Spon's International Construction Costs Handbook*, covering thirty-two countries worldwide. That was intended to be the first in a series of such handbooks which would become progressively more detailed and extensive. It has now been decided to produce regional volumes; the first covered Europe and was published in 1992; this volume covers the Asia Pacific region. Both of these regional volumes include the UK, the USA and Japan.

The format has been modified to include considerably more information than was provided in the International book. In particular, detailed cost data is provided for individual items of construction work. Additionally, the section on unit costs for different building types, Approximate Estimating, has been greatly enlarged.

The book is designed to be a convenient reference. Its purpose is to present coherent snapshots of the economies and construction industries of the Asia Pacific region; it also puts this information in an international context with the inclusion of the United Kingdom. It is not a substitute for local knowledge and professional advice. It will, however, be extremely useful as an introduction to a country and its construction industry for clients, consultants, contractors, manufacturers of construction materials and equipment and others concerned with development, property and construction in the region.

Davis Langdon Consultancy
London
1993

Acknowledgements

The contents of this book have been gathered together from a variety of sources - individuals, organizations and publications. Construction cost data and general background information on local construction industries is based on contributions from a network of professional colleagues and associates worldwide. These include:

Davis Langdon Australia
Davis Langdon & Seah, Brunei
Davis Langdon & Seah, Hong Kong Ltd.
Davis Langdon & Seah, China Ltd.
Davis Langdon & Seah, Indonesia Pt.
Davis Langdon & Seah, Malaysia
Davis Langdon & Seah, Philippines, Inc.
Davis Langdon & Seah, Singapore
Davis Langdon & Seah (Thailand) Ltd.
Davis Langdon & Everest, UK.
Futaba Quantity Surveyors, Tokyo, Japan
RS Means Company Inc, USA
Alastair Law, MMP International Inc, Washington DC, USA
Fletcher Construction, New Zealand
Professor Helen Tippett, Victoria University of Wellington, New Zealand
Dr Jacques Poot, Victoria University of Wellington, New Zealand
Goran Runeson, University of New South Wales, Australia
Mr Jae Yong Choi, South Korea
Leroux Chauchan Ouimet & Associates, Canada

Much of the statistical data is from World Bank Development Reports, the *Economist World in Figures* and official published statistics. The background on individual countries has come from local sources, national yearbooks, annual reports and *Economist Intelligence Unit Reports*.

Important sources of general and construction industry data have been various Embassies, High Commissions, Trade Missions, statistical offices, and government departments in the UK and overseas. Information on international contracting is largely based on surveys undertaken by *Engineering News Record* magazine. Data on exchange rates and consumer price indices come mainly from the *Financial Times* or International Monetary Fund publications. Information on development control and standards in China and on liability and insurance in Hong Kong have been supplied by Baker McKenzie, Hong Kong.

The published sources of data for the general statistics are:

The Economist, *World in Figures*, London: Hutchinson, 1991
The World Bank, *World Development Report 1990: Poverty*, Oxford: OUP, 1990
The Statesman Yearbook 1990/91
OECD in Figures
UN Construction Statistics Yearbook, 1985.

Specific acknowledgements and sources are given where appropriate in each country. The research and compilation of this book were undertaken by Davis Langdon Consultancy. Special acknowledgements are due to Dr Patricia Hillebrandt.

How to use this book

This book is in three parts - *Part One: Regional Overview*; *Part Two: Individual Countries*; and *Part Three: Comparative Data*. The fifteen countries covered in the book are listed in the Contents. The United Kingdom is outside the region but is included for comparative purposes.

Part One: Regional Overview

Part One comprises an essay - *The construction industry in the Asia Pacific region* - which describes the current situation and main trends in the construction industries covered in this publication.

Part Two: Individual Countries

In Part Two the fifteen countries are arranged in alphabetical order, and each is presented in a similar format under the following main headings:

* *Key data* provides main national, economic and construction indicators.
* *The construction industry* outlines the structure of the industry, tendering and contract procedures plus the regulations and standards.
* *Construction cost data* includes data on labour and material costs, measured rates for items of construction work and approximate estimating costs per square metre for different building types.
* *Exchange rates and inflation* presents data on exchange rates with the pound sterling, US$ and Japanese yen, and includes data on the main indices of price movements for retail prices and construction.
* *Useful addresses* gives the names and addresses of public and private organizations associated with construction.

Part Three: Comparative Data

To allow comparison between countries covered in the book, Part Three brings together data from Part Two and presents them under three main headings:

* *Key national indicators* including financial and demographic data.
* *Construction output indicators* including output per capita.
* *Construction cost data* including labour and material costs and costs per square metre.

Abbreviations

LENGTH
kilometre	km
metre	m
decimetre	dm
millimetre	mm
yard	yd
foot	ft
inch	in

AREA
hectare	ha

VOLUME
kilolitre	kl
hectolitre	hl
litre	l
millilitre	ml

WEIGHT (MASS)
tonne	t
kilogram	kg
gram	g
hundredweight	cwt
pound	lb
ounce	oz

FORCE
kilonewton	kN
newton	N

not available	n.a.

Conversion factors

LENGTH

Metric		Imperial equivalent
1 kilometre	1000 metres	0.6214 miles
		1093.6 yards
1 metre	100 centimetres	1.0936 yards
	1000 millimetres	3.2808 feet
		39.370 inches
1 centimetre	10 millimetres	0.3937 inches
1 millimetre		0.0394 inches

Imperial		Metric equivalent
1 mile	1760 yards	1.6093 kilometres
	5280 feet	1609.3 metres
1 yard	3 feet	0.9144 metres
	36 inches	914.40 millimetres
1 foot	12 inches	0.3048 metres
		304.80 millimetres
1 inch		25.400 millimetres

AREA

Metric		Imperial equivalent
1 square kilometre	100 hectares	0.3861 square miles
	10^6 square metres	247.11 acres
1 hectare	10 000 square metres	2.4711 acres
		11 960 square yards
1 square metre	10 000 square centimetres	1.1960 square yards
		10.764 square feet
1 square centimetre	100 square millimetres	0.1550 square inches
1 square millimetre		0.0016 square inches

Imperial		Metric equivalent
1 square mile	640 acres	2.5900 square kilometres
		259.00 hectares
1 acre	4840 square yards	0.4047 hectares
		4046.9 square metres
1 square yard	9 square feet	0.8361 square metres
1 square inch		6.4516 square centimetres
		645.16 square millimetres

VOLUME

Metric		**Imperial equivalent**
1 cubic metre or	10 hectolitres	1.3080 cubic yards
1 kilolitre	1000 cubic decimetres	35.315 cubic feet
	1000 litres	
1 hectolitre	100 litres	3.5315 cubic feet
		21.997 gallons
1 cubic decimetre	1000 cubic centimetres	61.023 cubic inches
or 1 litre	1000 millilitres	0.2200 gallons
		1.7598 pints
		0.2642 US gallons
		2.1134 US pints
1 cubic centimetre	1000 cubic millimetres	0.0610 cubic inches
or 1 millilitre		

Imperial		**Metric equivalent**
1 cubic yard	9 cubic feet	0.7646 cubic metres
1 cubic foot	1728 cubic inches	28.317 litres
	6.2288 gallons	
	7.4805 US gallons	
1 cubic inch		16.387 cubic centimetres
1 gallon	8 pints	4.5461 litres
1 pint		0.5683 litres

US		
1 barrel	42 gallons	158.99 litres
1 gallon	8 pints	3.7854 litres
1 pint		0.4732 litres

WEIGHT (MASS)

Metric		**Imperial equivalent**
1 tonne	1000 kilograms	0.9842 tons
		1.1023 US tons
		2204.6 pounds
1 kilogram	1000 grams	2.2046 pounds
		35.274 ounces
1 gram		0.0353 ounces

Imperial		**Metric equivalent**
1 ton	20 hundredweights	1.0160 tonnes
	2240 pounds	1016.0 kilograms
1 hundredweight	112 pounds	50.802 kilograms
1 pound	16 ounces	0.4536 kilograms
		453.59 grams
1 ounce		28.350 grams

US		
1 ton	20 hundredweights	0.9072 tonnes
	2000 pounds	907.18 kilograms
1 hundredweight	100 pounds	45.359 kilograms

FORCE

Metric		**Imperial equivalent**
1 kilonewton	1000 newtons	0.1004 tons force
		0.1124 US tons force
1 newton		0.2248 pounds force

Imperial		**Metric equivalent**
1 ton force	2240 pounds force	9.9640 kilonewtons
1 pound force		4.4482 newtons

US		
1 ton force	2000 pounds force	8.8964 kilonewtons

PRESSURE

Metric	**Imperial equivalent**
1 newton per square millimetre	145.04 pounds force per square inch
1 kilonewton per square metre	20.885 pounds force per square foot

Imperial	**Metric equivalent**
1 pound force per square inch	6.8948 kilonewtons per square metre
	0.0069 newtons per square millimetre
1 ton force per square inch	107.25 kilonewtons per square metre
	0.1073 newtons per square millimetre

US	
1 ton force per square foot	95.761 kilonewtons per square metre
	0.9576 newtons per square millimetre

Davis Langdon & Seah International

Practice Profile

Davis Langdon & Seah International (DLSI) is an independent firm of Chartered Quantity Surveyors, Project and Construction Managers, which operates throughout the Asia Pacific region, Australia, the Middle East, the UK and mainland Europe and has associations with firms in the USA, Canada, Africa, New Zealand and Japan. The overall DLSI group employs some 1,500 staff managed by 114 Partners in 54 offices in 21 countries around the world.

In the Asia Pacific region and Australia these offices are:

- in Singapore : Davis Langdon & Seah
- in Hong Kong : Davis Langdon & Seah Hong Kong Ltd
- in Malaysia : Davis Langdon & Seah Malaysia
- in Brunei : Davis Langdon & Seah
  Petrojaya SDN BHD
  Petrokon Utama SDN BHD
- in Indonesia : Davis Langdon & Seah Indonesia PT
- in the Philippines : Davis Langdon & Seah Philippines Inc
- in Thailand : Davis Langdon & Seah (Thailand) Ltd
  LECE Thailand Ltd
- in China : Davis Langdon & Seah China Ltd
  Shanghai Genius Quantity Surveying Ltd
- in Australia : Davis Langdon & Ash
  Davis Langdon & Beattie

and elsewhere in the world:

- in the UK : Davis Langdon & Everest
  Davis Langdon Consultancy
  Davis Langdon Management
- in Germany : Davis Langdon & Weiss
- in Spain : Davis Langdon Edetco
- in Italy : Davis Langdon & Copper
- in France : Davis Langdon Economistes
- in the Czech Republic : Davis Langdon Cesko*Slovensko
- in the Middle East : Davis Langdon Arabian Gulf

The firm is also engaged on projects in Holland, Belgium, Luxembourg and Russia.

In addition to the financial management of construction projects we also, through Davis Langdon Consultancy, undertake varied construction industry research and consultancy assignments worldwide, ensuring that Davis Langdon & Seah International provides a broadly based and truly international service to its clients.

We recognize the value of our international experience, research and information, which is distilled into the strategic advice and services we provide to our individual clients and also forms the basis for publications, such as this current *Asia Pacific Construction Price Handbook*.

Professional Services

We specialize in the financial management of construction projects, from inception to completion and our range of services includes:

- Feasibility Studies
- Construction Financial Services
- Cost Planning
- International Procurement
- Tender and Contract Documentation
- Project Management
- Construction Management
- Claims Negotiation
- Development Economics and Appraisals
- Value Analysis and Management Services
- Quality Management Reviews
- Construction Litigation Services
- Premises and Facilities Management
- Construction Insolvency Services
- Research and Consultancy

Our experience extends to managing a wide range of construction projects including:

- Airports and Airport Buildings
- Arts and Cultural Buildings
- Business Park Developments
- Civic Buildings
- Civil Engineering and Infrastructure Works
- Educational Buildings
- Health and Hospital Buildings
- Historic Buildings
- Hotels
- Industrial/Warehouse Developments
- Leisure Projects
- Office Buildings and Fit-outs
- Petro-chemical Projects
- Power Generation Projects
- Public Buildings
- Residential Developments
- Retail Developments
- Sports Centres
- Transportation
- Water and Waste Projects

Practice Statement

Davis Langdon & Seah International is an independent firm of Chartered Quantity Surveyors, Project and Construction Managers, which is committed to representing, protecting and enhancing client interests on construction projects, large or small, locally, nationally or internationally.

The strategic and integrated management of cost, time and quality - the client 'risk' areas of a contract - are essential functions, which are necessary to ensure the satisfactory planning, procurement, execution and operation of construction projects.

We specialise in the financial management of construction projects and their risk areas, from project inception to completion.

We employ highly qualified and skilled professional staff, with specialist experience in all sectors of the construction industry, including international cost variables, procurement options and management structures.

We operate a sophisticated information support system, based on the latest computer technology, enabling large-scale capture and retrieval of cost and relevant market data.

We observe the highest operational standards to ensure quality of product and are Quality Assured in respect of our services in those countries where formal accreditation is available.

We draw upon our international network of offices but work in manageable teams under direct Partner leadership and maintain personal client contact at all stages of a project.

We concentrate on:

- being positive and creative in our advice, rather than simply reactive;
- providing value for money via efficient management, rather than by superficial cost monitoring;
- giving advice that is matched to the Client's specific requirements, rather than imposing standard or traditional solutions;
- paying attention to the life-cycle costs of constructing and occupying a building, rather than to the initial capital cost only.

Our aim is to provide our clients with risk assurance, cost control and value for money, via effective advice, cost planning and management.

DLSI MANAGES AND LIMITS CLIENT RISK

- ADDING VALUE -

EVERYTHING YOU WANTED TO KNOW ABOUT QUANTITY SURVEYORS

BUT WERE TOO AFRAID TO ASK

What exactly do
Quantity Surveyors do?

- They manage client risk, control costs, add value.

What areas of client risk?

- Those risks associated with financial assessment and investment.

On what?

- All types of construction projects

When do these risks arise?

- At all stages of projects from inception to completion.

How do they deal with these risks?

- By effective advice, cost planning and management.

What is achieved as a result?

- Risk limitation, cost control and added-value for clients.

Who are the clients?

- Anyone contemplating, planning or carrying out a construction project.

Does the client come first and is confidentiality ensured?

- Yes

How can we be sure?

- Ask one of our clients

Do quantity surveyors charge much?

- Much less than you would think

IF YOU HAVE ANY MORE QUESTIONS - ASK DLSI

DAVIS LANGDON & SEAH INTERNATIONAL

SOUTH EAST ASIA

BRUNEI
DAVIS LANGDON & SEAH
No. 1 First Floor, Block H
Abdul Razak Complex Gadong
P O Box 313
Bandar Seri Begawan 1903
Brunei Darussalam
Tel: (010 6732) 446888
Fax: (010 6732) 445555

PETROKON UTAMA SDN. BHD
No. 3 First Floor, Block H
Abdul Razak Complex Gadong
P O Box 1188
Bandar Seri Begawan 1911
Brunei Darussalam
Tel : (010 6732) 441384
Fax : (010 6732) 441382

CHINA
DAVIS LANGDON & SEAH
CHINA LTD
Shanghai Representative Office
2203 Shartex Plaza
88 Zhun Yi Nan Road
Shanghai 200335, China
Tel : (010 8621)219 1107
Fax : (010 8621) 219 3680

SHANGHAI GENIUS
QUANTITY SURVEYING LTD
1111 Yan An Road (M)
Shanghai, China
Tel : (010 8621) 2477149 ext 329
Fax : (010 8621) 3291790

HONG KONG
DAVIS LANGDON & SEAH
HONG KONG LTD
21st Floor, Leighton Centre
77 Leighton Road, Hong Kong
Tel : (010 852) 576 3231
Fax : (010 852) 576 0416

INDONESIA
DAVIS LANGDON & SEAH
INDONESIA PT
Wisma Metropolitan 1, Level 13
Jalan Jendral Sudirman Kav. 29
PO Box 3139/Jkt
Jakarta 10001, Indonesia
Tel : (010 6221) 514745
Fax : (010 6221) 514764

MALAYSIA
DAVIS LANGDON & SEAH
MALAYSIA
124 Jalan Kasah
Damansara Heights
50490 Kuala Lumpur
Tel : (010 603) 254 3411
Fax : (010 603) 255 9660

DAVIS LANGDON & SEAH
MALAYSIA
Suite 8A, 8th Floor
Wisma Pendidikan
Jalan Padang
PO Box 11598
88817 Kota Kinabalu
Tel : (010 6088) 223369
Fax : (010 6088) 216537

DAVIS LANGDON & SEAH
MALAYSIA
2nd Floor, Lot 142
Bangunan WSK
Jalan Abell
93100 Kuching, Sarawak
Tel : (010 6082) 429861
Fax : (010 6082) 426416

DAVIS LANGDON & SEAH
MALAYSIA
2nd Floor
10 Bishop Street
10200 Penang
Tel : (010 604) 619051
Fax : (010 604) 619028

DAVIS LANGDON & SEAH
MALAYSIA
3rd Floor Wisma Zainah
95 Jalan Tun Abdul Razak
8000 Johor Bahru
Tel : (010 607) 236229
Fax : (010 607) 235975

PHILIPPINES
DAVIS LANGDON & SEAH
PHILIPPINES INC
7th Floor, Electra House
Esteban Street
Legaspi Village, Makati
Metro Manila, Philippines
Tel : (010 632) 812 2679
Fax : (010 632) 815 6460

SINGAPORE
DAVIS LANGDON & SEAH
135 Cecil Street # 12 - 00
LKN Building
Singapore 0106
Tel : (010 65) 2223888
Fax : (010 65) 2247089

THAILAND
DAVIS LANGDON & SEAH
(THAILAND) LTD
8th Floor, Kian Gwan Building
140 Wireless Road
Bangkok 10330, Thailand
Tel : (010 662) 253 7390
Fax : (010 662) 253 4977

AUSTRALIA

VICTORIA
DAVIS LANGDON & BEATTIE
1st Floor, 79-81 Franklin Street
Melbourne
Victoria 3000
Tel : (010 613) 663 1277
Fax : (010 613) 663 8039

DAVIS LANGDON QUALITY
MANAGEMENT PTY LTD
1st Floor, 79-81 Franklin Street
Melbourne
Victora 3000
Tel : (010 613) 663 4925
Fax : (010 613) 663 8039

M.H.B. PROJECT SERVICES
PTY LTD
2 Victoria Road
Hawthorn
Victoria 3122
Tel : (010 613) 882 7044
Fax : (010 613) 882 8612

NEW SOUTH WALES
DAVIS LANGDON & BEATTIE
1st Floor
146 Arthur Street
North Sydney
NSW 2060
Tel : (010 612) 956 8822
Fax : (010 612) 956 8848

DAVIS LANGDON & SEAH INTERNATIONAL

AUSTRALIA (Cont'd)

QUEENSLAND
DAVIS LANGDON & ASH
19th Floor
141 Queen Street
Brisbane
QLD 4000
Tel : (010 617) 221 1788
Fax : (010 617) 221 3417

TASMANIA
DAVIS LANGDON & BEATTIE
53 Salamanca Place
Hobart
Tasmania 7000
Tel : (010 6102) 34 8788
Fax : (010 6102) 31 1429

MIDDLE EAST

DAVIS LANGDON
ARABIAN GULF

BAHRAIN
PO Box 640
Manama
State of Bahrain
Arabian Gulf
Tel : (010 973) 251755
Fax : (010 973) 232291

UNITED ARAB EMIRATES
PO Box 7856
Deira
Dubai
United Arab Emirates
Tel : (010 9714) 227424
Fax : (010 9714) 220069

QATAR
PO Box 3206
Doha
State of Qatar
Tel : (010 974) 328440
Fax : (010 974) 437349

MAINLAND EUROPE

SPAIN
DAVIS LANGDON EDETCO

GERONA
Calle Figuerola 56, 2°
17001 - Gerona
Spain
Tel : (010 34) 72 221878
Fax : (010 34) 72 223545

MADRID
C/Ferrer del Rio, 14
28028 - Madrid
Spain
Tel: (010 34) 1 3611805
Fax: (010 34) 1 3612951

BARCELONA
C/Avinyó, 52, pral.
08002 - Barcelona
Spain
Tel : (010 34) 34 123108
Fax : (010 34) 34 122664

BILBAO
C/Victor, 2 1
48005 - Bilbao
Spain
Tel : (010 34) 4 416 67 93
Fax : (010 34) 4 416 67 93

SEVILLE
C/Salado, 45
41010 - Seville
Spain
Tel: (010 34) 95 4281858
Fax: (010 34) 95 4458706

FRANCE
DAVIS LANGDON
ECONOMISTES
16, Rue Albert Einstein
Champs sur Marne
77436 Marne la Valle
Cedex 2, France
Tel: (010 33) 1 64620724
Fax: (010 33) 1 64119087

ITALY
DAVIS LANGDON & COPPER
via Nomentana 263
Rome 00161
Italy
Tel : (010 39) 6 835 00082
Fax : (010 39) 6 440 4351

GERMANY
DAVIS LANGDON & WEISS

STUTTGART
Böblinger Strasse 63
70199 Stuttgart - 1
Germany
Tel : (010 49) 711 602225
Fax : (010 49) 711 609812

FRANKFURT
Altkönigstrasse 124
61440 Oberursel
Nr Frankfurt
Germany
Tel : (010 49) 6171 26213
Fax : (010 49) 6171 24928

BERLIN
Gotlandstrasse 16
010439 Berlin
Germany
Tel: (010 49)30 4175710
Fax: (010 49) 30 4175715

THE CZECH REPUBLIC
DAVIS LANGDON
CESKO*SLOVENSKO
Sokolovská 22
180 00 Prague 8
The Czech Republic
Tel: (010 422) 2360876
Fax: (010 422) 2360878

DAVIS LANGDON & SEAH INTERNATIONAL

UNITED KINGDOM

DAVIS LANGDON & EVEREST
DAVIS LANGDON MANAGEMENT
DAVIS LANGDON CONSULTANCY

LONDON
Princes House
39 Kingsway
London
WC2B 6TP
Tel : 071-497 9000
Fax : 071-497 8858

BRISTOL
St Lawrence House
29/31 Broad Street
Bristol
BS1 2HF
Tel : 0272-277832
Fax : 0272-251350

CAMBRIDGE
36 Storey's Way
Cambridge
CB3 ODT
Tel : 0223-351258
Fax : 0223-321002

CARDIFF
3 Raleigh Walk
Brigantine Place
Atlantic Wharf
Cardiff
CF1 5LN
Tel : 0222-471306
Fax : 0222-471465

CHESTER
Ford Lane Farm
Lower Lane
Aldford
Chester
CH3 6HP
Tel : 0244-620222
Fax : 0244-620303

EDINBURGH
74 Great King Street
Edinburgh
EH3 6QU
Tel : 031-557 5306
Fax : 031-557 5704

GATESHEAD
11 Regent Terrace
Gateshead
Tyne and Wear
NE8 1LU
Tel : 091-477 3844
Fax : 091-490 1742

GLASGOW
Cumbrae House
15 Carlton Court
Glasgow
G5 9JP
Tel : 041-429 6677
Fax : 041-429 2255

IPSWICH
17 St Helens Street
Ipswich
IP4 1HE
Tel : 0473-253405
Fax : 0473-231215

LEEDS
Duncan House
14 Duncan Street
Leeds
LS1 6DL
Tel : 0532-432481
Fax : 0532-424601

LIVERPOOL
Cunard Building
Water Street
Liverpool
L3 1JR
Tel : 051-236 1992
Fax : 051-227 5401

MANCHESTER
Boulton House
Chorlton Street
Manchester
M1 3HY
Tel : 061-228 2011
Fax : 061-228 6317

MILTON KEYNES
6 Bassett Court
Newport Pagnell
Buckinghamshire MK16 OJN
Tel : 0908-613777
Fax : 0908-210642

NEWPORT
34 Godfrey Road
Newport
Gwent NP9 4PE
Tel : 0633-259712
Fax : 0633-215694

NORWICH
63A Thorpe Road
Norwich NR1 1UD
Tel : 0603-628194
Fax : 0603-615928

OXFORD
Avalon House
Marcham Road
Abingdon
Oxford OX14 1TZ
Tel : 0235-555025
Fax : 0235-554909

PLYMOUTH
Barclays Bank Chambers
Princess Street
Plymouth PL1 2HA
Tel : 0752-668372
Fax : 0752-221219

PORTSMOUTH
Kings House, 4 Kings Road
Portsmouth
Hampshire PO5 3BQ
Tel : 0705-815218
Fax : 0705-827156

SOUTHAMPTON
Clifford House, New Road
Southampton SO2 OAB
Tel : 0703-333438
Fax : 0703-226099

PART ONE
REGIONAL OVERVIEW

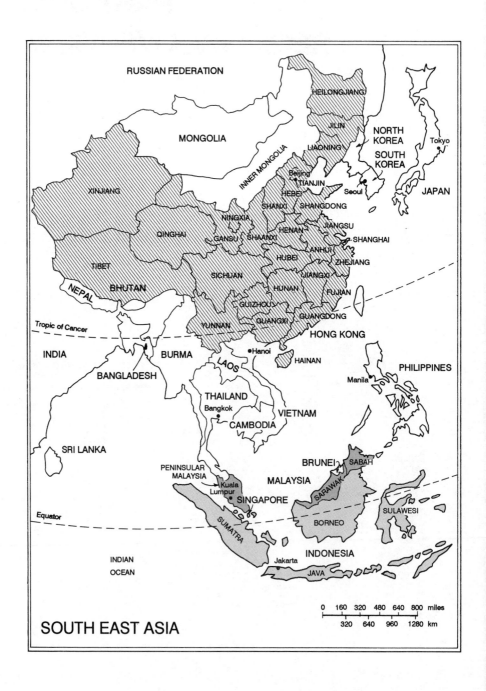

SOUTH EAST ASIA

1. The construction industry in the Asia Pacific region

INTRODUCTION

Unlike, say, Europe or America, the Asia Pacific region is not an easily defined entity. From a formal point of view the closest to a comprehensive regional grouping is the Pacific Rim, the provisional name for a proposed trading group linking countries with a Pacific seaboard. Potential member countries who attended an initial meeting in November 1989 are Australia, Brunei, Canada, Indonesia, Japan, Malaysia, New Zealand, the Philippines, Singapore, South Korea, Thailand and the USA; other potential members are China, Hong Kong and Taiwan. The Association of South East Asian Nations (ASEAN) is the main active regional grouping - it comprises Brunei, Indonesia, Malaysia, Philippines, Singapore and Thailand. Although the final list of countries included in this book has as much to do with availability of data and contacts as eligibility, it omits only Taiwan from the Pacific Rim grouping and adds the UK. Table A lists the countries, indicates their membership of international groupings and whether they have formal Davis Langdon & Seah International (DLSI) offices or representation by a firm associated with the DLSI group.

Table A: MEMBERSHIP OF FORMAL OR EMBRYONIC
ORGANIZATIONS OF COUNTRIES IN THE BOOK

Country	OECD	Pacific Rim	ASEAN	DLSI offices (X) or associates (*)
Australia	X	X		X
Brunei		X	X	X
Canada	X	X		*
China		X		X
Hong Kong		X		X
Indonesia		X	X	X
Japan	X	X		*
Malaysia		X	X	X
New Zealand	X	X		*
Philippines		X	X	X
Singapore		X	X	X
South Korea		X		
Thailand		X	X	X
UK	X			X
USA	X	X		*

The map opposite is of the area traditionally known as South East Asia. In addition to the ASEAN nations covered by this book the map also shows the location of China, Japan and South Korea.

The 15 countries covered in the book are a fascinating mixture of large and small, rich and poor, developed and developing, with planned and market economies. From Singapore and Hong Kong as prime examples of rapidly developing city states to China, also developing rapidly, but with a quarter of the world's population; from Brunei with one of the highest per capita incomes in the world to China and Indonesia with amongst the lowest; from Malaysia and Indonesia representing the developing world to Japan and the USA as the most developed countries in the world. Table B summarizes key characteristics of the countries - population, land area, population density, Gross Domestic Product (GDP) and Gross National Product (GNP) per capita arranged in order of GNP per capita. Definitions of these and other statistical terms are discussed in Part Two, section 2 (see pages 17-18).

Table B : KEY CHARACTERISTICS OF COUNTRIES

Country	Population m	Land area 000 km²	Population per km²	GDP US$bn 1990	GNP per capita US$ 1990
Low Income Economies					
China	1,133.7	9,561	117	365	370
Indonesia	183	1,919	95	107	570
Middle Income Economies					
Philippines	64.6	300	215	44	730
Thailand	60	513	117	80	1,420
Malaysia	17.6	330	53	42	2,320
South Korea	42.8	99	432	236	5,400
High Income Economies					
Singapore	2.8	0.7	4,382	35	11,160
Hong Kong	5.8	1.1	5,395	60	11,490
New Zealand	3.4	269	13	43	12,680
United Kingdom	57.1	244	234	975	16,100
Brunei	0.26	5.3	49	5*	17,000*
Australia	17.1	7,689	2	296	17,000
Canada	26.5	9,976	2	570	20,470
USA	248.7	9,373	27	5,392	21,790
Japan	123.5	378	327	2,943	25,430

* *approximately.*
Principal Source: World Bank, World Development Report 1992, Oxford University
                Press 1992.

Because of the need to use monetary values and exchange rates for conversion to a common currency, GDP and GNP are not always the best indicators of economic development. Table C shows, where available, other selected indicators for the 16 countries in order of GNP per capita. Brunei appears amongst the high income economies based on oil wealth. China appears low - economic experts suggest that GNP understates the stage of development - and should thus appear with the middle income economies. Apart from China (statistics for Korea not being available), the UN Development Index rises more or less in line with GNP per capita. South Korea stands out as exceptionally high for secondary school enrolment and telephones. Singapore is low on doctors and the UK is low on telephones.

Table C : SELECTED NON-MONETARY INDICATORS OF DEVELOPMENT

Country	Population per telephone line	Secondary school enrolment*	Doctors per million persons	UN Human Development Index+
Low Income Economies				
China	149.8	43	839	71.6
Indonesia	n.a.	46	95	59.1
Middle Income Economies				
Philippines	n.a.	66	138	71.4
Thailand	52.6	28	148	78.3
Malaysia	11.7	59	292	80.0
South Korea	5.4	89	850	90.3
High Income Economies				
Singapore	2.3	71	410	89.9
Hong Kong	2.2	74	906	93.6
New Zealand	1.5	85	1,747	96.6
United Kingdom	3.7	83	1,615	97.0
Brunei	6.5	n.a.	483*	n.a.
Australia	1.8	98	2,215	97.8
Canada	1.3	104	1,883	98.3
USA	1.3	98	2,035	96.1
Japan	1.8	95	1,477	99.6

* Percentage of relevant age group. Percentages greater than 100 indicates some attendance outside normal age group.
+ Based on life expectancy, literacy and whether average income based on PPP estimates is sufficient to meet basic needs.
Principal Source: Economist, Book of Vital World Statistics 1990.

However, none of these statistics shows the financial viability of the economies. Pointers in this direction include foreign debt and aid receipts and the proportion of GDP which is invested. Generally low foreign debt and high investment are favourable factors. Aid receipts may be taken in several ways. They show a degree of dependence; further than this it all depends on what type of aid is being given. If it is for capital projects then in theory that should strengthen the economy in the future though in practice this is not always the case. If the aid is for consumption then it has little effect on the long term future of the economy.

Table D shows some of the statistics on the economy and its dependence on outside help. It will be seen that in general investment is higher in the poorer countries than in the richer countries. The great exception is Japan which has in the past invested to bring its industry to a high standard and is now turning its attention to housing and social infrastructure. Both aid receipts and external debt are low by world standards where some countries have debt far in excess of annual GNP. It must be concluded that the developing countries of the Pacific Rim are managing to develop without over dependence on the rest of the world.

Table D : INVESTMENT, AID AND FOREIGN DEBT

Country	Investment as % of GDP 1990	Aid receipts as % of GNP	External debt as % of GNP 1990
Low Income Economies			
China	39	0.6	13
Indonesia	36	1.6	64
Middle Income Economies			
Philippines	22	2.9	75
Thailand	37	1.0	39
Malaysia	34	1.1	59
South Korea	37	0.0	27
High Income Economies			
Singapore	39	0.0	20 (1988)
Hong Kong	28	0.1	18 (1988)
New Zealand	22	-	6
United Kingdom	19	-	4
Australia	21	-	4
Canada	21	-	3
USA	16	-	1
Japan	33	-	nil

Principal Sources: World Bank, World Development Report 1992, Oxford University Press 1992, and The Economist, Vital World of Statistics 1990.

CONSTRUCTION OUTPUT AND THE ECONOMY

Gross construction output normally accounts for 10 to 20% of GDP and net construction output for about half this amount. Table E overleaf shows total investment, gross and net output of the construction industry and net output as a percentage of gross output (total investment includes gross output). It will be seen from Table E that gross construction output accounts for a high proportion of total investment - up to nearly 70% but on average around half.

Table E : INVESTMENT AND CONSTRUCTION OUTPUT RELATED TO GDP

Country	Investment % of GDP	Gross output as % of GDP	Net output as % of GDP	Net output as % of gross output
Low Income Economies				
China	39	22	6.5	30
Indonesia	36	n.a.	5.5	n.a.
Middle Income Economies				
Philippines	22	10	4.7	47
Thailand	37	19.0*	7.1	38
Malaysia	34	n.a.	3.8	n.a.
South Korea	37	29	15.5	53
High Income Economies				
Singapore	39	14.5	6.8	47
Hong Kong	28	12.6*	5.8	46
New Zealand	22	n.a.	4.3	n.a.
United Kingdom	19	8.8	6.8	77
Brunei		n.a.	2.9	n.a.
Australia	21	n.a.	6.5	n.a.
Canada	21	14.6	8.5	58
USA	16	8.8	4.4	50
Japan	33	19.1	9.5	50

* *approximately*

The relationship of net output to gross output (see statistical notes, page 18) is affected by the relative prices of labour and materials, the level of profits and overheads, and the mix of output in terms of those which are labour intensive compared with those which are material intensive. The statistics are often based on broad methods of assessment of gross output and net output and therefore need to be treated with reserve, but on average net output is a little under half gross output.

Despite these reservations the last column of Table E follows the expected relationships: in general the lower the GNP per capita, the lower the percentage of value added in construction to gross output. This is because at low income levels, wages are low in relation to the costs of materials which on average do not vary as greatly from one type of economy to another because the high costs of imported materials in developing countries tend to offset the low costs of locally produced materials. Wages on the other hand are much lower in developing than in developed economies. Indeed construction wages in most developing countries are less than average wages while in many developed countries they are higher than average wages. Even if productivity is low the total cost of labour is still less in low income countries than in high income countries.

At high levels of GNP per capita the net output as a percentage of gross output percentage continues to rise partly because of the relatively high repair and maintenance component which is labour intensive and therefore has a high value added. More specifically, the only low income country in the group for which we have data - China - has a low percentage of net output of gross output of 30. The simple average for the next group is 46 and the simple average for the high income economies is 55.

Korea stands out as having high net output in relation to gross output but this may be a reflection of the reliability of the statistics; data for earlier years suggests that it is nearer to 46 to 48%. The United Kingdom ratio is remarkably high. However, the content of the two sets of figures is not identical. The net output figure is that of value added used in the national income accounts and is compiled by the Central Statistical Office. The gross output is that collected by the Department of the Environment from contractors. Moreover, the UK has a very high output on repair and maintenance which has a high value added.

An important component of output in any construction industry is housing and the production of dwellings in the various countries considered with the supply of dwellings gives interesting insights into the objectives of governments and the state of the economy. In order to obtain consistency over a wide range of countries the figures for production in Table F overleaf are for 1985.

Population per dwelling generally decreases with increases in income. The exception is Singapore where population per dwelling is currently being tackled by the government with a high level of dwelling completions per 1,000 persons. Japan regards its supply of dwellings and particularly space standards as unsatisfactory and is also trying to remedy the situation with a high rate of construction.

THE ORGANIZATION OF THE CONSTRUCTION SECTOR

The organization of the construction sector varies greatly from planned economies to market economies. China is the only planned economy covered in this book. Table G shows data on establishments for 1985, the last year for which data are generally available. It will be seen from Table G that China is very different from the other countries with construction firms in market economies serving few persons and a small area. 1988 data suggest that there has been a decrease rather than an increase in the number of firms in China. By contrast the number of firms in the UK has increased although the current recession is once again reducing numbers.

Table F : THE HOUSING STOCK AND CONSTRUCTION

Country	Dwelling stocks 000s	Population per dwelling	Dwelling completion	Completions per 1000 persons
Low Income Economies				
China	290,456	3.6	n.a.	n.a.
Indonesia	40,920	4.1	n.a.	n.a.
Middle Income Economies				
Philippines	8,972	5.6	20.2 Pp	0.3
Thailand	9,200	5.1	n.a.	n.a.
Malaysia	2,850	3.4	n.a.	n.a.
South Korea	n.a.	n.a.	227.0	5.3
High Income Economies				
Singapore	552	5.7	67.0	23.9
Hong Kong	1,348	4.1	84.4	14.6
New Zealand	1,250	2.6	19.1	5.6
United Kingdom	23,055	2.6	197.0	3.4
Australia	5,690	2.8	143.0	8.4
Canada	8,906	1.7	139.1	5.2
USA	88,073	2.7	1,703.0 P	6.8
Japan	40,125	3.0	1,236.0 S	10.0

P Private
p permits
S starts
Sources: The Economist, Vital World Statistics, 1990 and UN Construction Statistics
*   Yearbook, 1985, 1988.*

Table G :   NUMBER AND SIZE OF CONSTRUCTION ESTABLISHMENTS
            IN RELATION TO AREA AND POPULATION

Country	Number of establishments 1985	Average person per establishment	Area per establishment in m²	Population per establishment
Brunei	474	41	11.1	549
China	93,750	181	102.0	12,093
Hong Kong	6,779	14	0.2	856
Japan (1981)	550,798	10	0.7	224
United Kingdom	175,044	7	1.4	328
USA (1982)	1,389,309	4	6.7	179

Source: Department of International Economic and Social Affairs, Construction
*   Statistics Yearbook 1985, UK, 1988.*

Many of the large construction companies have some part to play in exporting construction services to other parts of the world. The role of companies in various countries in exporting is shown in Table H.

Table H :   NUMBER OF CONSTRUCTION COMPANIES IN *ENGINEERING NEWS RECORD* 1991 LIST OF INTERNATIONAL COMPANIES

Country	Number in top 100 companies	Number in top 225 companies
Australia	1	2
Brunei	-	-
Canada	3	8
PRC	2	4
Hong Kong	-	-
Japan	16	30
Malaysia	-	-
New Zealand	1	1
Philippines	-	2
Singapore	-	2
South Korea	3	4
UK	6	13
USA	20	53
All	52	119

It is clear from this table that the main countries in the area whose contractors play a prominent part in international contracting are Japan and the USA. In many countries - Canada for example - the contractors who are important in the domestic market do not participate internationally and vice versa.

PART TWO
INDIVIDUAL COUNTRIES

International Dictionary of Heating, Ventilating and Air Conditioning

2nd Edition

REHVA, Federation of European Heating and Ventilating Associations

The International Dictionary of Heating, Ventilating and Air Conditioning is the result of a collaborative effort by an international panel of professional engineers set up by REHVA. Each member of the panel has considerable experience in this specialist engineering field and is responsible for the terms in his own mother tongue, thus ensuring the accuracy and general acceptability of the terms and translations given.

The dictionary comprises two major divisions. The main sequence of the book consists of some *4,000 terms* (covering heating, ventilation, air conditiong and related mechanical/electrical comonents), given in English, in alphabetical order, with their translations. The remainder of the book consists of alphabetical indexes for the other eleven languages covered:

* **Danish, Dutch,**
  French, Finnish,
  German,
  Hungarian,
  Italian
  Polish,
  Russian,
  Spanish, and Swedish,

Each alphabetical index is keyed to serial numbers which refer the user to the correct item in the main sequence. The book will be an invaluable reference for all manufacturers, contractors and consulting engineers engaged in heating, ventilating and air conditioning.

September 1993: 234x156: c.792pp
Hardback: 0-419-15390-X

For further information and to order please contact: **The Promotion Dept., E & F N Spon,** 2-6 Boundary Row, London SE1 8HN Tel 071 865 0066 Fax 071 522 9623

2. Introductory notes to country sections

INTRODUCTION

In this part of the book, fifteen countries are arranged alphabetically, and each country is presented as far as possible in a similar format, under five main headings - Key data, The construction industry, Construction cost data, Exchange rates and inflation, and Useful addresses. These notes introduce the five main sets of information presented on the individual countries and provide, in one place, general notes, definitions and explanations, in order to keep the individual country sections as succinct as possible. A final heading, Statistical notes, discusses and explains the statistical definitions and concepts adopted in the book.

KEY DATA

The key data sheet at the start of each country lists main population, geographic, economic and construction indicators and thus provides a brief statistical overview of that country. In many cases data produced by national statistical offices have been used; in other cases, UN or World Bank sources have been relied on. In Part Three, Comparative Data, international agency data has been used throughout in order to ensure consistency. Further notes on economic indicators are provided below in the Statistical notes.

THE CONSTRUCTION INDUSTRY

The main topics covered in this section are the contribution of the industry to the economy; the structure of the industry; the availability of and constraints on construction labour and materials; tendering and contract procedures and standards.

Although construction is often fragmented and tends to be labour intensive with low capital investment, it is invariably the single largest industry in a country. In most countries it contributes between 5% and 15% to Gross Domestic Product (GDP) and a similar percentage to direct construction employment (indirect employment - in the construction materials industries and other related activities - can more than double the contribution).

CONSTRUCTION COST DATA

This section includes both construction costs incurred by contractors and the costs they charge their clients. The costs of labour and materials are input costs of construction, i.e. the costs incurred by contractors.

Unit costs, measured rates for construction work and approximate estimating costs per square metre are output costs, i.e. the costs contractors charge their clients. Problems of definition make meaningful and consistent presentation of unit rates extremely difficult. For unit rates to be useful it is essential to be clear what is included and what excluded. Notes are provided in each country section, for example, on the treatment of preliminary items and on the methods of measurement adopted for approximate estimating rates per square metre.

Cost of labour and materials

Typical costs for construction labour and materials are given in most country sections. Two figures are generally given for each grade of labour. The wage rate is the basis of an employee's income - his basic weekly wage will be the number of hours worked multiplied by his wage rate. The cost of labour, on the other hand, is the cost to the employer of employing that employee; it is also based on the wage rate but includes (where applicable) allowances for:

- incentive payments
- travelling time and fares
- lodging and subsistence
- public and annual holidays with pay
- training levies
- employer's liability and third party insurances
- health insurance
- payroll taxes
- other mandatory and voluntary payments.

The costs of main construction materials are given as delivered to site in quantities appropriate to a reasonably substantial building project. It is presumed that there are no particular difficulties of access etc. which would significantly affect costs. Generally tax, and particularly any value added tax, is excluded from material costs mainly because the rate of tax to be levied may depend on the type of work the material is to be incorporated in.

Unit rates

Rates for a variety of commonly occurring construction items are provided for most countries. They are usually based on a major, if not the capital, city and the relevant date is always first quarter 1993. Rates generally include all necessary labour, materials, plant and equipment and, where appropriate, allowances for contractors' overheads and profit, preliminary and general items associated with site set-up, etc. and contractors' profit and attendance on specialist trades. Where the basis of rates is different from this, notes are provided in the text in each country section. Value added tax and other taxes are excluded. The rates are appropriate to a reasonably substantial building project.

In the country sections abbreviated descriptions are given for each work item; a full description of each work item is presented in section 4.

Approximate estimating

Approximate estimating costs per unit area (square metres and square feet) are given for most countries for a variety of building types. Notes on the method of measurement and what is or is not included in unit rates are provided in each country section. Areas generally are measured on all floors inside external walls and with no deduction for internal walls, columns, etc. Where this is not the case it is noted. Generally tax, and particularly value added tax, is excluded in approximate estimating costs.

When making comparisons of construction costs between countries it is important to be clear about what is being compared. There are two main methods of comparison: first the comparison of identical buildings in each country and, second, the comparison of functionally similar buildings in each country. In the country sections, the approximate estimating rates given are for the standard of building of each type normally built in that country. Rates are therefore closer to the 'functionally similar' approach. The rate per square metre given for an office building, for example, or a warehouse in any particular country refers to the normal type of office building or warehouse built in that country. In country sections they are presented in national currencies. A selection of approximate estimating costs are also presented in pound sterling, US dollar and yen equivalents in Part Three thus enabling comparisons on a common currency basis to be made.

EXCHANGE RATES AND INFLATION

Exchange rates

Currency exchange rates are important when comparing costs between one country and another. While it is most useful to consider costs within a country in that country's currency, it is necessary, from time to time, to use a common currency in order to compare one country's costs with another. But exchange rates fluctuate dramatically and few currencies (even those considered strong) can be considered really stable. It can be risky to think in terms, for example, of one country being consistently a set percentage more or less expensive than another.

Different rates of internal inflation affect the relative values of currencies and, therefore, the rates of exchange between them. However, the reasons behind exchange rate fluctuations are complex and often political as much as economic; they include such factors as interest rates, balance of payments, trade figures and, of course, government intervention in the foreign exchange markets, and, for that matter, other government actions.

Graphs of exchange rates since 1980 against the US dollar, the pound sterling and the Japanese yen are included for most countries. They have been calculated by averaging the published weekly values in each quarter. The values given are therefore smoothed - the most dramatic peaks and troughs have been ironed out. They are, however, useful for indicating long term trends. As far as possible, the form of the graph is kept the same, hence the vertical scale is adjusted to accommodate different currencies. It should always be checked whether marked movement in a graph is a result of erratic exchange rates or merely the selected vertical scale.

If a line moves up from left to right (for example, the Philippine peso against the pound sterling to 1991 - see below) it indicates that the subject currency (the peso) is declining in value against the currency of the line (the pound sterling). The higher the line is, the more subject currency is required to purchase the line currency. If, on the other hand, a line moves down from left to right (for example, the Japanese yen against the pound sterling) it indicates the subject currency is strengthening against the line currency. Where there is virtually no movement at all, that is the line is horizontal, this usually indicates a currency effectively 'tied' or 'pegged' to the line currency.

EXCHANGE RATE GRAPH

 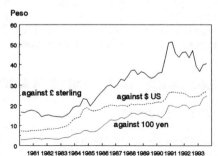

Inflation

General inflation has been measured using consumer or retail price indices. These reflect price changes in a basket of goods and services weighted according to the spending patterns of a typical family. Weights are changed periodically, and new items inserted. General inflation indices usually rise and, in so doing erode the purchasing power of a given currency unit. Other measures of inflation tend to be related to specific items. The two most commonly prepared for the construction industry are discussed below.

Cost and tender price indices measure different types of inflation which occur within the construction industry. Building costs are the costs actually incurred by a contractor in the course of his business, the major ones being labour and materials; tender prices are the prices for which a contractor offers to erect a building. Tender prices include building costs but also take into account the prevailing market situation. When there is plenty of construction work tender prices may increase at a greater rate than building costs while, when work is scarce, tender prices may actually fall even if building costs are rising.

Most countries have building cost indices - the method of compilation is generally relatively simple, basically comprising a weighted basket of the main inputs to construction. Rather fewer countries have tender price indices - their method of compilation is more complex usually involving a detailed analysis of accepted tenders for construction work and comparing these with a common base schedule of prices. When construction indices are described as price indices it is not always clear what these are.

USEFUL ADDRESSES

At the end of each country section, a list of addresses is given. This usually comprises main government, contracting, professional, standards and research organizations involved in the construction industry.

STATISTICAL NOTES

Gross Domestic Product (GDP) is the total value of all the goods and services produced in a country. Thus it shows the wealth generated within a country. *Gross National Product* (GNP) is the total value of all the goods and services produced in a country plus or minus net income from outside. Thus it represents the total amount of income available to the population. Reasons why GNP can be greater than GDP include that nationals abroad send back money, that the country receives aid or that the country has an income from investment abroad. Debt repayment and payment of interest can make GNP less than GDP.

It is appropriate to use GNP as a measure of wealth when income is being considered, e.g. in allocation for various purposes. GDP is more appropriate where productive capacity is being considered. Because a primary focus of this book is on the productive capacity of the construction industry in the key data sheets for each country the emphasis is on GDP, although there are a few countries where only statistics of GNP are available.

In considering expenditure the data for *private and public consumption and investment* are expressed as a proportion of GDP. This is partly because the main source for this expresses it this way and use of this one source gives a consistent picture. Because expenditure is made out of GNP the three percentages do not always total to 100, e.g. Philippines receives remittances from abroad which make its GNP greater than GDP and hence it is able to spend more than its own production on consumption and investment. *Central government expenditure* is, however, expressed as a percentage of GNP as in the World Development Report published by the World Bank.

Data on construction output for most countries are available in the form of *net output* or value added, that is, broadly, *gross value* of construction output minus the value of the material input, and the cost of hiring plant and equipment. However, the method of arriving at this data and gross value of construction output varies from country to country and is sometimes so indirect that it is of dubious value. Nevertheless it is all that is available. Both gross and net construction output are given where possible. Where no figure of net output is available it has been estimated using ratios from earlier years.

The *exchange rates* given in the key data are those which are appropriate for use with the cost data. For conversion of figures for a year, e.g. GDP in 1990, the average exchange rate for that year has been used. Because a single yen has a small value compared to the US dollar or the pound sterling, a rate for 100 yen is given in each case. *Purchasing power parity* (PPP) is the exchange rate which would be appropriate to express an income in one country in terms of its purchasing power in another country.

The United Nations Development Programme (UNDP) in 1990 published its first attempt at constructing *a human development index*. It uses three measures: life expectancy, literacy and whether average income based on PPP measures is sufficient to meet basic needs. A country's score for each component is scaled according to where it falls between the minimum and maximum country scores. It is not an index of quality of life and takes no account of basic freedoms in each country. It is quoted in the Introduction.

All the statistics are subject to considerable margins of error but particularly so for the less developed countries. As soon as they are converted from national currencies to US$ in order to permit comparison, the difficulty arises that the exchange rate may not reflect the purchasing power parity (PPP). In using exchange rates to convert value of construction output the difficulty is greater because of the greater specificity of production. In one case - that of China - a comment has been made in the text that the statistics do not reflect the real situation, but the problems exist in a greater or lesser degree for all countries. Indeed even taking authoritative sources, variations of a factor of two are possible. The statistics in this volume are those considered by the editors to be as accurate and as representative of the real situation as possible.

3. Individual countries

In Australia:

DAVIS LANGDON & BEATTIE
DAVIS LANGDON & ASH
DAVIS LANGDON QUALITY MANAGEMENT PTY LTD
M.H.B. PROJECT SERVICES PTY LTD

The strategic and integrated management of cost, time and quality - the client "risk" areas of a contract - are essential functions, which are necessary to ensure the satisfactory planning, procurement, execution and operation of construction projects.

We specialise in the financial management of construction projects and their risk areas, from project inception to completion and we concentrate on:

* being positive and creative in our advice, rather than simply reactive;

* providing value for money via efficient management, rather than on superficial cost monitoring;

* giving advice that is matched to the Client's requirements, rather than imposing standard or traditional solutions;

* paying attention to the life-cycle costs of constructing and occupying a building, rather than to the initial capital cost only.

Our aim is to provide our clients with risk assurance, cost control and value for money, via effective advice, cost planning and management.

Melbourne, Brisbane, Sydney, Hobart

DAVIS LANGDON & SEAH INTERNATIONAL

MANAGE AND LIMIT CLIENT RISK - ADDING VALUE

Australia

KEY DATA

Population

Population	17.1m
Urban population	86%
Population under 15	22%
Population over 65	11%
Average annual growth rate (1980 to 1990)	1.5%

Geography

Land area	7,687,000 km²
Agricultural area	63%
Capital city	Canberra (population 0.3m)
Largest city	Sydney (population 3.7m)

Economy

Monetary unit	Australian dollars (A$)
Exchange rate (average first quarter 1993) to:	
the pound sterling	A$ 2.17
the US dollar	A$ 1.47
the yen x 100	A$ 1.19
Average annual inflation (1981 to 1991)	7.1%
Inflation rate (1992)	0.8%
Gross Domestic Product (GDP) (1991)	A$ 378.3bn
GDP per capita (1991)	A$ 22,123
Real GDP growth (1980 to 1990)	3.4%
Private consumption as a proportion of GDP	61%
Public consumption as a proportion of GDP	18%
Investment as a proportion of GDP	21%
Central government expenditure as a proportion of Gross National Product	26%

Construction

Net value of construction output (1991)	A$ 24.6bn
Net value of construction output per capita (1991)	A$ 1,438
Net value of construction output as a proportion of GDP	6.5%

Note: All data relate to 1990 unless otherwise indicated.

THE CONSTRUCTION INDUSTRY

Construction output

The value added of construction in Australia in 1991 was A$24.6 billion equivalent to US$19.2 billion. This represents about 6.5% of GDP. The construction industry is in depression with a continued fall in activity since 1988/9.

In recent years in broad terms residential work has been about 40 to 50% of total output, about 30 to 35% has been non-residential building and 25 to 30% non-building construction (which includes some industrial plant). Comprehensive output data are not up to date. However, detailed information on work approved and work commenced is available for building and there is some information for civil engineering.

Building approvals since 1985/6 have developed as shown in the table.

BUILDING APPROVALS, AUSTRALIA 1985/86
TO 1990/91 IN A$bn

	Dwellings *	Other building	Total
1985/86	8.3	8.4	16.8
1986/87	8.0	8.5	16.5
1987/88	10.9	11.3	22.2
1988/89	13.3	15.5	28.9
1989/90	13.1	13.2	26.3
1990/91	12.1	9.0	21.1

Notes: There were expected to be further declines in 1991/92
* includes alterations and additions
Sources: ABS. Australian Economic Indicators

The percentages of building work commenced and of population in each state are shown below.

BUILDING WORK COMMENCED AND POPULATION,
AUSTRALIA, 1991

Regions	% of value of work commenced 1991	% of population
New South Wales	36	34
Victoria	21	26
Queensland	22	17
South Australia	7	8
Western Australia	8	9
Tasmania	2	3
Northern Territory	1	1
Australian Capital Territory	3	2
Total	100	100

Although distribution of work broadly follows that of the population Victoria shows evidence of faster development while Queensland is falling behind. All regions have suffered from the recession with the exception of the Northern Territory where approvals are small. Victoria is the worst hit.

There is evidence of a recent upturn in residential building but not in non-residential. The non building construction has maintained its output over the period of the recent depression; most of it is in the public sector.

The table below shows the distribution of work by type in Australia as a whole and in the five states with the largest building programmes - 94% of the total. It will be seen that new dwellings account for between 44 and 57% of the building total. Offices are most important in New South Wales and Victoria. Hotels are important in Queensland and starts in 1991 were 57% of those in all Australia.

BUILDING WORK BY TYPE AND STATE, AUSTRALIA, 1991 (1984/85 prices)

	Australia A$m	%	New South Wales % of total	Victoria % of total	Queensland % of total	South Australia % of total	Western Australia % of total
Residential							
New dwellings	6,265	49	44	44	57	50	62
Alterations and additions	1,154	9	12	11	4	8	7
Total	7,419	58	55	55	61	58	70
Other buildings							
Offices	1,493	12	11	18	7	7	5
Shops	634	5	5	5	5	9	3
Hotels	305	2	2	1	6	1	1
Other business premises	599	5	6	4	4	5	4
Factories	584	5	6	7	3	5	2
Education and health	1,029	8	7	6	10	8	9
Other social	773	6	7	4	5	8	6
Total	5,418	42	44	45	39	42	30
Grand total	12,837	100	100	100	100	100	100

The distribution of civil engineering work in New South Wales and Victoria is shown in the table overleaf.

CIVIL ENGINEERING WORK, NEW SOUTH WALES AND VICTORIA

	New South Wales 1988/89 %	Victoria 1991 1st Quarter %
Roads, highways etc	31.3	20.5
Water storage and supply and sewerage and drainage	11.7	12.7
Electricity generation, transmission and distribution	14.3	18.3
Heavy industry	9.1	8.8
Other	33.1	39.7*
Total	100	100
of which: public	77.6	81.7
private	22.4	18.3

Note: * 26.1% of other is Telecommunications

Characteristics and structure of the industry

There are a number of large contractors in terms of turnover but because subcontracting is so prevalent in the building industry, the largest has personnel of less than 2,000. In total there are about 20 contractors who operate all over Australia out of a total of some 100,000 firms. Average employment is 2.6 persons; 85% of construction firms have less than 5 employees. Some subcontractors, especially in the mechanical and electrical services, are large. On an average contract for a high rise office building, the number of subcontracts may be 100 to 150 while on very large projects it may be 250. There is some labour-only subcontracting, for example in bricklaying.

Two Australian contractors are in the *Engineering News Record*'s 1991 list of 225 top international contractors compared with four in 1990.

MAJOR AUSTRALIAN INTERNATIONAL CONTRACTORS

Contractor	Location	Place in ENR list	1991 contracts Total A$ mn	% foreign
McConnell Dowel Corp Ltd	Sydney, NSW	73	401	94
Leighton Holdings Ltd	St Leonards, NSW	107	1,089	23

Architects usually undertake a complete design service. On large projects they are seldom responsible for supervision of work on site.

Civil engineers are the dominant profession for civil works. Quantity surveyors are slowly moving away from work on bills of quantities towards cost control and advice to clients. Quantity surveyors are regulated by the Australian Institute of Quantity Surveyors which approves the course content of various educational institutions as a qualification and carries out assessment of professional competence.

Clients and finance

In 1991 in Australia 93% of dwellings commenced were for private clients, only 7% being for government bodies; 70 to 80% of other building is privately funded but in civil engineering work 75 to 85% is publicly funded. There will be an increase in private funding because of the privatisation of some public sector organisations.

Selection of design consultants

There is not uniformity across Australia in the way consultants are appointed. In the states of New South Wales, Victoria and Queensland the architect is always appointed directly by the client but in Victoria this is usually after some form of competition whereas there is a mixture of direct and competitive selection in New South Wales and Queensland. Other consultants may be appointed by the client or by a main consultant and, again in Victoria, some competition is likely to be held. Price is most important in New South Wales and Victoria but contacts and recommendations are more critical in Queensland. Track record is taken into account everywhere and, together with contacts, is more important in the private sector than in the public sector where price is significant save that in Tasmania competition is rare and price least important in selection.

Some states have more formal systems than others. In Tasmania the State Government keeps a register of consultants and has standard conditions of engagement and there are State Government Purchasing Guidelines for Queensland.

Professional bodies all publish fee scales but they are not mandatory and are not usually used except in Tasmania.

Contractual arrangements

Contractual arrangements are influenced both by State and by Federal Governments and there are some 20 contract types in use. The Federal Government has recently carried out an inquiry into the operation of the construction industry and the Government of New South Wales set up a Royal Commission on the Building Industry whose report was published in 1992. Contractual arrangements were covered in these investigations but there has not been time for implementation and discussion must take place on the precise changes which will be made. Thus the arrangements are in a state of flux.

Government departments regularly publish invitations for construction companies to join approved lists for various categories of work. Evidence of financial stability, experience in similar work and extent of turnover are usually the type of information required. In Federal Government work and for the majority of State contracts there is some prequalification and companies have to satisfy the client on their training record, meeting of contract obligations etc. However, as public works departments are being privatized these conditions are likely to become less important but there are considerable uncertainties about future developments following the inquiries referred to above.

After preselection, competitive lump sum tender is the most common form of contractor selection. Construction management and cost plus fee arrangements are used occasionally.

A retention of 5% of contract value may be withheld until the maintenance period has expired. This is retained at the rate of 10% until the level of 5% of the contract sum has been reached.

Liability and insurance

Several insurances are required by contract.

Development control and standards

The planning system is based on a fairly detailed land usage designation for many areas in the country. This might specify, for example, single family housing or industrial development for the chemical industry. If proposed development conforms to this land usage, planning permission is not necessary.

For building in an area where there is no land usage designation or where the proposed project does not conform to it then planning permission is necessary. If the proposed development does not present problems approval would be given within six months and most problems would be resolved within a year. However, there are cases which receive publicity where it may take years to agree, with proposals and counter proposals going to and fro.

Building design standards are set by the Standards Association of Australia and incorporated in the Building Codes which are administered by local municipal councils. Building approval is necessary for all projects. They used to be based on local building regulations but these are slowly being developed into a code for all Australia.

CONSTRUCTION COST DATA

Cost of labour

The figures below are typical of labour costs in Melbourne as at the first quarter 1993. The wage rate is the basis of an employee's income, while the cost of labour indicates the cost to a contractor of employing that employee. The difference between the two covers a variety of mandatory and voluntary contributions - a list of items which could be included is given in section 2.

	Wage rate (per week) AU$	Cost of labour (per hour) AU$	Number of hours worked per year
Site operatives			
Mason/bricklayer	460	20	1,656
Carpenter	470	21	1,656
Plumber	500	22	1,656
Electrician	500	22	1,656
Structural steel erector	470	21	1,656
HVAC installer	480	22	1,656
Semi-skilled worker	425	19	1,656
Unskilled labourer	390	18	1,656
Equipment operator	425	19	1,656
Watchman/security	420	19	1,656
Site supervision			
General foreman	-	35	1,656
Trades foreman	-	32	1,656
Clerk of works	-	32	1,656
	(per year)	*(per hour)*	
Contractors' personnel			
Site manager	85,000	60	1,760
Resident engineer	65,000	45	1,760
Resident surveyor	45,000	35	1,760
Junior engineer	38,000	30	1,654
Junior surveyor	30,000	24	1,654
Planner	38,000	30	1,654
Consultants' personnel			
Senior architect	60,000	85	1,760
Senior engineer	80,000	80	1,760
Senior surveyor	55,000	75	1,760
Qualified architect	42,000	65	1,654
Qualified engineer	42,000	50	1,654
Qualified surveyor	38,000	60	1,654

Cost of materials

The figures that follow are the costs of main construction materials, delivered to site in the Melbourne area, as incurred by contractors in the first quarter 1993. These assume that the materials would be in quantities as required for a medium sized construction project and that the location of the works would be neither constrained nor remote.

	Unit	Cost AU$
Cement and aggregate		
Ordinary portland cement in 50kg bags	tonne	185.00
Coarse aggregates for concrete	m³	22.50
Fine aggregates for concrete	m³	27.00
Ready mixed concrete (Grade 40)	m³	95.00
Ready mixed concrete (Grade 10)	m³	82.00
Steel		
Mild steel reinforcement	tonne	880.00
High tensile steel reinforcement	tonne	880.00
Structural steel sections	tonne	1,200.00
Bricks and blocks		
Common bricks (230 x 110 x 76)	1000	335.00
Good quality facing bricks (230 x 110 x 76mm)	1000	435.00
Hollow concrete blocks (400 x 200 x 100mm)	1000	1,280.00
Solid concrete blocks (400 x 200 x 100mm)	1000	1,980.00
Precast concrete cladding units with exposed aggregate finish	m²	280.00
Timber and insulation		
Softwood sections for carpentry	m³	760.00
Softwood for joinery	m³	763.00
Hardwood for joinery	m³	789.00
Exterior quality plywood (6mm)	m²	26.00
Plywood for interior joinery (6mm)	m²	23.00
Softwood strip flooring (17mm)	m²	23.00
Chipboard sheet flooring (19mm)	m²	23.00
100mm thick quilt insulation	m²	9.00
Softwood internal door complete with frames and ironmongery	each	285.00
Glass and ceramics		
Float glass (6mm)	m²	90.00
Sealed double glazing units	m²	210.00
Plaster and paint		
Good quality ceramic wall tiles (150 x 150mm)	m²	28.00
Plaster in 50 kg bags	tonne	30.00
Plasterboard (10mm thick)	m²	12.00

	Unit	Cost AU$
Emulsion paint in 4 litre tins	litre	9.00
Gloss oil paint in 4 litre tins	litre	9.50

Tiles and paviors

	Unit	Cost AU$
Clay floor tiles (150 x 150mm)	m^2	28.00
Vinyl floor tiles (300 x 300 x 3mm)	m^2	20.00
Precast concrete paving slabs (400 x 400 x 25mm)	m^2	40.00
Clay roof tiles	m^2	14.00
Precast concrete roof tiles	m^2	10.00

Drainage

	Unit	Cost AU$
WC suite complete	each	1,400.00
Lavatory basin complete	each	1,400.00
100mm diameter clay drain pipes	m	13.00
150mm diameter cast iron drain pipes	m	20.00

Unit rates

The descriptions below are generally shortened versions of standard descriptions listed in full in section 4. Where an item has a two digit reference number (e.g. 05 or 33), this relates to the full description against that number in section 4. Where an item has an alphabetic suffix (e.g. 12A or 34B) this indicates that the standard description has been modified. Where a modification is major the complete modified description is included here and the standard description should be ignored; where a modification is minor (e.g. the insertion of a named hardwood) the shortened description has been modified here but, in general, the full description in section 4 prevails.

The unit rates below are for main work items on a typical construction project in the Melbourne area in the first quarter 1993. The rates include all necessary labour, materials, equipment and contractors' overheads and profit. Allowances of 8 to 12% should be added to cover preliminary and general items.

		Unit	Rate AU$
Excavation			
01	Mechanical excavation of foundation trenches	m^3	35.00
02	Hardcore filling making up levels	m^2	8.30
03	Earthwork support	m^2	12.00
Concrete work			
04	Plain insitu concrete in strip foundations in trenches	m^3	125.00
05	Reinforced insitu concrete in beds	m^3	125.00
06	Reinforced insitu concrete in walls	m^3	125.00
07	Reinforced insitu concrete in suspended floor or roof slabs	m^3	125.00
08	Reinforced insitu concrete in columns	m^3	130.00

		Unit	Rate AU$
09	Reinforced insitu concrete in isolated beams	m^3	125.00
10	Precast concrete slab	m^3	220.00

Formwork

		Unit	Rate AU$
11	Metal formwork to concrete walls	m^2	70.00
12	Metal formwork to concrete columns	m^2	80.00
13	Metal formwork to horizontal soffits of slabs	m^2	64.00

Reinforcement

		Unit	Rate AU$
14	Reinforcement in concrete walls	tonne	1,250.00
15	Reinforcement in suspended concrete slabs	tonne	1,250.00
16	Fabric reinforcement in concrete beds	m^2	8.50

Steelwork

		Unit	Rate AU$
17	Fabricate, supply and erect steel framed structure	tonne	2,200.00

Brickwork and blockwork

		Unit	Rate AU$
18	Precast lightweight aggregate hollow concrete block walls	m^2	55.00
19	Solid (perforated) concrete blocks	m^2	60.00
20	Sand lime bricks	m^2	60.00
21	Facing bricks	m^2	65.00

Roofing

		Unit	Rate AU$
22	Concrete interlocking roof tiles 430 x 380mm	m^2	22.00
23	Plain clay roof tiles 260 x 160mm	m^2	30.00
24	Fibre cement roof slates 600 x 300mm	m^2	45.00
25	Sawn softwood roof boarding	m^2	20.00
26	Particle board roof coverings	m^2	32.00
27	3 layers glass-fibre based bitumen felt roof covering	m^2	60.00
28	Bitumen based mastic asphalt roof covering	m^2	62.00
29	Glass-fibre mat roof insulation 100mm thick	m^2	10.00
31	Troughed galvanised steel roof cladding	m^2	24.00

Woodwork and metalwork

		Unit	Rate AU$
32	Preservative treated sawn softwood 50 x 100mm	m	7.50
33	Preservative treated sawn softwood 50 x 150mm	m	9.00
34A	Single glazed casement window in local hardwood, size 650 x 900mm	each	300.00
35A	Two panel glazed door in local hardwood, size 850 x 2000mm	each	720.00
36	Solid core half hour fire resisting hardwood internal flush doors, size 800 x 2000mm	each	430.00
37	Aluminium double glazed window, size 1200 x 1200mm	each	460.00
38A	Aluminium single glazed door, size 850 x 2100mm	each	1,500.00
39	Hardwood skirtings	m	7.00
40	Framed structural steelwork in universal joist sections	tonne	2,400.00
41	Structural steelwork lattice roof trusses	tonne	3,200.00

	Unit	Rate AU$
Plumbing		
42 Steel half round eaves gutter	m	15.00
43 UPVC rainwater pipes	m	15.00
44 Light gauge copper cold water tubing	m	12.00
45 High pressure plastic pipes for cold water supply	m	14.00
46 Low pressure plastic pipes for cold water		
distribution	m	12.00
47 UPVC soil and vent pipes	m	20.00
48 White vitreous china WC suite	each	850.00
49 White vitreous china lavatory basin	each	650.00
50 Glazed fireclay shower tray	each	550.00
51 Stainless steel single bowl sink and double drainer	each	750.00
Electrical work		
52 PVC insulated and copper sheathed cable	m	3.00
53 13 amp unswitched socket outlet	each	18.00
54 Flush mounted 20 amp, 1 way light switch	each	18.00
Finishings		
55 2 coats gypsum based plaster on brick walls	m^2	35.00
56 White glazed tiles on plaster walls	m^2	65.00
57 Red clay quarry tiles on concrete floor	m^2	70.00
58 Cement and sand screed to concrete floors	m^2	30.00
59 Thermoplastic floor tiles on screed	m^2	35.00
60 Mineral fibre tiles on concealed suspension system	m^2	49.00
Glazing		
61 Glazing to wood	m^2	80.00
Painting		
62 Emulsion on plaster walls	m^2	6.00
63 Oil paint on timber	m^2	8.00

Approximate estimating

The building costs per unit area given below are averages incurred by building clients for typical buildings in the Melbourne area as at the first quarter 1993. They are based upon the total floor area of all storeys, measured between external walls and without deduction for internal walls.

Approximate estimating costs generally include mechanical and electrical installations but exclude furniture, loose or special equipment, and external works; they also exclude fees for professional services. The costs shown are for specifications and standards appropriate to Australia and this should be borne in mind when attempting comparisons with similarly described building types in other countries. A discussion of this issue is included in section 2. Comparative data for countries covered in this publication, including construction cost data, are presented in Part Three.

Approximate estimating costs must be treated with caution; they cannot provide more than a rough guide to the probable cost of building.

	Cost m² AU$	Cost ft² AU$
Industrial buildings		
Factories for letting	385	36
Factories for owner occupation (light industrial use)	435	40
Factories for owner occupation (heavy industrial use)	510	47
Factory/office (high-tech) for letting (ground floor shell, first floor offices)	700	65
Factory/office (high tech) for owner occupation (controlled environment, fully finished)	900	84
High tech laboratory workshop centres (air conditioned)	1,600	149
Warehouses, low bay (6 to 8m high) for letting	350	33
Warehouses, low bay for owner occupation (no heating)	430	40
Warehouses, high bay for owner occupation (no heating)	495	46
Administrative and commercial buildings		
Civic offices, fully air conditioned	900	84
Offices, fully air conditioned	900	84
Offices for letting, 5 to 10 storeys, air conditioned	1,200	111
Offices for letting, high rise, air conditioned	1,400	130
Offices for owner occupation, high rise, air conditioned	1,800	167
Prestige/headquarters office, 5 to 10 storeys, air conditioned	1,550	144
Prestige/headquarters office, high rise, air conditioned	2,000	186
Health and education buildings		
General hospitals (150 beds)	1,700	158
Teaching hospitals (200 beds)	2,000	186
Private hospitals (100 beds)	1,500	139
Health centres	1,000	93
Nursery schools	750	70
Primary/junior schools	800	74
Secondary/middle schools	1,000	93
University (arts) buildings	1,300	121
University (science) buildings	1,700	158
Management training centres	1,500	139
Recreation and arts buildings		
Theatres (over 500 seats) including seating and stage equipment	2,000	186
Theatres (less than 500 seats) including seating and stage equipment	2,200	204
Sports halls including changing and social facilities	900	84
Swimming pools (international standard) excluding changing and social facilities	each	550,000

	Cost m^2 AU\$	Cost ft^2 AU\$
Swimming pools (schools standard) excluding changing facilities	each	350,000
National museums including full air conditioning and standby generator	2,700	251
Local museums including air conditioning	1,500	139
Branch/local libraries	1,400	130
Residential buildings		
Social/economic single family housing (multiple units)	500	46
Private/mass market single family housing 2 storey detached/semidetached (multiple units)	600	56
Purpose designed single family housing 2 storey detached (single unit)	900	84
Social/economic apartment housing, low rise (no lifts)	800	74
Social/economic apartment housing, high rise (with lifts)	1,000	93
Private sector apartment building (standard specification)	1,100	102
Private sector apartment buildings (luxury)	1,600	149
Student/nurses halls of residence	1,300	121
Homes for the elderly (shared accommodation)	700	65
Homes for the elderly (self contained with shared communal facilities)	1,000	93
Hotel, 5 star, city centre	2,200	204
Hotel, 3 star, city/provincial	1,800	167
Motel	1,200	111

Regional variations

The approximate estimating costs are based on projects in Melbourne. For other parts of Australia, adjust these costs by the following factors:

      Sydney   : +2.5%
      Brisbane   : -10%
      Perth   : -6%
      Adelaide   : -7%
      Hobart   : -8%
      Canberra   : +5%
      Darwin   : +8%

EXCHANGE RATES AND INFLATION

The combined effect of exchange rates and inflation on prices within a country and price comparisons between countries is discussed in section 2.

Exchange rates

The graph below plots the movement of the Australian Dollar against sterling, the US dollar and the Japanese Yen since 1980. The figures used for the graph are quarterly and the method of calculating these, and other related issues are discussed in section 2. The exchange rate at the first quarter 1993 was AU$2.17 to the pound sterling, AU$1.47 to the US dollar and AU$1.19 to 100 Japanese Yen.

THE AUSTRALIAN DOLLAR AGAINST STERLING, THE US DOLLAR
AND THE JAPANESE YEN

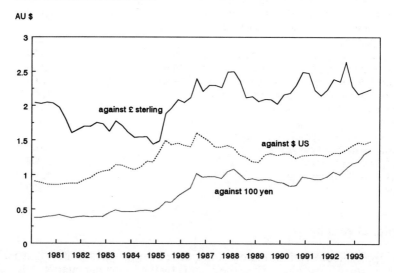

Price inflation

The table opposite presents general price and building cost and price inflation in Australia since 1980. Building costs have increased at a similar but slower rate than general prices. Building prices show even slower growth and have declined since 1989.

CONSUMER PRICE AND BUILDING COST AND PRICE INFLATION

Year	Consumer price inflation average index	average change %	Building cost index average index	average change %	Building price index average index	average change %
1981	74.7	-				
1982	82.9	11.0			77	-
1983	90.1	8.6			80	3.9
1984	92.4	2.6	97	-	85	6.3
1985	100.0	8.2	100	3.1	100	17.6
1986	109.8	9.8	106	6.0	99	-1.0
1987	117.6	7.1	112	5.7	107	8.1
1988	126.5	7.6	120	7.1	115	7.5
1989	136.5	7.8	130	8.3	124	7.8
1990	145.8	6.9	138	6.2	114	-8.1
1991	148.0	1.5			110	-3.5
1992	148.0	0.0			93	-15.5

USEFUL ADDRESSES

Public Organizations

Australian Industry Development Corporation - AIDC
POB 1483
Canberra ACT 2601
Tel: (062) 479411
Telex: 62307

Canberra Commercial Development Authority
Belconnen Mall
3rd Floor, Benjamin Way
Belconnen ACT 2617
Tel: (062) 51433

Department of Employment and Industrial Relations
1 Farrell Place
Canberra ACT 2601
Tel: (062) 437333
Fax: (062) 437598
Telex: 62210

Australian Bureau of Statistics
Cameron Offices
Chandler Street
Belconnen ACT 2616

Trade and Professional Associations

Australian Federation of Construction Contractors
    PO Box 320
    St Leonards
    NSW 2065

Australian Institute of Building
    PO Box 1467
    Canberra City
    ACT 2601

Housing Industry Association
    79 Constitution Avenue
    Campbell
    ACT 2601

ACT Civil Engineering Contractors Association
    PO Box 364
    Canberra City
    ACT 2601

Association of Consulting Engineers
    PO Box 1002
    North Stanet
    NSW 2060

Royal Australian Institute of Architects (RAIA)
    PO Box 373
    Manuka
    ACT 2603

Australian Institute of Quantity Surveyors
    PO Box 534
    Crows Nest
    NSW 2065

Australian Chamber of Commerce (ACC)
    Commerce House
    Brisbane Avenue, Barton
    ACT 2600

Royal Australian Planning Institute Inc (RAPI)
    POB 263
    Canberra ACT 2601

Confederation of Australian Industry (CAI)
    Industry House
    National Circuit
    Barton
    Canberra ACT 2600

Spon's European Construction Costs Handbook

Edited by **Davis Langdon & Everest**, Chartered Quantity Surveyors, UK

A unique source of information on the world's largest construction market.
27 countries arranged in alphabetical order, each have their own chapter containing the following information.

* key data on the main economic and construction industries

* an outline of the national construction industry, covering structure, tendering and contract procedures, regulations and standards

* labour and material costs data

* measured rates (in local currency) for up to 63 construction operations

* costs per unit area for a range of building types from housing to offices and factories

* regional variations percentages, tax details, cost and price indices, exchange rates with £ sterling and $US

* addresses of authorities, professional institutions, trade associations etc.

* multilingual glossary with fully detailed specifications, in 5 languages for the operations priced as measured rates

Countries covered in detail: Austria * Belgium * Cyprus * Denmark * Finland * France * Germany * Greece * Hungary * Ireland * Italy * Japan * Luxembourg * Malta * Netherlands * Norway * Poland * Portugal * Spain * Sweden * Switzerland * Turkey * UK * USA * USSR(CIS) * Yugoslavia *
Japan and the USA are included for the purpose of comparison

March 1992: 234x156: 544pp
Hardback: 0-419-17480-X

For further information and to order please contact: **The Promotion Dept.**, **E & F N Spon**, 2-6 Boundary Row, London SE1 8HN Tel 071 865 0066 Fax 071 522 9623

In Brunei:

DAVIS LANGDON & SEAH
PETROJAYA SDN BHD
PETROKON UTAMA SDN BHD

The strategic and integrated management of cost, time and quality - the client "risk" areas of a contract - are essential functions, which are necessary to ensure the satisfactory planning, procurement, execution and operation of construction projects.

We specialise in the financial management of construction projects and their risk areas, from project inception to completion and we concentrate on:

*   being positive and creative in our advice, rather than simply reactive;

*   providing value for money via efficient management, rather than on superficial cost monitoring;

*   giving advice that is matched to the Client's requirements, rather than imposing standard or traditional solutions;

*   paying attention to the life-cycle costs of constructing and occupying a building, rather than to the initial capital cost only.

Our aim is to provide our clients with risk assurance, cost control and value for money, via effective advice, cost planning and management.

DAVIS LANGDON & SEAH	**PETROJAYA SDN BHD**
No. 1 First Floor, Block H	**PETROKON UTAMA SDN BHD**
Abdul Razak Complex Gadong	No. 3 First Floor, Block H
P O Box 313	Abdul Razak Complex Gadong
Bandar Seri Begawan 1903	P O Box 1188
Brunei Darussalam	Bandar Seri Begawan 1911
Tel: (010 6732) 446888	Brunei Darussalam
Fax: (0106732) 445555	Tel : (010 6732) 441384
	Fax : (010 6732) 441382

═══ DAVIS LANGDON & SEAH INTERNATIONAL ═══

MANAGE AND LIMIT CLIENT RISK - ADDING VALUE

Brunei

KEY DATA

Population
Population	0.26m
Average annual growth rate (estimate)	3.5%

Geography
Land area	5,765 km²
Agricultural area	2%
Capital city	Bandan Seri Begawan
	(population 0.06 m 1983 estimate)

Economy
Monetary unit	Brunei dollar (B$)
	at par with Singapore dollar
Exchange rate (average first quarter 1993) to:	
the pound sterling	B$ 2.45
the US dollar	B$ 1.65
the yen x 100	B$ 1.34
Gross Domestic Product (GDP)	B$ 6.5bn
GDP per capita	B$ 25,327
Central government expenditure as a proportion of Gross National Product	22%

Construction
Net value of construction output	B$ 0.28bn
Net value of construction output per capita	B$ 1,079
Net value of construction output as a proportion of GDP	4.3%

Notes: All data relate to 1990 unless otherwise indicated.
Brunei is known also as Negara Brunei Darussalam or Brunei Darussalam.

THE CONSTRUCTION INDUSTRY

Construction output

The value of the net output of the construction industry in 1990 was about B$277.4 million equivalent to US$171.23. This represented 4.3% of GDP. Although this percentage is relatively small the importance of construction is very great in absolute terms. Brunei is one of the richest countries in the world with a per capita income approaching the OECD average. In 1990 54% of the national income came from the oil and liquefied natural gas industries. Construction is in fact the second largest industry. It employs about 40% of the private sector labour force. This is because the oil and gas industries employ very little labour in relation to their contribution to GDP.

Since 1979, in line with falling oil prices worldwide, real GDP in Brunei has declined. In 1990 real GNP was approximately 85% of the figure in 1980. The non-oil sector of the economy represents an increasingly high percentage of GDP, from 12% (1974) to 46% (1990). The major contribution to this has come from the service sector.

Statistics of GNP and construction in current prices are shown below.

GROSS NATIONAL PRODUCT AND CONSTRUCTION
IN BRUNEI, 1980 TO 1990

Year	Gross national product B$ billion	Construction B$ million	%
1980	10.6	168.1	1.59
1981	9.2	216.5	2.35
1982	9.1	264.6	2.90
1983	8.1	265.5	3.27
1984	8.1	207.6	2.56
1985	7.8	159.2	2.05
1986	5.1	170.1	3.34
1987	5.8	183.1	3.16
1988	5.4	195.7	3.62
1989	5.8	254.6	4.39
1990	6.5	277.4	4.26

The above figures are as provided by the National Accounts Section and Statistics Division, Economic Planning Unit, Ministry of Finance. Figures are provided under other categories including the oil sector and transport, storage and communication. It is probable therefore that the figure against construction may be low.

There was a great boom in construction activity up to independence in 1984, with many large projects being erected. Shortages of building materials are commonplace as almost all have to be imported. Aggregate supplies from the normal local quarries are progressively being depleted;

timber is in short supply because of government conservation policies and a consequent reduction in tree felling.

Characteristics and structure of the industry

The majority of projects are undertaken by a main contractor through single stage competitive tendering on the basis of drawings and measured bills of quantities. Construction management and management contracting are rarely used in Brunei. There is some design and build but it is not very widespread.

The number of larger locally based contractors capable of undertaking multi-million dollar contracts is less than twenty. Architectural firms maintain a fairly high profile, with a handful of locally owned practices undertaking the majority of public sector work. Others are mainly confined to small scale private sector developments. Engineers and surveyors are in a similar position to architects, although there are currently slightly fewer locally-owned practices.

Most of the construction workers in Brunei are Filipinos, Thais and members of the Chinese community. Construction employs around 20,000 persons or 40% of the private sector work force.

The sponsoring ministry for the construction industry is the Ministry of Development set up in 1984, with a number of functional departments - public works, electrical services, housing development, land, survey, town and country planning, and construction planning and research.

- The Public Works Department (PWD) is responsible for the design and construction of various government projects such as bridges, roads, water and sewerage. It also promotes *Bumiputra* (local) contractors and keeps a register of consultants and contractors.
- The Electrical Services Department is in charge of electricity provision and registering electrical contractors.
- The Housing Development Department is charged with implementing the government's objective for every citizen to own a house. The department builds between 500 and 600 houses each year under its housing and resettlement programme.
- The Land Department is responsible for registration of privately owned land, the Survey Department is responsible for surveys throughout the country.
- The Town and Country Planning Department is responsible for land use planning and control, covering both structure and local development plans, as well as setting and monitoring minimum environmental standards. The department is showing increasing concern for the conservation and protection of the natural environment.

Clients and finance

The industry is very dependent on public sector projects. Government expenditure plans are set out in National Development Plans usually covering five years. Most construction and civil engineering work from the public sector is administered by the Ministry of Development. In 1990 the total expenditure of the Ministry was B$269.7 million. Of private sector clients, however, the most prominent are members of the Royal Family, Brunei Shell Petroleum Company (though they are not very active in on-shore construction work) and a few local property developers who concentrate on providing retail and commercial space. All these developers are mainly self-financed.

CONSTRUCTION COST DATA

Cost of labour

The figures below are typical of labour costs in Bandar Seri Begawan as at the first quarter 1993. The wage rate is the basis of an employee's income, while the cost of labour indicates the cost to a contractor of employing that employee. The difference between the two covers a variety of mandatory and voluntary contributions - a list of items which could be included is given in section 2.

	Wage rate (per day) B$	Cost of labour (per day) B$	Number of hours worked per year
Site operatives			
Mason/bricklayer	40	-	2,625
Carpenter	45	-	2,625
Plumber	40	-	2,625
Electrician	50	-	2,625
Structural steel erector	60	-	2,625
Semi-skilled worker	30	-	2,625
Unskilled labourer	20	-	2,625
Equipment operator	60	-	2,625
Watchman/security	40	-	2,625
	(Month B$)	*(Month B$)*	
Site supervision			
General foreman	3,000	3,500	2,040
Trades foreman	2,300	2,800	2,040
Clerk of works	2,500	3,500	2,040
Contractors' personnel			
Site manager	4,500	6,000	2,040
Resident engineer	4,000	5,500	2,040
Resident surveyor	3,500	5,000	2,040
Junior engineer	2,500	4,000	2,040
Junior surveyor	2,500	4,000	2,040
Planner	3,500	5,000	2,040

	Wage rate (per month) B$	Cost of labour (per month) B$	Number of hours worked per year
Consultants' personnel			
Senior architect	5,000	7,000	2,040
Senior engineer	5,000	7,000	2,040
Senior surveyor	4,500	6,500	2,040
Qualified architect	3,500	5,500	2,040
Qualified engineer	3,500	5,500	2,040
Qualified surveyor	3,500	5,500	2,040

Cost of materials

The figures that follow are the costs of main construction materials, delivered to site in the Bandar Seri Begawan area, as incurred by contractors in the first quarter 1993. These assume that the materials would be in quantities as required for a medium sized construction project and that the location of the works would be neither constrained nor remote.

	Unit	Cost B$
Cement and aggregate		
Ordinary portland cement in 50kg bags	tonne	180.00
Coarse aggregates for concrete	m^3	38.00
Fine aggregates for concrete	m^3	15.00
Ready mixed concrete (1:1.5:3)	m^3	175.00
Ready mixed concrete (1:2:4)	m^3	155.00
Steel		
Mild steel reinforcement	tonne	680.00
High tensile steel reinforcement	tonne	680.00
Structural steel sections	tonne	1,000.00
Bricks and blocks		
Common bricks (4" x 9" x 3")	1,000	170.00
Good quality facing bricks (4" x 9" x 3")	1,000	600.00
Hollow concrete blocks (6" x 9" x 4")	1,000	450.00
Solid concrete blocks (4" x 9" x 3")	1,000	200.00
Timber and insulation		
Softwood for joinery	m^3	2,275.00
Hardwood for joinery	m^3	700.00
Exterior quality plywood (12mm)	m^2	11.00
Plywood for interior joinery (6mm)	m^2	6.50
Softwood strip flooring (12mm)	m^2	70.00
Chipboard sheet flooring (12mm)	m^2	30.00
100mm thick quilt insulation	m^2	6.00
Softwood internal door complete with frames and ironmongery	each	700.00

	Unit	Cost B$
Glass and ceramics		
Float glass (6mm)	m²	30.00
Sealed double glazing units (50mm)	m²	380.00
Plaster and paint		
Good quality ceramic wall tiles (8" x 8")	m²	35.00
Plasterboard (12mm thick)	m²	6.75
Emulsion paint in 5 litre tins	litre	8.00
Gloss oil paint in 5 litre tins	litre	10.00
Tiles and paviors		
Clay floor tiles (8" x 4" x 0.5")	m²	30.00
Vinyl floor tiles (12" x 12" x 0.125")	m²	15.00
Precast concrete paving slabs (12" x 12" x 3")	m²	30.00
Clay roof tiles	1,000	2,800.00
Precast concrete roof tiles	1,000	1,400.00
Drainage		
WC suite complete	each	200.00
Lavatory basin complete	each	150.00
100mm diameter clay drain pipes	m	14.50
150mm diameter cast iron drain pipes	m	30.00

Unit rates

The descriptions below are generally shortened versions of standard descriptions listed in full in section 4. Where an item has a two digit reference number (e.g. 05 or 33), this relates to the full description against that number in section 4. Where an item has an alphabetic suffix (e.g. 12A or 34B) this indicates that the standard description has been modified. Where a modification is major the complete modified description is included here and the standard description should be ignored; where a modification is minor (e.g. the insertion of a named hardwood) the shortened description has been modified here but, in general, the full description in section 4 prevails.

The unit rates below are for main work items on a typical construction project in the Bandar Seri Begawan area in the first quarter 1993. The rates include all necessary labour, materials and equipment. Allowances of 10 to 15% to cover preliminary and general items and 10% to cover contractors' overheads and profit should be added to the rates.

	Unit	Rate B$
Excavation		
01 Mechanical excavation of foundation trenches	m³	9.20
02 Hardcore filling making up levels	m²	6.90
03 Earthwork support	m²	11.50

	Unit	Rate B$
Concrete work		
04 Plain insitu concrete in strip foundations in trenches	m³	180.00
05 Reinforced insitu concrete in beds	m³	180.00
06 Reinforced insitu concrete in walls	m³	180.00
07 Reinforced insitu concrete in suspended floor or roof slabs	m³	180.00
08 Reinforced insitu concrete in columns	m³	180.00
09 Reinforced insitu concrete in isolated beams	m³	180.00
10 Precast concrete slab	m²	92.00
Formwork		
11 Softwood or metal formwork to concrete walls	m²	19.00
12 Softwood or metal formwork to concrete columns	m²	20.00
13 Softwood or metal formwork to horizontal soffits of slabs	m²	18.00
Reinforcement		
14 Reinforcement in concrete walls	tonne	1,200.00
15 Reinforcement in suspended concrete slabs	tonne	1,200.00
16 Fabric reinforcement in concrete beds	m²	5.50
Steelwork		
17 Fabricate, supply and erect steel framed structure	tonne	3,500.00
Brickwork and blockwork		
19 Solid (perforated) concrete blocks	m²	25.30
20 Sand lime bricks	m²	24.15
21 Facing bricks	m²	51.80
Roofing		
22 Concrete interlocking roof tiles 430 x 380mm	m²	45.00
23 Plain clay roof tiles 260 x 160mm	m²	63.30
24 Fibre cement roof slates 600 x 300mm	m²	51.80
25 Sawn softwood roof boarding	m²	23.00
27 3 layers glass-fibre based bitumen felt roof covering	m²	50.00
28 Bitumen based mastic asphalt roof covering	m²	46.00
31 Troughed galvanised steel roof cladding	m²	28.80
Woodwork and metalwork		
32 Preservative treated sawn softwood 50 x 100mm	m	5.00
33 Preservative treated sawn softwood 50 x 150mm	m	7.50
34A Single glazed casement window in Nyatoh hardwood, size 650 x 900mm	each	265.00
35A Two panel glazed door in Nyatoh hardwood, size 850 x 2000mm	each	900.00
36 Solid core half hour fire resisting hardwood internal flush doors, size 800 x 2000mm	each	900.00
37 Aluminium double glazed window, size 1200 x 1200mm	each	598.00

		Unit	Rate B$
38	Aluminium double glazed door, size 850 x 2100mm	each	437.00
39	Hardwood skirtings	m	8.50
40	Framed structural steelwork in universal joist sections	tonne	3,000.00
41	Structural steelwork lattice roof trusses	tonne	3,500.00

Plumbing

		Unit	Rate B$
42	UPVC half round eaves gutter	m	27.60
43	UPVC rainwater pipes	m	18.40
44	Light gauge copper cold water tubing	m	18.40
45	High pressure plastic pipes for cold water supply	m	9.20
46	Low pressure plastic pipes for cold water distribution	m	11.50
47	UPVC soil and vent pipes	m	20.70
48	White vitreous china WC suite	each	322.00
49	White vitreous china lavatory basin	each	276.00
50	Glazed fireclay shower tray	each	230.00
51	Stainless steel single bowl sink and double drainer	each	345.00

Electrical work

		Unit	Rate B$
52	PVC insulated and copper sheathed cable	m	2.88
53	13 amp unswitched socket outlet	each	69.00
54	Flush mounted 20 amp, 1 way light switch	each	173.00

Finishings

		Unit	Rate B$
55	2 coats gypsum based plaster on brick walls	m^2	13.80
56	White glazed tiles on plaster walls	m^2	40.30
57	Red clay quarry tiles on concrete floor	m^2	57.50
58	Cement and sand screed to concrete floors	m^2	9.20
59	Thermoplastic floor tiles on screed	m^2	34.50
60	Mineral fibre tiles on concealed suspension system	m^2	27.60

Glazing

		Unit	Rate B$
61	Glazing to wood	m^2	46.00

Painting

		Unit	Rate B$
62	Emulsion on plaster walls	m^2	5.00
63	Oil paint on timber	m^2	10.00

Approximate estimating

The building costs per unit area given below are averages incurred by building clients for typical buildings in the Bandar Seri Begawan area as at the first quarter 1993. They are based upon the total floor area of all storeys, measured between external walls and without deduction for internal walls.

Approximate estimating costs generally include mechanical and electrical installations but exclude furniture, loose or special equipment, and external works; they also exclude fees for professional services. The costs shown are for specifications and standards appropriate to Brunei and this should be borne in mind when attempting comparisons with similarly described building types in other countries. A discussion of this issue is included in section 2. Comparative data for countries covered in this publication, including construction cost data, is presented in Part Three.

Approximate estimating costs must be treated with caution; they cannot provide more than a rough guide to the probable cost of building.

	Cost m² B$	Cost ft² B$
Industrial buildings		
Factories for letting	525	49
Factories for owner occupation (light industrial use)	685	64
Factories for owner occupation (heavy industrial use)	815	76
Factory/office (high-tech) for letting (shell and core only)	625	68
Factory/office (high-tech) for letting (ground floor shell, first floor offices)	715	66
Factory/office (high tech) for owner occupation (controlled environment, fully finished)	1,150	107
High tech laboratory workshop centres (air conditioned)	1,350	125
Warehouses, low bay (6 to 8m high) for letting (no heating)	650	60
Cold stores/refrigerated stores	1,250	116
Administrative and commercial buildings		
Civic offices, non air conditioned	625	58
Civic offices, fully air conditioned	750	70
Offices for letting, 5 to 10 storeys, non air conditioned	925	86
Offices for letting, 5 to 10 storeys, air conditioned	1,100	102
Offices for owner occupation 5 to 10 storeys, non air conditioned	1,050	98
Offices for owner occupation 5 to 10 storeys, air conditioned	1,170	109
Prestige/headquarters office, 5 to 10 storeys, air conditioned	1,490	138
Health and education buildings		
General hospitals (500 beds)	1,650	153
Teaching hospitals (100 beds)	1,400	130
Private hospitals (100 beds)	1,500	139
Health centres	1,200	112
Nursery schools	700	65
Primary/junior schools	750	70
Secondary/middle schools	1,100	102
Management training centres	1,100	102

	Cost m^2 B$	Cost ft^2 B$
Recreation and arts buildings		
Theatres (over 500 seats) including seating and stage equipment	3,350	311
Theatres (less than 500 seats) including seating and stage equipment	3,150	293
Concert halls including seating and stage equipment	2,000	186
Sports halls including changing and social facilities	1,690	157
Swimming pools (schools standard) including changing facilities	each 650,000	
National museums including full air conditioning and standby generator	2,800	260
City centre/central libraries	2,000	186
Branch/local libraries	1,350	125
Residential buildings		
Social/economic single family housing (multiple units)	750	70
Private/mass market single family housing 2 storey detached/semidetached (multiple units)	900	84
Purpose designed single family housing 2 storey detached (single unit)	1,100	102
Social/economic apartment housing, low rise (no lifts)	720	67
Social/economic apartment housing, high rise (with lifts)	840	78
Private sector apartment building (standard specification)	1,050	98
Private sector apartment buildings (luxury)	1,200	116
Student/nurses halls of residence	870	81
Hotel, 5 star, city centre	3,260	303
Hotel, 3 star, city/provincial	2,630	244
Motel	1,890	176

Regional variations

The approximate estimating costs are based on projects in the Bandar Seri Begawan area. For other parts of Brunei, adjust these costs by the following factors:

    Kuala Belait   +5%
    Temburong   +7.5%

EXCHANGE RATES

The graph opposite plots the movement of the Brunei dollar against sterling, the US dollar and the Japanese yen since 1980. The figures used for the graph are quarterly and the method of calculating these and other related issues are discussed in section 2. The exchange rate at the first quarter 1993 was B$2.45 to the pound sterling, B$1.65 to the US dollar and B$1.34 to 100 Japanese yen.

THE BRUNEI DOLLAR AGAINST STERLING, THE US DOLLAR
AND THE JAPANESE YEN

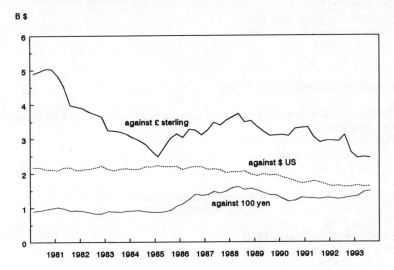

USEFUL ADDRESSES

Public Organizations

Construction Planning and Research Unit
    Ministry of Development
    Bandar Seri Begawan 1190
    Negara Brunei Darussalam
    Tel: 02 241911
    (Comprising Departments of Town and Country Planning,
    Survey, Land, Housing Development, Public Works and Electrical
    Services)

Industry Unit
    Ministry of Industry and Primary Resources
    Bandar Seri Begawan 1220
    Negara Brunei Darussalam
    Tel: 02 244822

Economic Planning Unit
  Ministry of Finance
  PO Box 2222
  Bandar Seri Begawan 1922
  Negara Brunei Darussalam
  Tel: 02 241991

Trade and Professional Associations

The Brunei Darussalam International Chamber of Commerce and Industry
  PO Box 2246
  Bandar Seri Begawan 1922
  Negara Brunei Darussalam
  Tel: 02 236601

Association of Surveyors, Engineers and Architects
  Pentubuhan Ukur Jurutera dan Arkitek (PUJA)
  PO Box 1069
  Bandar Seri Begawan 1910
  Negara Brunei Darussalam
  Tel: 02 424261

Frank Lloyd Wright and Japan

The role of traditional Japanese art and architecture in the work of Frank Lloyd Wright

K H Nute, Architect, Cambridge, UK

A unique combination of text and graphics to illustrate the influence of Japan on Wright's work

Supported by The Japan Foundation

Frank Lloyd Wright's admiration for traditional Japanese art is well known, as is his insistence that neither the art nor the architecture had any direct *formal* influence on his own work. This book examines the evidence that, quite apart from their philosophical lessons, certain forms of Japanese art and architecture did in fact have a significant formal impact on Wright's formal vocabulary, and one which may cast light on his general approach to design.

The book also explains Wright's particular perception of tradtional Japanese art and architecture in terms of his own "organic" design principles, and by illustrating how he brought together disparate forms and ideas in new creative syntheses it attempts to clarify the nature of his artistic originality.

Contents: Acknowledgements. Forewords. Introduction. 'Japanism' and the Boston orientalists. Japanese homes: the Japanese house dissected. The Ho-O-den: the temple and the villa married in south Chicago. Fenollosa and the "organic" nature of Japanese art. Composition: the picture, the plan, and the pattern, as aesthetic line-ideas. The wookblock print and the geometric abstraction of natural, man-made and social forms. Okakura and the social and aesthetic *Ideals of the East*. Jaean itself: giving and receiving in "Yedo". Japan as inspiration: analogies with Japanese built-forms. Japan as confirmation: the universal manifested in the particular. Appendices: summary of events; biographical sketches; Kakuzo Okakura's catalogue of the Ho-o-den; Ernest Fenollosa's essay on "The Nature of Fine Art"; Frederick Gookin's reviews of Kakuzo Okakura's books; glossary. Bibliography. Illustration acknowledgements. Index.

September 1993: 297x210: 256pp, 133 line illus, 92 halftone illus, 11colour illus
Hardback: 0-412-57420-9

Chapman & Hall

For further information and to order, please contact: The Promotion Dept., Chapman & Hall, 2-6 Boundary Row, LONDON SE1 8HN
Tel 071 865 0066 Fax 071 522 9623

COST DATA ON BUILDINGS
AND
INDUSTRIAL PROJECTS
THROUGHOUT CANADA

Leroux, Chauhan, Ouimet provides services to the following Clients:

Institutional
Commercial
Residential
Petro-Chemical
Mettallurgical
Heavy Civil
Pulp and Paper

Types of Services

Feasibility Studies

Conceptual Estimates

Cost Planning

Planning & Scheduling

Resource Planning

Expert Witness

Progress Measurement of Engineering
& Construction

Claims analysis

Project Management

Contract Administration

Owners Representatives

Cost Engineering

Project Cost & Schedule
Auditing

Leroux,	Construction Cost		
Chauhan,	Consultants	4115 Sherbrooke St. West	177 Nepean Street
Ouimet	Project Management	Suite 210	Suite 503
& Associates	Services	Westmount (Québec)	Ottawa (Ontario)
	Quantity Surveyors	H3Z 1K9	K2P 0B4
		Tel. (514) 846-8914	Tel. (613) 564-0562
		Fax. (514) 846-8913	Fax. (613) 564-9753

Canada

KEY DATA

Population
Population	26.5m
Urban population	77%
Population under 15	17%
Population over 65	22%
Average annual growth rate (1980 to 1990)	1.0%

Geography
Land area	9,976,000 km²
Agricultural area	8%
Capital city	Ottawa
	(population 0.3m)
Largest city	Toronto
	(population 2.2m)

Economy
Monetary unit	Canadian dollar (C$)
Exchange rate (average first quarter 1993) to:	
the pound sterling	C$ 1.88
the US dollar	C$ 1.27
the yen x 100	C$ 1.03
Average annual inflation (1980 to 1990)	4.4%
Inflation rate (1991)	1.6%
Gross Domestic Product (GDP) (1991)	C$ 658.0bn
GDP per capita (1991)	C$ 24,830
Real GDP growth (1980 to 1990)	3.4%
Private consumption as a proportion of GDP	59%
Public consumption as a proportion of GDP	20%
Investment as a proportion of GDP	21%
Central government expenditure as a proportion of Gross National Product	23%

Construction
Gross value of construction output (1991)	C$96.1bn
Net value of construction output (1991)*	C$ 56.0bn
Net value of construction output per capita (1991)*	C$ 2,113
Net value of construction output as a proportion of GDP (1991)*	8.5%

Note: All data relate to 1990 unless otherwise indicated.
* estimate

THE CONSTRUCTION INDUSTRY

Construction output

The gross value of output of the construction industry in 1991 was C$96 billion equivalent to US$84 billion. It represented 14.6% of GDP. Output had fallen in money terms and in real terms since 1990. A breakdown by type of work is shown in the table below.

CONSTRUCTION WORK PURCHASED BY TYPE OF WORK, CANADA, 1991

Type of work	Value C$ billion	Percentage of total
New work		
Residential	32.8	34.1
Non-residential	20.4	21.2
Engineering construction	27.9	29.0
Total	81.1	84.4
Repair and maintenance		
Residential	3.9	4.1
Non-residential	5.2	5.4
Engineering construction	5.9	6.1
Total	15.0	15.6
Overall total	96.1	100.0

A breakdown of the total of new and repair work for non-residential buildings is shown below:

TOTAL NON-RESIDENTIAL BUILDING BY TYPE OF WORK, CANADA, 1991

Type of work	Value C$ billion	Percentage of total
Industrial	3.4	13.3
Commercial	14.0	54.7
Institutional	5.6	21.9
Other	2.6	10.2
Total	25.6	100.0

The breakdown of output by regions in 1991 is shown below compared with population.

CONSTRUCTION WORK PURCHASED AND POPULATION
IN THE CANADIAN PROVINCES* 1991

Province	Percentage of population	Percentage of construction work
Newfoundland	2.3	2.0
Prince Edward Island	0.5	0.4
Nova Scotia	3.5	2.7
New Brunswick	2.8	2.3
Quebec	25.9	22.5
Ontario	36.1	35.6
Manitoba	4.2	3.1
Saskatchewan	4.0	3.7
Alberta	9.4	13.1
British Columbia	11.4	14.7
Total	100.0	100.0

*excludes territories and some incompletely enumerated Indian Reserves

Characteristics and structure of the industry

In 1989 the leading construction firms had turnovers ranging from about C$290 million to over C$1,300 million as shown in the table below.

MAJOR CANADIAN CONSTRUCTION COMPANIES, 1989

Company	Location	Volume (C$mn)
PCL Construction Group	Edmonton, Alberta	1,321
Ellis-Don Ltd	London, Ontario	1,025
Banister Continental Ltd	Edmonton, Alberta	648
Canron Inc	Toronto, Ontario	483
Magil Construction Ltd	Montreal, Province of Quebec	370
Matthews Group	London, Ontario	336
Groupe Herve Pomerleau Inc	St Georges, Province of Quebec	323
Dominion Bridge AMCA International	Etobicoke, Ontario	300
Commonwealth Construction Co Ltd	Burnaby, British Columbia	292
Eastern Construction Co Ltd	Toronto, Ontario	289

Source: Construction Record, June 1990

In 1991 eight Canadian contractors shared export contracts of US$1.2 billion (C$1.4 billion) similar to 1990 but small by international standards. 72% of the value of these contracts were in the USA and another 19% in the Middle East, the remainder being spread over the rest of the world.

The number of architectural firms in Canada in 1988 was 2,513 averaging five employees per firm. The great majority of firms are in Quebec and Ontario.

ARCHITECTS BY PROVINCE, CANADA, 1988

Province	No of firms	No of employees	Average per firm
Newfoundland	21	84	4
Prince Edward Island	8	51	6
Nova Scotia	48	303	6
New Brunswick	49	233	5
Quebec	683	3,046	4
Ontario	919	4,820	5
Manitoba	70	391	6
Saskatchewan	53	293	6
Alberta	224	1,000	4
British Columbia	438	1,372	3
Total	2,513	11,593	5

Source: Statistics Canada Catalogue 63-234

The distribution of the 5,375 consulting engineers is similarly shown in the table below.

CONSULTING ENGINEERS BY PROVINCE, CANADA, 1988

Province	No of firms	No of employees	Average per firm
Newfoundland	77	648	8
Prince Edward Island	6	87	15
Nova Scotia	141	1,186	8
New Brunswick	79	685	9
Quebec	759	19,060	25
Ontario	1,753	20,668	12
Manitoba	86	1,120	13
Saskatchewan	118	1,030	9
Alberta	1,360	7,960	6
British Columbia	996	9,551	10
Total	5,375	61,995	12

Source: Statistics Canada Catalogue 63-234

Quantity surveying firms vary in number and size from region to region but are widely used in the construction process throughout Canada. The size of firm can vary from one individual to as many as 30 professionals in various branches throughout Canada.

Clients and finance

The main public sector clients are the public utilities. Private sector work is promoted by property developers such as Trizec and Bramerlea, insurance companies (notably Sun Life and Commercial Union) and pension funds of which Canadian National, Canadian Pacific and Alcan are all very important.

Financing can be arranged through banks and/or trust companies. There is normally a fee charged by these lending institutions of 1 to 1.5% of the construction cost for drawing up the loan agreement and for conducting a feasibility study of the project.

Selection of design consultants

Most projects are designed by private consultants selected by some form of competition. It is not common practice to find in-house design organizations. Selection of consultants in the public sector is normally based on company experience with price being a major factor. Projects are advertised in the local press and professionals may bid either by themselves or through a consortium. Design competitions are used for government or municipal projects but have not proved to be very successful over the years.

The private sector tends to select design consultants on large projects on the basis of a successful record, with once again price being an important element. On smaller projects the private developers may select solely on the basis of price and will play an important role in the design of the project.

There are large differences in size and in capability between consultants and it is, therefore important to select very carefully depending on the scale, complexity and type of structure proposed.

Contractual arrangements

Most projects are let to main contractors. The majority are tendered on a lump sum basis and the process is as follows:

- All working drawings are completed to 100% and co-ordinated between the various consultants.
- Contractors are invited to bid or the project is open to public tender provided that certain qualifications are met such as requirements for performance bonds, etc.
- Each contractor calls his own bids on trade packages and reviews all specifications to ensure that all trades are covered.

- Contractors have three to four weeks in which to submit bids.
- In the public sector, bids are opened in public.

Civil engineering projects are usually bid on a unit price basis. All bids are normally accompanied by a bid bond which guarantees that the contractor, if awarded the contract, will sign the contract document. A labour and material bond or performance bond may also be a requirement of the contract.

The private sector may select a general contractor by using either a lump sum approach or through negotiation. This negotiation process may require the contractor to submit his credentials in conjunction with a list of proposed savings.

The lien laws which are similar to those in the USA (see section on USA) provide a substantial degree of protection to the contractors and subcontractors working on a project.

Management contracting has become relatively popular in recent years and more and more contractors use the term 'project managers'. The project manager takes a fee for calling bids for trades and for ensuring the final completion of the project. Construction management is not widely used in Canada on smaller projects but has been successful on 'megatype' developments. Design and build is not a normal process in Canada.

The process known as 'maximum upset price (guaranteed)' is cost plus fee with a ceiling. For large projects it is not used but it is becoming more popular for smaller projects as work can commence before working drawings are complete. Costs can be controlled through supervision of all signed contracts awarded to subcontractors. The quantity surveyor reviews all contracts, confirms all extras or savings, prepares monthly status reports showing the revised upset price and approves the final certificate.

The most common form of contract is the Canadian Construction Association document which is used throughout Canada.

Liability and insurance

All design consultants are advised to carry liability insurance for all types of buildings and engineering projects for an average term of five years. The general contractor should obtain and maintain during the contract period certain policies of insurance in the names of the owner, the general contractor, architect and all subcontractors. This includes the following:

- Insurance during the course of construction - provides all-risks builders' risk coverage for the project. The limit insured by this policy will be the estimated completed insurable value of the whole project.
- Commercial (wrap-up) general liability insurance. This insurance has a limit of liability not less than $2 million dollars per occurrence and in the annual aggregate. The amount will vary depending on the size of the project.

These policies include coverages commonly referred to as: premises and operations, products and completed operations, blanket contractual, broad form property damage, owners' and contractors' protective, personal injury liability, incidental medical malpractice cross liability, and explosion, collapse and underground damage.

The memorandum of insurance requires each subcontractor to procure certain prescribed minimum levels of insurance covering his own construction equipment, automobiles and employees.

The construction equipment policy and automobile policy must include a waiver of subrogation in favour of the owner and the general contractor, and all policies must include an undertaking to give the owner at least 30 days prior written notice of cancellation or material change. Alternatively, if any subcontractor elects to self-insure his construction equipment or automobiles for physical damage with the consent of the owner, the owner and general contractor must be held harmless for any damage thereto.

Subcontractors of every tier are subject to, and obligated to comply with, these requirements. Each subcontractor is required to confirm to the owner that these policies have been procured by completing the prescribed certificate of insurance which must also be executed by or for the insurers concerned. Certificates must be provided to the general contractors prior to the commencement of any work by the subcontractor, and must be provided on the prescribed certificate form. No other certificate will be acceptable.

Construction claims can be settled by an independent cost consultant or by arbitration as described in the contract document.

Development control and standards (Montreal - Quebec)

The local city authority is responsible for the zoning and planning approvals for all land within the Montreal area. All codes and regulations are governed by the National Building Code of 1985. Approval of plans may take from two to three months provided no major re-zoning is contemplated. City inspectors will visit the project during construction and will issue reports stating deviations from the codes. A final city permit will be issued upon final completion of the project.

CONSTRUCTION COST DATA

Cost of labour

The figures below are typical of labour costs in the Montreal area of Quebec, as at the first quarter 1993. The wage rate is the basis of an employee's income, while the cost of labour indicates the cost to a contractor of employing that employee. The difference between the two covers a variety of mandatory and voluntary contributions - a list of items which could be included is given in section 2.

	Wage rate (per hour) C$	Cost of labour (per hour) C$	Number of hours worked per year
Site operatives			
Mason/bricklayer	23.12	32.44	1,856
Carpenter	22.67	31.87	1,856
Plumber	23.78	32.99	1,856
Electrician	23.78	33.43	1,856
Structural steel erector	23.78	36.05	1,856
HVAC installer	23.78	32.41	1,856
Semi-skilled worker	18.47	26.48	1,856
Unskilled labourer	17.91	25.77	1,856
Equipment operator	21.22	30.01	1,856
	(per week)	*(per week)*	
Watchman/security	585.00	899.40	1,856
Site supervision			
General foreman	1,100	1,375	1,856
Trades foreman	950	1,190	1,856
	(per month)	*(per month)*	
Clerk of works	2,500	3,100	1,856
Contractors' personnel			
Site manager	5,000	6,250	1,740
Resident engineer	4,200	5,250	1,740
Resident surveyor	3,300	4,125	1,740
Junior engineer	2,900	3,625	1,740
Junior surveyor	2,500	3,100	1,740
Planner	3,300	4,125	1,740
Consultant personnel			
Senior architect	6,700	8,375	1,740
Senior engineer	5,400	6,750	1,740
Senior surveyor	5,000	6,250	1,740
Qualified architect	4,200	5,250	1,740
Qualified engineer	4,200	5,250	1,740
Qualified surveyor	4,200	5,250	1,740

Cost of materials

The figures that follow are the costs of main construction materials, delivered to site in the Montreal area, as incurred by contractors in the first quarter 1993. These assume that the materials would be in quantities as required for a medium sized construction project and that the location of the works would be neither constrained nor remote.

All the rates in this section exclude sales tax (see below).

	Unit	Cost C$
Cement and aggregate		
Ordinary portland cement in 40kg bags	tonne	121.50
Coarse aggregates for concrete	tonne	9.00
Fine aggregates for concrete	tonne	9.00
Ready mixed concrete (mix 30)	m^3	85.51
Ready mixed concrete (mix 20)	m^3	80.89
Steel		
Mild steel reinforcement	tonne	600.00
High tensile steel reinforcement	tonne	650.00
Structural steel sections	tonne	800.00
Bricks and blocks		
Common bricks (200 x 100 x 75mm)	1,000	125.00
Good quality facing bricks (200 x 100 x 75mm)	1,000	550.00
Hollow concrete blocks (400 x 200 x 200mm)	1,000	1,500.00
Solid concrete blocks (400 x 200 x 100mm)	1,000	850.00
Precast concrete cladding units with exposed aggregate finish	m^2	140.00
Timber and insulation		
Softwood for carpentery	m^3	227.50
Softwood for joinery	m^3	910.00
Hardwood for joinery	m^3	1,365.00
Exterior quality plywood (12mm)	m^2	6.75
Plywood for interior joinery (12mm)	m^2	15.13
Softwood strip flooring (12mm)	m^2	43.00
Chipboard sheet flooring (12mm)	m^2	2.35
100mm thick quilt insulation	m^2	2.65
100mm thick rigid slab insulation	m^2	21.00
Softwood internal door complete with frames and ironmongery	each	350.00
Glass and ceramics		
Float glass (5mm)	m^2	45.00
Sealed double glazing units (22mm)	m^2	150.00
Plaster and paint		
Good quality ceramic wall tiles (100 x 100mm)	m^2	30.00
Plaster in 50kg bags	tonne	240.00
Plasterboard (12mm thick)	m^2	2.00
Emulsion paint in 5 litre tins	litre	8.00
Gloss oil paint in 5 litre tins	litre	9.00
Tiles and paviors		
Clay floor tiles (200 x 200 x 12mm)	m^2	60.00
Vinyl floor tiles (300 x 300 x 3mm)	m^2	5.00

	Unit	Cost C$
Precast concrete paving slabs (300 x 300 x 38mm)	m²	32.00
Clay roof tiles	1,000	3,000.00
Precast concrete roof tiles	1,000	800.00

Drainage

	Unit	Cost C$
WC suite complete	each	250.00
Lavatory basin complete	each	100.00
100mm diameter clay drain pipes	m	4.00
150mm diameter cast iron drain pipes	m	21.00

Unit rates

The descriptions below are generally shortened versions of standard descriptions listed in full in section 4. Where an item has a two digit reference number (e.g. 05 or 33), this relates to the full description against that number in section 4. Where an item has an alphabetic suffix (e.g. 12A or 34B) this indicates that the standard description has been modified. Where a modification is major the complete modified description is included here and the standard description should be ignored; where a modification is minor (e.g. the insertion of a named hardwood) the shortened description has been modified here but, in general, the full description in section 4 prevails.

The unit rates below are for main work items on a typical construction project in the Montreal area in the first quarter 1993. The rates include all necessary labour, materials, equipment and allowances to cover preliminary and general items and contractors' overheads and profit. All the rates in this section exclude sales tax (see below).

		Unit	Rate C$
Excavation			
01	Mechanical excavation of foundation trenches	m³	8.50
02	Hardcore filling making up levels	m²	14.50
03	Earthwork support	m²	16.20
Concrete work			
04	Plain insitu concrete in strip foundations in trenches	m³	53.00
05	Reinforced insitu concrete in beds	m³	96.00
06	Reinforced insitu concrete in walls	m³	96.00
07	Reinforced insitu concrete in suspended floor or roof slabs	m³	98.00
08	Reinforced insitu concrete in columns	m³	105.00
09	Reinforced insitu concrete in isolated beams	m³	105.00
10	Precast concrete slab	m²	76.80

		Unit	Rate C$
Formwork			
11	Softwood or metal formwork to concrete walls	m²	32.00
12	Softwood or metal formwork to concrete columns	m²	60.00
13	Softwood or metal formwork to horizontal soffits of slabs	m²	33.48
Reinforcement			
14	Reinforcement in concrete walls	tonne	1,000.00
15	Reinforcement in suspended concrete slabs	tonne	920.00
16	Fabric reinforcement in concrete beds	m²	5.94
Steelwork			
17	Fabricate, supply and erect steel framed structure	tonne	1,700.00
Brickwork and blockwork			
18	Precast lightweight aggregate hollow concrete block walls	m²	70.20
19	Solid (perforated) concrete blocks	m²	88.00
20	Sand lime bricks	m²	91.00
21	Facing bricks	m²	93.96
Roofing			
22	Concrete interlocking roof tiles 430 x 380mm	m²	38.00
23	Plain clay roof tiles 260 x 160mm	m²	48.40
24	Fibre cement roof slates 600 x 300mm	m²	31.00
25	Sawn softwood roof boarding	m²	13.00
26	Particle board roof coverings	m²	4.10
27	3 layers glass-fibre based bitumen felt roof covering	m²	38.88
28	Bitumen based mastic asphalt roof covering	m²	27.70
29	Glass-fibre mat roof insulation 100mm thick	m²	23.76
30	Rigid sheet loadbearing roof insulation 75mm thick	m²	16.20
31	Troughed galvanized steel roof cladding	m²	35.00
Woodwork and metalwork			
32	Preservative treated sawn softwood 50 x 100mm	m	7.40
33	Preservative treated sawn softwood 50 x 150mm	m	3.13
34A	Single glazed casement window in hardwood, size 650 x 900mm	each	220.00
35A	Two panel glazed door in hardwood, size 850 x 2000mm	each	1,400.00
36	Solid core half hour fire resisting hardwood internal flush doors, size 800 x 2000m	each	410.00
37	Aluminium double glazed window, size 1200 x 1200mm	each	342.00
38	Aluminium double glazed door, size 850 x 2100mm	each	1,400.00
39A	Hardwood skirtings	m	8.20
40	Framed structural steelwork in universal joist sections	tonne	1,600.00
41	Structural steelwork lattice roof trusses	tonne	1,720.00

		Unit	Rate C$
Plumbing			
42	UPVC half round eaves gutter	m	10.10
43	UPVC rainwater pipes	m	11.35
44	Light gauge copper cold water tubing	m	31.83
45	High pressure plastic pipes for cold water supply	m	23.80
46	Low pressure plastic pipes for cold water distribution	m	19.30
47	UPVC soil and vent pipes	m	27.10
48	White vitreous china WC suite	each	420.16
49	White vitreous china lavatory basin	each	247.18
50	Glazed fireclay shower tray	each	710.28
51	Stainless steel single bowl sink and double drainer	each	376.35
Electrical work			
52	PVC insulated and copper sheathed cable	m	8.10
53	13 amp unswitched socket outlet	each	60.00
54	Flush mounted 20 amp, 1 way light switch	each	45.00
Finishings			
55	2 coats gypsum based plaster on brick walls	m^2	33.00
56	White glazed tiles on plaster walls	m^2	70.20
57	Red clay quarry tiles on concrete floor	m^2	81.00
58	Cement and sand screed to concrete floors	m^2	29.00
59	Thermoplastic floor tiles on screed	m^2	27.00
60	Mineral fibre tiles on concealed suspension system	m^2	19.44
Glazing			
61	Glazing to wood	m^2	88.00
Painting			
62A	Latex on plaster walls	m^2	4.32
63	Oil paint on timber	m^2	4.90

Approximate estimating

The building costs per unit area given below are averages incurred by building clients for typical buildings in the Montreal area as at the first quarter 1993. They are based upon the total floor area of all storeys, measured between external walls and without deduction for internal walls.

Approximate estimating costs generally include mechanical and electrical installations but exclude furniture, loose or special equipment, and external works; they also exclude fees for professional services. The costs shown are for specifications and standards appropriate to Canada and this should be borne in mind when attempting comparisons with similarly described building types in other countries. A discussion of this issue is included in section 2. Comparative data for countries covered in this publication, including construction cost data, is presented in Part Three.

Approximate estimating costs must be treated with caution; they cannot provide more than a rough guide to the probable cost of building. All the rates in this section exclude sales tax (see below).

	Cost m² C$	Cost ft² C$
Industrial buildings		
Warehouses for letting	269	25
Warehouse for owner occupation (light industrial use)	336	31
Warehouse for owner occupation (heavy industrial use)	529	49
Warehouse/office (high-tech) for letting (shell and core only)	307	29
Warehouse/office (high-tech) for letting (ground floor shell, first floor offices)	433	40
Warehouse/office (high tech) for owner occupation (controlled environment, fully finished)	461	43
High tech laboratory workshop centres (air conditioned)	1,202	112
Warehouses, low bay (6 to 8m high) for letting (no heating)	231	21
Warehouses, low bay for owner occupation (including heating)	269	25
Warehouses, high bay for owner occupation (including heating)	336	31
Cold stores/refrigerated stores	320	30
Administrative and commercial buildings		
Civic offices, non air conditioned	529	49
Civic offices, fully air conditioned	625	58
Offices for letting, 5 to 10 storeys, non air conditioned	577	54
Offices for letting, 5 to 10 storeys, air conditioned	625	58
Offices for letting, high rise, air conditioned	769	71
Offices for owner occupation 5 to 10 storeys, non air conditioned	721	67
Offices for owner occupation 5 to 10 storeys, air conditioned	757	70
Offices for owner occupation high rise, air conditioned	837	78
Prestige/headquarters office, 5 to 10 storeys, air conditioned	817	76
Prestige/headquarters office, high rise, air conditioned	921	86
Health and education buildings		
General hospitals (200 beds)	1,298	121
Teaching hospitals (30 beds)	1,057	98
Private hospitals (100 beds)	1,371	127
Health centres	801	74
Nursery schools	721	67
Primary/junior schools	596	55
Secondary/middle schools	614	57
University (arts) buildings	776	72
University (science) buildings	1,184	107
Management training centres	774	72

	Cost m^2 C$	Cost ft^2 C$
Recreation and arts buildings		
Theatres (over 500 seats) including seating and stage equipment	1,291	120
Theatres (less than 500 seats) including seating and stage equipment	1,380	128
Concert halls including seating and stage equipment	1,655	154
Sports halls including changing and social facilities	913	85
Swimming pools (international standard) including changing facilities	1,175	109
Swimming pools (schools standard) including changing facilities	1,068	99
National museums including full air conditioning and standby generator	1,771	165
Local museums including air conditioning	1,602	149
City centre/central libraries	1,157	98
Branch/local libraries	1,009	94
Residential buildings		
Social/economic single family housing (multiple units)	336	31
Private/mass market single family housing 2 storey detached/semidetached (multiple units)	384	36
Purpose designed single family housing 2 storey detached (single unit)	625	58
Social/economic apartment housing, low rise (no lifts)	529	49
Social/economic apartment housing, high rise (with lifts)	625	58
Private sector apartment building (standard specification)	653	61
Private sector apartment buildings (luxury)	749	70
Student/nurses halls of residence	673	63
Homes for the elderly (shared accommodation)	625	58
Homes for the elderly (self contained with shared communal facilities)	653	61
Hotel, 5 star, city centre	1,059	98
Hotel, 3 star, city/provincial	817	76
Motel	623	58

Sales tax

There is a general sales tax (GST) of 7% and in addition in Quebec a public services tax (PST) of 4%. There are also regional sales taxes varying from zero in Alberta to 11% in Newfoundland. These are accounted for in the following regional variations.

Regional variations

The approximate estimating costs are based on national average costs. Adjust these costs by the following factors for regional variations (including regional sales taxes):

Montreal	:	0%
Quebec	:	1%
Toronto	:	15%
Halifax	:	-3%
Vancouver	:	7%
Edmonton	:	0%
Calgary	:	1%
St Johns	:	16%
Winnipeg	:	0%

EXCHANGE RATES AND INFLATION

The combined effect of exchange rates and inflation on prices within a country and price comparisons between countries is discussed in section 2.

Exchange rates

The graph overleaf plots the movement of the Canadian dollar against sterling, the US dollar and the Japanese yen since 1980. The figures used for the graph are quarterly and the method of calculating these, and other related issues, are discussed in section 2. The exchange rate at the first quarter 1993 was C$1.88 to the pound sterling and C$1.27 to the US dollar and CS1.03 to 100 Japanese yen.

Price inflation

The table overleaf presents general price, non-residential building cost and industrial average price inflation in Canada since 1980. All three are similar.

THE CANADIAN DOLLAR AGAINST STERLING, THE US DOLLAR
AND THE JAPANESE YEN

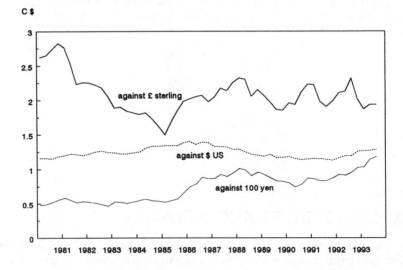

CONSUMER PRICE AND BUILDING COST AND PRICE INFLATION

Year	Consumer price inflation average index	average change %	Construction price index non-residential average index	average change %	Construction price index industrial average index	average change %
1980	100		100		100	
1981	113	13.0	109	9.0	110	10.0
1982	125	10.6	119	9.2	120	9.1
1983	132	5.6	127	6.7	128	6.7
1984	138	4.5	134	5.5	135	5.5
1985	143	3.6	140	4.5	142	5.2
1986	149	4.2	146	4.3	148	4.2
1987	n.a.		152	4.1	156	5.4
1988	n.a.		159	4.6	163	4.5
1989	n.a.		166	4.4	170	4.3
1990	178		175	5.4	179	5.3
1991	188	5.6	181	3.4	185	3.4
1992	191	1.6	187	3.3	192	3.8

USEFUL ADDRESSES

Public Organizations

Government of Canada
    Public Works Canada
    200 René-Lévesque
    Montreal (Quebec) H2Z 1X4
    Tel: (514) 496 3700
    Fax: (514) 396 3722

Trade and Professional Associations

Royal Architectural Institute of Canada (RAIC)
    328 Somerset St W
    Ottawa (Ontario) K2P 0JP
    Tel: (613) 232 7165

Canadian Construction Association (CCA)
    2nd Floor, 85 Albert Street
    Ottawa (Ontario) K1P 6A4
    Tel: (613) 236 9455

The Association of Consulting Engineers of Canada
    130 Albert Street, # 616
    Ottawa (Ontario) K1P 5G4
    Tel: (613) 236 0569

Canadian Council of Professional Engineers
    116 Albert St, # 401
    Ottawa (Ontario) K1P 5G3
    Tel: (613) 232 2474

Canadian Institute of Quantity Surveyors
    Box 124 Station Road
    Toronto (Ontario) M4G 3Z3
    Tel: (416) 731 3800

Standards Council of Canada
    International Standardisation Branch
    2000 Argentia Road, Suite 2-401
    Mississauga
    Ontario

Association Committee on the National Building Code
    National Research Council of Canada
    Ottawa (Ontario) K1A 0R6

Canadian Real Estate Association
  99 Duncan Mill Road, # 1400
  Don Mills (Ontario) M3B 1Z2
  Tel: (416) 445 9910

Institute of Surveying
  512 Rochester Street
  Ottawa (Ontario) K15 4L9

Statistics Canada
  Ottawa (Ontario) K1A 0T6
  Tel: (613) 992 4734

In China:

DAVIS LANGDON & SEAH CHINA LTD
SHANGHAI GENIUS QUANTITY SURVEYING LTD

The strategic and integrated management of cost, time and quality - the client "risk" areas of a contract - are essential functions, which are necessary to ensure the satisfactory planning, procurement, execution and operation of construction projects.

We specialise in the financial management of construction projects and their risk areas, from project inception to completion and we concentrate on:

* being positive and creative in our advice, rather than simply reactive;

* providing value for money via efficient management, rather than on superficial cost monitoring;

* giving advice that is matched to the Client's requirements, rather than imposing standard or traditional solutions;

* paying attention to the life-cycle costs of constructing and occupying a building, rather than to the initial capital cost only.

Our aim is to provide our clients with risk assurance, cost control and value for money, via effective advice, cost planning and management.

DAVIS LANGDON & SEAH CHINA LTD
Shanghai Representative Office
2203 Shartex Plaza
88 Zhun Yi Nan Road
Shanghai 200335, China
Tel : (010 8621)219 1107
Fax : (010 8621) 219 3680

SHANGHAI GENIUS QUANTITY SURVEYING LTD
1111 Yan An Road (M)
Shanghai
China
Tel : (010 8621) 2477149 ext 329
Fax : (010 8621) 3291790

DAVIS LANGDON & SEAH INTERNATIONAL

MANAGE AND LIMIT CLIENT RISK - ADDING VALUE

People's Republic of China

KEY DATA

Population

Population	1,158.2m
Urban population	26%
Population under 15	27%
Population over 65	6%
Growth rate (1991)	1.4%

Geography

Land area	9,600,000 km²
Agricultural area	42%
Capital city (1990)	Beijing
	(population 10.8m)

Economy

Monetary unit	Renminbi (Rmb)
	also known as yuan
Exchange rate (average first quarter 1993) to:	
the pound sterling	Rmb 8.59
the US dollar	Rmb 5.79
the yen x 100	Rmb 4.71
Average annual inflation (1980 to 1990)	9%
Inflation rate	10%
Gross National Product (GNP) (1991)	Rmb 1,985bn
GNP per capita (1991)	Rmb 1,725
Real Gross Domestic Product (GDP)	
growth (1980 to 1990)	9.5%
Private consumption as a proportion of GDP	49%
Public consumption as a proportion of GDP	8%
Investment as a proportion of GDP	39%

Construction

Gross value of construction output	Rmb 385bn
Net value of construction output	Rmb 114.2bn
Net construction output per capita	Rmb 100
Net construction output as a	
proportion of GNP	6.5%

Note: All data relate to 1990 unless otherwise indicated.

THE CONSTRUCTION INDUSTRY

Construction output

There are three main measures of national production in the People's Republic of China (PRC):

1. Gross Social Product (sum total of gross output of five sectors of which construction is one and involves some double counting).
2. National Income or Net Material Product (value added of the five sectors).
3. Gross National Product (value added of both 'productive' sectors and non-productive or service sectors plus net exports).

Housing is classified as non-productive as are some other social and cultural buildings.

The 1990 figures for the total economy and for construction are:

MEASURES OF NATIONAL PRODUCTION AND CONSTRUCTION IN THE PRC

Measures of production	Total Rmb bn current prices	Construction Rmb bn current prices
Gross Social Product	3,799.6	300.9
National Income	1,442.9	82.2
Gross National Product	1,768.6	114.2*

*   estimate based on productive construction being 72% of total construction output. See following table.

Source: based on Economist Intelligence Unit Country Profiles and Reports

The nearest equivalent to net value of output of construction is that used for the measure of Gross National Product (GNP) at Rmb 114.2 billion equivalent at the official exchange rate to US$239 million. This represents 6.5% of GNP. However, although the gross value of output is probably Rmb 300 billion plus say Rmb 85 billion for non-productive products (Rmb 385 billion), this cannot be related to Gross Social Product in a meaningful way because this total includes double counting. In fact the gross output is probably about 22% of total GNP. Construction includes much of the production plant and equipment installed in buildings.

It is believed, however, that all the statistics measuring production are grossly understated though the relationship between construction and national income may not be too far out. It seems that the standard of living in the PRC is higher than the national income would indicate partly because the rate of exchange to the dollar and other currencies bears little relationship to purchasing power. Because of excess demand for construction work and for investment funds, government has restricted non-productive construction. It has fallen from nearly 40% of the total in 1984, and even 38% in 1989, to 28% in 1990. The figures for selected years are as follows:

IMPORTANCE OF VARIOUS CATEGORIES OF CONSTRUCTION
IN THE PRC, 1985 TO 1990

Categories of construction	1985 %	1987 %	1989 %	1990 %
Productive construction e.g. factories	61	63	62	72
Non-productive construction	39	37	38	28
- of which residential	(25)	(24)	(26)	n.a.
Total	100	100	100	100

Source: based on Economist Intelligence Unit Country Profile

New works constituted 94.1% of the total work, building maintenance 2.6%, manufacturing of pre-fabricated products (fully or semi fabricated) 2.3%; research, geological investigation and surveying and design constituted 0.1%.

The gross floor area under construction in 1990 was 232 million m² (inclusive of 92 million m² or 40% for residential purposes) and the gross floor area practically completed was 112 million m² (inclusive of 48 million m² or 43%, for residential purposes).

Later figures are not available because the PRC is slow to produce statistics but the indications are that since then construction has been booming. Growth in GDP has been high, 7% in 1991 and probably around 13% in 1992 and consumer spending has been rising rapidly. Construction has been buoyant in rural and urban housing, tourism, education, energy, transport and the industrial Special Enterprise Zones (see below). Housing targets for the future are ambitious. The rate of house construction is planned to double to create 200 million m² per annum.

Special Enterprise Zones are islands of capitalism. The first at Shenzhen - just over the border from Hong Kong - was established in 1979 followed by three others in the southern PRC. In particular, the zones are intended to be areas for foreign investment through joint ventures. Special arrangements exist regarding taxation, import levies and incentives to foreign investment. The impact of the zones has now spread to the entire Pearl River delta in southern Guangdong (Canton) province. This is Asia's fastest growing economy with 13% to 15% growth last year. This is generating an increasing demand for construction for which Hong Kong is well placed to respond not only because of its geographical position but also because Cantonese, the language of Hong Kong, is also spoken in the south of China. There are also many Mandarin speakers which is both the official and written language in the region.

The regional distribution of construction output and of population in 1987 is shown in the table on the next page. (For a map see page 2) Apart from Beijing, the regions of high construction compared to population are coastal areas - east of Beijing, Liaoning and Tianjin, round Shanghai and in the South, at Guangdong. The current developments in Guangdong will put it higher in the construction per capita figures than was recorded in 1987. Indeed almost all the major growth areas of the PRC are on the coast. Fourteen coastal cities have been designated for investment of which Dahan, Tianjin, Shanghai and Guangzhou have been selected for priority in funding. Increased autonomy in these four cities has also helped account for over 60% of industrial and other enterprise in the coastal areas. However, now the Government of the PRC helped by the United Nations Industrial Development Organization (UNIDO) is currently assisting in the development of inland areas in the North West of the PRC. Investment in infrastructure has already taken place. Preferential policies to encourage foreign investment there have been instituted or are under consideration by the State Council.

The most important regions are Jiansu, Shandong, Guangdong, Sichuan and Liaoning, but both Beijing and Shanghai have a much higher share of construction output than of population, as would be expected for a metropolitan area.

Characteristics and structure of the industry

The table below shows the main types of construction enterprises and their employment in 1990.

CONSTRUCTION ENTERPRISES AND EMPLOYMENT, PRC, 1990

Type of construction enterprise	Enterprise numbers	Employment thousands	Average employment number
State-owned	4,275	6,210	1,453
Urban collective-owned	9,052	3,897	431
Rural construction teams	60,818	7,060	116
Total	74,145	17,167	232

Source: based on China Statistical Yearbook

POPULATION AND VALUE OF CONSTRUCTION OUTPUT BY REGION, PRC, 1990

Region	Percentage of population	Percentage of construction output	Rank by population	Rank by construction output
Beijing	1.0	8.6	25	3
Tianjin	0.8	1.7	26	22
Hebei	5.4	4.2	7	8
Shanxi	2.5	2.1	19	17
Inner Mongolia	1.9	2.5	22	13
Liaoning	3.5	11.3	12	1
Jilin	2.2	3.2	20	11
Heilongjiang	3.1	5.4	15	7
Shanghai	1.2	5.5	24	6
Jiangsu	5.9	5.7	4	5
Zhejiang	3.7	4.2	10	9
Anhui	5.0	2.0	8	17
Fujian	2.7	2.0	18	18
Jiangxi	3.3	1.8	13	21
Shandong	7.4	3.8	3	10
Henan	7.6	2.2	2	15
Hebei	4.8	2.9	9	12
Hunan	5.4	2.5	6	13
Guangdong	5.5	11.1	5	2
Guangxi	3.7	1.7	11	29
Hainan	0.6	0.7	27	27
Sichuan	9.5	6.2	1	4
Guizhou	2.9	1.1	16	27
Yannan	3.3	1.7	13	22
Tibet	0.2	0.2	30	29
Shaanxi	2.9	1.6	16	16
Gansu	2.0	1.4	21	26
Qinghai	0.4	0.6	28	29
Ningxia	0.4	0.7	28	28
Xinjiang	1.3	1.6	23	25

Source: Based on China Statistical Yearbook

State-owned enterprises consist of local Units (effectively construction companies) spread throughout the country and account for 59% of the work done by the state: the Ministry of Affiliated Units undertakes the remaining 41%. The most important ministries for construction output (which may include plant and machinery) are the Ministry of Energy Resources and the Ministry of Railways (which together account for 63% of the work), plus the Ministries of Metallurgical Industry and Communications, and the China State Construction Engineering Corporation. State enterprises also do some geotechnical investigation, surveying and design both in the local Units and in the Ministries. Government departments act both as developers and contractors.

The China State Construction Engineering Corporation (CSCEC) is the nearest equivalent that the PRC has to a construction company on the western model. It employs about 1.5 million persons of whom 150,000 are administrative and professional staff. It is organized into eight construction companies and undertakes large projects all over the country. It also has an overseas division which has been involved in 400 projects in 50 countries. This company undertakes the majority of the overseas construction work of the PRC. In 1991 it was ranked 60 in the Engineering News Record's (ENR) list of 225 international contractors - its total contracts were given as US$1,162.5 million of which US$492.9 were foreign. Other Chinese contracting organizations in the ENR's list are the China Metallurgical Construction Group (ranked 96) also with a turnover of over a billion US$ but only US$212 million abroad, the China Road and Bridge Corporation (ranked 141) and the China International Water and Electrical Corp (ranked 188).

Within the state enterprises three main parties are involved in the construction industry: the Development Unit, the Design Unit and the Construction Unit. The Development Unit is the project developer, and is responsible for initiating a project, organizing the team members and making sure that the project is satisfactorily completed. The Design Unit prepares conceptual and detail drawings, and supervises construction of the project. The Construction Unit carries out the construction work with, usually, separate construction units for specialist work such as mechanical and electrical installations. It is similar to a main contractor, though the contracts between the various parties are usually simple, setting out the benefits, duties and obligations of the various units.

Contractors are licensed and classified into four categories on the basis of fixed assets, expertise and previous experience. Apart from the national contractors, they normally work locally in their region and must obtain permission to go outside that region. All contractors have to register with their Local Construction Commission. Only the state authorities can give permission to work abroad.

Joint ventures

Increasingly, projects are carried out as joint ventures with foreigners, in particular firms from Hong Kong. The law on joint ventures was introduced in 1979, since when the PRC has had an open door policy towards foreign investment and gives preference to foreign investors.

Expatriate construction and professional personnel operate in the PRC under the general laws that govern foreign investment. Participation in joint ventures has the advantage to Chinese partners that modern equipment can be imported tax free.

Although there is no shortage of labour in the PRC, the domestic construction industry is hampered by a lack of modern know-how and engineering ability and is therefore anxious to acquire skills from abroad. It is this deficiency that has created a niche for international contractors and specialist subcontractors in the PRC. Foreign construction involvement, however, tends to be limited to the provision of the design and construction management techniques required for complex projects plus technology transfer connected with the installation of sophisticated plant and machinery. The construction work itself is invariably carried out by domestic contractors. The state is involved in all contracts, though this can be at a variety of levels, depending upon the nature of the project. Large projects usually result in a foreign contractor contracting directly with a national or provincial organization. However, the majority of foreign investment in the PRC is carried out using co-operative joint ventures. Essentially, these consist of agreements between State bodies - professional units, tourist corporations, etc., whereby the Chinese party usually provides resources such as land and labour whilst the foreign party provides capital, advanced technology and key equipment. The joint venture parties agree to co-operate for a period of years after which the whole of the enterprise will come under Chinese ownership.

Contractors may become involved in joint venture projects in one of two ways, either as the foreign party to the joint venture or as a contractor employed by the joint venture to construct the project. The first involves a long-term commitment that goes beyond simple contracting. The second is the most common, and the contractor is likely to find that his negotiations are largely with the foreign party to the joint venture as it is often that party's obligation to provide the management contractor and the finance to pay him. However, the final contract will have to be approved and registered with the State. The *China Investment Guide* (4th edition, 1989) gives comprehensive information on joint ventures.

Basic building materials are available in the PRC but many finishing materials and engineering and mechanical systems have to be imported. Material production has not always kept up with the increase in demand and shortages have occurred. To meet demand, even some basic materials have sometimes to be imported. The PRC is a vast country and delays in the delivery of building materials due to transport difficulties are common. The State no longer controls the supply of materials by stockpiling them in each region; instead they are sent direct to the construction unit that contracts for a project.

Clients and finance

Of the 1990 capital investment in construction 21% is funded from state budgets, 31% is self-financed, 22% is from bank loans, 13% from foreign capital and the remaining 13% from other sources.

In 1990, 24% of total government capital spending was on construction. The market for constructing by joint ventures was Rmb 14 billion (US$2.5 billion) in 1988. In the mid 1980s the boom in non-government work led to a shortage of building materials and to higher prices. Restrictions on extra-budgetary projects were introduced and access to loans limited.

However, joint venture companies comprising a partner from the PRC and one or more foreign partners are now responsible for a large proportion of development in the PRC. The usual arrangement is for the PRC to provide the land whilst finance and technical expertise come from the foreign partner.

The Construction Bank of China is responsible for providing funds to the various construction departments or units. The State allocates a total sum to the Bank which will in turn issue it to the departments or units as required. Savings achieved as a result of better efficiency or shorter construction periods may be retained by the construction department while any extra cost due to delays must be repaid.

Funds for extra-budgetary projects must now be placed with the Construction Bank for six months before they can be used. Non-productive (e.g. housing and social projects) outside the State Plan are subject to a special 30% tax and in practice it is difficult to get approval of funds. Priority is given to key construction projects. In spite of these and other moves to control projects there is still a major increase in investment.

Selection of design consultants

It is compulsory for a foreign design consultant to work together with a local design institute because only the latter can provide the authorized person required for the submission of drawings to the local authority for approval. In addition to this, local knowledge of their staff is invaluable. A joint venture company, therefore, can have its design completed by one of the following arrangements:

* the employment of a local PRC design institute
* the employment of a foreign design consultant working with a PRC design institute or vice versa
* the employment of a JV design consultant.

The selection of a foreign design consultant is based on the same criteria as in other parts of the world. Similar criteria are used when selecting a local PRC design institute. There is a wide variation in the size, scope and abilities of design institutes. Most of them are involved mainly in local projects and have no experience of working with foreigners.

According to the Standards of Qualification Grouping of Design Institutes for Building and Civil Engineering Works promulgated in 1986, design institutes are divided into integrated or specialized institutes. Integrated ones cover all aspects of design including structural, mechanical and electrical engineering. Specialized units only undertake one or a limited number of aspects.

Design institutes are allocated to one of four classifications (see table on page 76), Class A being the highest of these. Institutes belonging to this class are authorized to work on any PRC project, no matter how complex that project might be, whereas class B institutes are able to work not only in their own region but outside of it. The smaller design institutes belong to classes C and D. Strict minimum qualifications and numbers of staff are laid down for each category. Class A for example must have at least five lead architects, five structural engineers and three other specialized designers of university or college standard with at least five years experience on major projects. Fifty per cent of their designers must be university or college trained with a minimum of five years experience. They will be working with sophisticated equipment. For Class B there must be at least three lead architects and the qualifications and experience can be slightly less. Only 40% of the staff of Class B must have university or college education and five years experience. Classes C and D may be at a lower level of qualification and experience. The table overleaf shows which projects each of the four classes is authorized to undertake. Some institutes are permitted to work on both building and civil engineering projects, whereas others are limited to one or the other.

Local institutes in the PRC have a good knowledge of structural design and civil engineering, but benefit from guidance in technological advances in the industry and the use of imported materials. In recent years they have started to make advances in these fields.

Many foreign firms have forged good working relationships with particular institutes, but should a developer need a suitable local connection, advice may be required on which one is most suitable for his needs.

Contractual arrangements

In 1984, the Sixth National People's Congress in Beijing called for shorter construction durations, and improved quality. In order to encourage competition and to prevent monopolies, open tendering was introduced. Construction and design units from all over the PRC can now bid for projects previously not available to them. The result is reported to be a reduction in construction costs. Now, open tendering is being practised in most areas of the PRC. Administrative procedures and the PRC regulations regarding tendering have been set. Negotiation occurs very frequently during the tendering period.

The involvement of American, European and Japanese companies, banks, architects and contractors has led to a great diversity in the way construction contracts are structured. There are no standard forms of contract and varieties of American, British and international forms such as FIDIC (*Fédération Internationale des Ingénieurs Conseils*), often substantially amended, are in use. All contracts have to be translated into Chinese and are generally expressed as subject to Chinese law though both versions are considered to be equally authentic for legal purposes. Usually the Chinese party prefers to sign a contract document in Chinese.

There are various government building regulations and specifications and the various provinces and cities have their own schedules of rates used for estimating and for valuing construction work. However, these

PROJECTS PERMITTED FOR GRADES OF DESIGN INSTITUTES

Public buildings	Residential buildings	Industrial buildings and warehouses	Other
Class A			
All types	All types	All types	All types
Class B			
High rise max height 50m grade 2 fireproofing	Max storeys 18	Single storey max span 30m max crane capacity 30 tons	Chimneys, water towers and tanks etc.
Single storey max span 30m		Multi storey max span 12m	
		Max storeys 6	
Class C			
Single storey max span 24m		High rise max height 24m	Medium chimneys, water towers, tanks, etc
		Single storey max span 24m max crane capacity 10 tons	
		Multi storey max span 9m max storeys 4	
Class D			
No basements	No basements	No basements	No basements
Framed buildings max span 7.5m max storeys 3	Houses, dormitories brick walls reinforced concrete floor max storeys 6	Single storey max span 15m max single beam crane capacity 5 tons	Medium and small chimneys, water towers, tanks, etc. with standardized drawings
Single storey max span 15m		Light buildings max span 75m max storeys 3	

max: maximum
min: minimum

rates might not be applicable directly to a joint-venture development depending on its type and location.

Development control and standards

Under Chinese law, all property is owned by the State. Individuals and companies are permitted to lease land under the concept of land use rights. In practical terms, the concept of land use rights granted for a specific period is very similar to a leasehold estate from the Crown in Hong Kong. Subject to payment of annual land use fees and observation of covenants in the grant contract, a holder of land use rights may exercise practically all the rights of an owner during the term of grant.

Under the Provisional Regulations of the People's Republic of China Concerning the Grant and Assignment of the Right to Use State Land in Urban Areas (*Urban Land Regulations*) promulgated in May 1990, the State may grant land use rights for a definite period of time and against payment of a grant premium. The grant of land use rights may be pursuant to a negotiated agreement, through the submission of tenders or by auction. Local governments at or above the county level may grant land. Their scope of authority varies in accordance with their position in the administrative hierarchy. However, the regulations set forth the maximum period of grant for different uses of land ranging from 40 years for commercial development and 50 years for industrial building and public facilities and mixed use to 70 years for residential development.

Under the Urban Land Regulations, land use rights which have been lawfully acquired will enjoy legal protection and the State generally may not resume possession prior to expiration of the term of grant. In the event that the public interest requires the resumption of possession by the State, compensation must be paid.

While the grant of land use rights for a premium implements the official policy of economic use of land, it is the ability of grantees to transfer land use rights through sale, exchange or gift which breathes real economic life into the system. The Urban Land Regulations require the registration of all transfers and the imposition of a certain degree of administrative market control. The government maintains the right to purchase if the transfer price is obviously below market price and the right to intervene if the market price rises unreasonably.

Assignment of land use rights from, or joint development with, current owners of land use rights are becoming more frequent. The Urban Land Regulations state that assignment or mortgage of allocated land in urban areas is subject to the approval of the relevant land and real estate departments. The relevant procedures are set forth in the Provisional Measures on the Management of Allocated Land Use Rights, promulgated on March 8 1992.

The PRC has a system of registration of title which is slowly recovering from chronic mismanagement. Most localities in the PRC still have two separate registration systems administered by separate departments, viz. one for land and one for buildings. Certificates issued following registration serve as legal evidence of ownership and other rights. However, it appears that their validity is not absolute. There have been cases where certificates have been successfully challenged in court and where certificates have been invalidated owing to corrupt practices or other irregularities at the time of issue.

Subject to the approval of the relevant real estate department, the sale of uncompleted buildings, known as pre-sale, is permitted. Standard pre-sale contracts and other documents must be submitted for approval. Contracts must be registered with the real estate registry.

A number of taxes and fees may be levied during the course of real estate development and on income derived from real estate development in the PRC. These include land use tax, turnover tax, income tax, real property tax, contract tax, stamp duty, transfer appreciation fee, registration fee, transaction fee and notarization fee.

CONSTRUCTION COST DATA

Cost of labour

The figures below are typical of labour costs in Guangdong Province as at the first quarter 1993. The wage rate is the basis of an employee's income, while the cost of labour indicates the cost to a foreign contractor of employing that employee. The difference between the two covers a variety of mandatory and voluntary contributions - a list of items which could be included is given in section 2.

	Wage rate (per month) Rmb	Cost of labour (per month) Rmb	Number of hours worked per year
Site operatives			
Mason/bricklayer	500 - 600	800	2,450
Carpenter	500 - 600	800	2,450
Plumber	500 - 600	800	2,450
Electrician	500 - 600	800	2,450
Structural steel erector	500 - 600	800	2,450
HVAC installer	500 - 600	800	2,450
Semi-skilled worker	200 - 300	500	2,450
Unskilled labourer	150 - 250	400	2,450
Equipment operator	500 - 600	800	2,450
Watchman/security	150 - 250	400	2,450
Site supervision			
General foreman	2,500 - 3,500		2,450
Trades foreman	1,500 - 2,500		2,450
Clerk of works	1,000 - 2,000		2,450
Contractors' personnel			
Site manager	2,500 - 3,500		2,450
Resident engineer	1,500 - 2,500		2,450

	Wage rate (per month) Rmb	Number of hours worked per year
Resident surveyor	1,500 - 2,500	2,450
Junior engineer	1,000 - 2,000	2,450
Junior surveyor	1,000 - 2,000	2,450
Planner	1,000 - 2,000	2,450
Consultants' personnel		
Senior architect	250 - 300	2,450
Senior engineer	250 - 300	2,450
Senior surveyor	250 - 300	2,450
Qualified architect	180 - 250	2,450
Qualified engineer	180 - 250	2,450
Qualified surveyor	180 - 250	2,450

Labour costs (for expatriates from Hong Kong, for example) incurred by joint venture developer are as follows.

	Wage rate (per day) HK$	Cost of labour (per day) HK$	Number of hours worked per year
Site operatives			
Mason/bricklayer	500 - 600	800 - 900	2,450
Carpenter	500 - 600	800 - 900	2,450
Plumber	500 - 600	800 - 900	2,450
Electrician	400 - 500	700 - 800	2,450
Structural steel erector	500 - 600	800 - 900	2,450
HVAC installer	450 - 550	780 - 850	2,450
Semi-skilled worker	300 - 400	550 - 650	2,450
Site supervision	*(per month)*		
General foreman	15,900 - 25,000		2,450
Trades foreman	10,000 - 20,000		2,450
Clerk of works	10,000 - 20,000		2,450
Contractors' personnel			
Site manager	20,000 - 30,000		2,450
Resident engineer	15,000 - 25,000		2,450
Resident surveyor	15,000 - 25,000		2,450
Junior engineer	10,000 - 20,000		2,450
Junior surveyor	10,000 - 20,000		2,450

	Wage rate (per day) HK$	Number of hours worked per year
Consultants' personnel		
Senior architect	40,000 - 50,000	2,200
Senior engineer	40,000 - 50,000	2,200
Senior surveyor	40,000 - 50,000	2,200
Qualified architect	25,000 - 35,000	2,200
Qualified engineer	25,000 - 35,000	2,200
Qualified surveyor	25,000 - 35,000	2,200

Labour cost is inclusive of overseas allowance, accommodation allowance, travelling expenses to and from Guangdong and profit and overheads (15%).

Cost of materials

The figures that follow are the costs of main construction materials, delivered to site in Guangdong Province, as incurred by contractors in the first quarter 1993. These assume that the materials would be in quantities as required for a medium sized construction project and that the location of the works would be neither constrained nor remote. All the costs in this section exclude tax (see below).

	Unit	Cost Rmb
Cement and aggregate		
Ordinary portland cement in 50kg bags	tonne	550
Coarse aggregates for concrete	tonne	90
Fine aggregates for concrete	tonne	50
Steel		
Mild steel reinforcement	tonne	3,700
High tensile steel reinforcement	tonne	3,800
Bricks and blocks		
Common bricks (240 x 115 x 53mm)	1,000	300
Good quality facing bricks (240 x 115 x 53mm)	1,000	350
Hollow concrete blocks	1,000	150
Precast concrete cladding units with exposed aggregate finish	m^2	550
Timber and insulation		
Softwood sections for carpentry	m^3	900
Softwood for joinery	m^3	1,500
Hardwood for joinery	m^3	1,300
Exterior quality plywood (18mm thick)	m^2	60
Plywood for interior joinery (12mm thick)	m^2	35
Hardwood strip flooring	m^2	120
100mm thick quilt insulation	m^2	150

	Unit	Cost Rmb
Hardwood internal door complete with frames and ironmongery	each	1,000

Glass and ceramics

	Unit	Cost Rmb
Float glass (4mm)	m^2	40
Sealed double glazing units	m^2	800

Plaster and paint

	Unit	Cost Rmb
Good quality ceramic wall tiles (152 x 152mm)	m^2	90
Plaster in 50kg bags	tonne	200
Plasterboard (12mm thick)	m^2	13
Emulsion paint in 5 litre tins	kg	5
Gloss oil paint in 5 litre tins	kg	10

Tiles and paviors

	Unit	Cost Rmb
Clay floor tiles (200 x 200 x 8mm)	m^2	50
Non-slip vinyl floor tiles (305 x 305 x 1.5mm)	m^2	20
Precast concrete paving slabs (490 x 490 x 40mm)	m^2	24
Clay roof tiles (200 x 500mm)	1,000	500
Precast concrete roof tiles (390 x 390 x 40mm)	1,000	3,800

Drainage

	Unit	Cost Rmb
WC suite complete	each	1,100
Lavatory basin complete	each	500
100mm diameter clay drain pipes (2500mm long)	m	100
150mm diameter cast iron drain pipes (1830mm long)	m	50

Unit rates

The descriptions below are generally shortened versions of standard descriptions listed in full in section 4. Where an item has a two digit reference number (e.g. 05 or 33), this relates to the full description against that number in section 4. Where an item has an alphabetic suffix (e.g. 12A or 34B) this indicates that the standard description has been modified. Where a modification is major the complete modified description is included here and the standard description should be ignored; where a modification is minor (e.g. the insertion of a named hardwood) the shortened description has been modified here but, in general, the full description in section 4 prevails.

The unit rates below are for main work items on a typical construction project in the Guangdong Province in the first quarter 1993. The rates include all necessary labour, materials, equipment and an allowance to cover preliminary and general items. Five per cent should be added to the rates to cover contractors' overheads and profit. All the rates in this section exclude tax (see below).

	Unit	Rate Rmb
Excavation		
01 Mechanical excavation of foundation trenches	m^3	11
02 Hardcore filling making up levels (150mm)	m^2	33
Concrete work		
04 Plain insitu concrete in strip foundations in trenches	m^3	450
05 Reinforced insitu concrete in beds	m^3	550
06 Reinforced insitu concrete in walls (200mm thick)	m^3	850
07 Reinforced insitu concrete in suspended floor or roof slabs	m^3	550
08 Reinforced insitu concrete in columns	m^3	550
09 Reinforced insitu concrete in isolated beams	m^3	550
10 Precast concrete slab	m^2	400
Formwork		
11 Softwood formwork to concrete walls	m^2	15
12 Softwood or metal formwork to concrete columns	m^2	20
13 Softwood or metal formwork to horizontal soffits of slabs	m^2	24
Reinforcement		
14 Reinforcement in concrete walls	tonne	4,500
15 Reinforcement in suspended concrete slabs	tonne	4,500
Steelwork		
17 Fabricate, supply and erect steel framed structure	tonne	12,500
Brickwork and blockwork		
21 Red brick wall (half brick thick)	m^2	50
21A Red brick wall (one brick thick)	m^2	75
Roofing		
22 Concrete interlocking roof tiles 490 x 490mm	m^2	30
27A Belt roof covering	m^2	55
Woodwork and metalwork		
32 Preservative treated sawn softwood 50 x 100mm	m	15
33 Preservative treated sawn softwood 50 x 150mm	m	20
35 Two panel glazed door in hardwood, size 850 x 2000mm	each	2,200
36 Solid core half hour fire resisting hardwood internal flush doors, size 800 x 2000mm	each	1,500
39 Hardwood skirtings	m	14
Plumbing		
44 Light gauge copper cold water tubing (20mm diameter)	m	100
Drainage		
48 White vitreous china WC suite	each	1,300
49 White vitreous china lavatory basin	each	600

	Unit	Rate Rmb
Electrical work		
52 PVC insulated and copper sheathed cable (4mm^2)	m	8
53 13 amp unswitched socket outlet	each	100
54 Flush mounted 20 amp, 1 way light switch	each	150
Finishings		
55 2 coats gypsum based plaster on brick walls	m^2	5
56 White glazed tiles on plaster walls	m^2	40
57 Red clay quarry tiles on concrete floor	m^2	60
59 Thermoplastic floor tiles on screed	m^2	55
60 Mineral fibre tiles on concealed suspension system	m^2	100
Glazing		
61 Glazing to wood	m^2	60
Painting		
62 Emulsion on plaster walls	m^2	5
63 Oil paint on timber	m^2	33

Approximate estimating

The building costs per unit area given below are expressed in US$ and are averages incurred by building clients for typical buildings in the Guangdong Province as at the first quarter 1993. They are based upon the total floor area of all storeys, measured between external walls and without deduction for internal walls.

Approximate estimating costs generally include mechanical and electrical installations but exclude furniture, loose or special equipment, and external works; they also exclude fees for professional services. The costs shown are for specifications and standards appropriate to China and this should be borne in mind when attempting comparisons with similarly described building types in other countries. A discussion of this issue is included in section 2. Comparative data for countries covered in this publication, including construction cost data, is presented in Part Three.

Approximate estimating costs must be treated with caution; they cannot provide more than a rough guide to the probable cost of building. All the rates in this section exclude tax (see below).

	Cost m^2 US$	Cost ft^2 US$
Administrative and commercial buildings		
Offices for letting, high rise, air conditioned	900	84
Prestige/headquarters office, high rise, air conditioned	1,200	110
Residential buildings		
Hotel, 5 star, city centre	1,500	140
Hotel, 3 star, city/provincial	1,100	102

Regional variations

The approximate estimating costs are based on projects in the Guangdong Province. For other parts of China, adjust these costs by the following factors:

> Beijing   +10%
> Shanghai   +5%

Tax

VAT is not applicable. The Consolidated Industrial and Commercial Tax (CICT) is currently 3.03%, chargeable on general building work.

EXCHANGE RATES AND INFLATION

The combined effect of exchange rates and inflation on prices within a country and price comparisons between countries is discussed in section 2.

Exchange rates

The graph opposite plots the movement of the renminbi against sterling, the US dollar and the Japanese yen since 1980. The figures used for the graph are quarterly and the method of calculating these and other related issues are discussed in section 2. The exchange rate at the first quarter 1993 was Rmb 8.59 to the pound sterling, Rmb 5.79 to the US dollar and Rmb 4.71 to 100 Japanese yen.

Consumer price inflation

The table opposite presents consumer price inflation in China since 1980.

THE CHINESE RENMINBI AGAINST STERLING, THE US DOLLAR
AND THE JAPANESE YEN

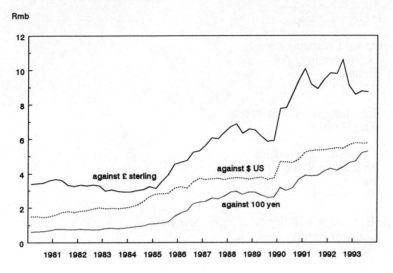

CONSUMER PRICE INFLATION

Year	Consumer price inflation average index	average change %
1980	100	
1981	102	2.0
1982	104	2.0
1983	106	1.9
1984	109	2.8
1985	118	8.3
1986	124	5.1
1987	135	8.9
1988	159	17.8
1989	188	18.2
1990	192	2.1

USEFUL ADDRESSES

Public Organizations

Ministry of Construction
Baiwanzhuang Av.
Beijing
Tel: 8992211

International Cooperation
Tel: 896927

State Planning Commission
38 Yuetan S. Street
Beijing
Tel: 868521

State Bureau of Building Materials Industry
Baiwanzhuang
Beijing
Tel: 8311144

Ministry of Foreign Economic Relations and Trade
Dong Chang Au Street
Beijing
Tel: 5126644

State Bureau of Standardization
Yuetan Beixiso Street
Beijing
Tel: 895148

Chinese Information Centre of Standardization
Rucheng Road
Beijing
Tel: 892236

Chinese Academy of Science (Construction Research)
Fuwai Sanlihe
Beijing
Tel: 868361

Chinese Construction Technology Development Research Centre
19 Donggongzhuang Ave
Beijing
Tel: 893289

Chinese Institute of Architectural Sciences
    Xiaohuangzhuang
    Beijing
    Tel: 4211133

Ministry of Construction, Urban Construction Research Institute
    Baiwanzhuang, North Building
    Beijing
    Tel: 8320626

Chinese Urban Planning Design Institute
    Baiwanzhuang,
    Beijing
    Tel: 8329944

Chinese Building Material Industry Planning Institute
    Xineibeishuncheng
    Beijing
    Tel: 6015877

Chinese Institute of Building Material Science
    Guanchuang
    Beijing
    Tel: 5761331

BJ Institute of Glass Fibre Reinforced Plastics
    State Bureau of Building Material Industry
    Yanqing County
    Beijing
    Tel: 334177/332872

Standardization Research Institute
    State Bureau of Building Material Industry
    Guanchoung
    Beijing
    Tel: 5762480

Institute of Geology Investigation
    Ministry of Construction
    177 Dongneidajai
    Beijing
    Tel: 4013366

Chinese Institute of Urban and Rural Construction and Economy
    Ministry of Construction
    Baiwanzhuang
    Beijing
    Tel: 8311336

State Bureau of Statistics
    38 Yuetan S Street
    Sanlihe
    Beijing
    Tel: 8322871

Trade and Professional Associations

Chinese Construction United Association
    Baiwanzhuang Av.
    Beijing
    Tel: 8319575

Chinese Overseas Contractors Association
    An Wai Donghouhang
    Beijing
    Tel: 4213959

Chinese Architectural Mechanization Association
    Baiwanzhuang
    Beijing
    Tel: 8327620

The Architectural Society of China
    W Suburbs
    Baiwanzhuang
    Beijing
    Tel: 8311585

China Exploration and Design Association
    Baiwanzhuang
    Beijing
    Tel: 8394207

China Civil Engineering Society
    Baiwanzhuang
    Beijing
    Tel: 8311313

Chinese Society of Mechanical Engineering
    Fuxingmenwai Sanlike
    Beijing
    Tel: 868441

Chinese Construction Enterprise Management Association
    Baiwanzhuang
    Beijing
    Tel: 8317693

State Bureau of Building Materials Industry
    Baiwanzhuang
    Beijing
    Tel: 8311144

State Bureau of Land Administration
    25 Daliushubeicun
    Beijing
    Tel: 8321166-3322

Chinese Property Development Corporation
    Haidianqu
    Beijing
    Tel: 8212079/8212077

In Hong Kong:

DAVIS LANGDON & SEAH HONG KONG LTD

The strategic and integrated management of cost, time and quality - the client "risk" areas of a contract - are essential functions, which are necessary to ensure the satisfactory planning, procurement, execution and operation of construction projects.

We specialise in the financial management of construction projects and their risk areas, from project inception to completion and we concentrate on:

*   being positive and creative in our advice, rather than simply reactive;

*   providing value for money via efficient management, rather than on superficial cost monitoring;

*   giving advice that is matched to the Client's requirements, rather than imposing standard or traditional solutions;

*   paying attention to the life-cycle costs of constructing and occupying a building, rather than to the initial capital cost only.

Our aim is to provide our clients with risk assurance, cost control and value for money, via effective advice, cost planning and management.

DAVIS LANGDON & SEAH HONG KONG LTD
21st Floor, Leighton Centre
77 Leighton Road
Hong Kong
Tel : (010 852) 576 3231
Fax : (010 852) 576 0416

DAVIS LANGDON & SEAH INTERNATIONAL

MANAGE AND LIMIT CLIENT RISK - ADDING VALUE

Hong Kong

KEY DATA

Population
Population	5.9m
Urban population	94%
Population under 15	21%
Population over 65	9%
Average annual growth rate (1982 to 1992)	1.0%

Geography
Land area	1,076 km²
Agricultural area	8%
Capital city	Victoria

Economy
Monetary unit	Hong Kong dollar (HK$)
Exchange rate (average first quarter 1993) to:	
the pound sterling	HK$ 11.48
the US dollar	HK$ 7.74
the yen x 100	HK$ 6.30
Average annual inflation (1983 to 1992)	7.8%
Inflation rate (1992)	9.4%
Gross Domestic Product (GDP) (1992)*	HK$ 742.6bn
GDP per capita (1992)*	HK$ 127,778
Real GDP growth (1982 to 1992)	6.5%
Private consumption as a proportion of GDP (1992)*	61%
Public consumption as a proportion of GDP (1992)*	9%
Investment as a proportion of GDP (1992)*	28%

Construction
Gross value of construction output (1991)*	HK$ 80.0bn
Net value of construction output (1991)*	HK$ 34bn
Net value of construction output per capita (1991)*	HK$ 5,763
Net value of construction output as a proportion of GDP (1991)*	5.3%

* estimate

THE CONSTRUCTION INDUSTRY

Construction output

In 1991 the value of the gross output of the Hong Kong construction industry is estimated at HK$80 billion, equivalent to US$10.3 billion, or about 12.5% of GDP. Of this, building including housing accounted for 75% of the total, and civil engineering, 25%. Expenditure on repair and maintenance is not known, though the Housing Authority has a substantial upgrading programme.

Over the period since 1984 private sector construction - mainly housing and other building - has grown steadily if slowly. Public sector work has been less buoyant. Overall there was a fall in output in real terms from 1984 to 1986 but since then there has been a rise bringing the total above 1984 levels by 1989. The current uncertainties make an assessment of the future very difficult. In 1989 a total of 91,655 residential units were completed of which 54,000 were public sector. The high public sector figure is not being maintained. The public sector housing authority had recently reduced its production target from 40,000 to 36,000 flats a year. The government has a major slum clearance programme to 2001 which was dependent on the 40,000 houses a year programme. The slum clearance programme will presumably now fall behind.

There are a number of major projects planned. The Port and Airport Strategy Project 1991 to 2000 is valued at US$20 billion with related major highway programmes. There is to be a third cross-harbour tunnel, waste treatment and other environmental projects and a major harbour land reclamation project.

Great opportunities are being created by modernization in the People's Republic of China (PRC). There are now as many people working for Hong Kong firms in the Shenzhen Special Enterprise Zone (SEZ) and in Guangdong Province as in Hong Kong itself. It is the gateway for Taiwan and for the People's Republic of China (see map on page 2).

Characteristics and structure of the industry

There are around 3,300 registered contractors and approved suppliers of materials in Hong Kong and the Hong Kong Government has lists of approved contractors for public works. Once registered, a company is designated by group with relation to any or all of five possible categories: building, port works, roads and drainage, site formation and waterworks. As at 31 December 1991 there were 54 contractors approved for building contracts of unlimited value (Group C), 51 contractors approved for contracts up to HK$30 million and 77 contractors approved for contracts up to HK$6 million. In addition there were 29 international contractors approved for contracts of unlimited value. In practice, private sector projects also usually employ only contractors who appear on the Government List of Approved Contractors.

For most projects a main contractor is chosen who is responsible for completing the project and employing approved subcontractors for major sections of works such as curtain walling or windows and building services.   These latter elements are tendered separately.   Main contractors tend to carry out very little construction work themselves, apart from possibly the concrete structure, and prefer to employ small subcontractors and labour-only gangs.   Recently design-and-build or turnkey contracts have been introduced, but it is too early to assess the success of these approaches.

Most major consultants and contractors in Hong Kong will, over the next few years, become involved in the new airport project set to become the largest building project in the world.   Many are also becoming involved in large projects in China, usually funded by Hong Kong developers.

During the 1980s, the number of foreign contractors in the market increased.   In 1982, for example, their market share in public housing projects was 9% but by 1986, 25%.   Most were from mainland China and Korea.   In 1988 the government tightened registration requirements for foreign contractors.

The majority of construction workers are engaged on a daily basis with only a very small percentage being employed by the month.   There is no unionization in construction.   If over four hours overtime is worked, an extra day's pay is usually due.   Restrictions on labour, especially supervisory staff, arise from immigration controls which apply to all contracts and the hiring of immigrants has to be justified and approved. This does not apply in the case of UK nationals.   Labour ordinances regulate the employment and termination of labour, and the observance of statutory holidays.

The Construction Industry Training Authority runs a training centre providing basic courses for craftsmen and technicians.   On completion of these, trainees are apprenticed to building contractors for a period of two or three years.   The Authority is funded by a special levy on newly completed construction works and the rate to be paid by contractors is currently 0.25% of the value of work exceeding HK$1 million.

The construction industry depends heavily on imported materials. Local quarries and plants can supply only a small portion of the aggregates and cement consumed each year.   Similarly the production of rolling mills in Hong Kong is too small to meet demand for iron and steel.   There is a wide variety of sources and qualities of materials available with correspondingly wide price variation.   Hong Kong is a free port and has no exchange controls and few import restrictions.   Import licences are generally not required.   No sales or purchase taxes apply to construction materials or equipment.   Because of the dependence of Hong Kong on imports the prices of materials are heavily influenced by exchange rates.

Hong Kong has a large number of well-established firms of architects, both of overseas and local origin and some foreign architects, mainly from Britain and America, are employed by them.   Small interior design and minor work practices proliferate on the back of the never-ending fitting out of offices, shops, flats, etc.   The Architectural Services Department is responsible for all public work, such as hospitals, schools, museums and council chambers.   The Housing Authority is responsible for government initiated housing in Hong Kong and the Housing Society supplements this (see under Clients and finance).

The main professional bodies in the construction industry are the Hong Kong Institute of Engineers with approximately 11,000 members, the Hong Kong Institute of Architects with approximately 1,400 members and the Hong Kong Institute of Surveyors with close to 3,100 members. On many large schemes a project manager has replaced the architect as the project co-ordinator, but in most cases the project manager himself will be a member of one of the above institutes.

The profession of quantity surveyor is recognized in Hong Kong but there is no compulsory registration scheme. The government set up a Hong Kong Institute of Surveyors in 1984 but there are no restrictions on membership. Anyone can set up as a quantity surveyor cost consultant by obtaining a Business Registration Certificate. There are as yet no Hong Kong surveying qualifications; the territory relies on RICS qualifications. However, the Hong Kong Institute of Surveyors does run a Test of Professional Competence (TPC) exercise.

Clients and finance

The private sector accounts for two thirds of all new works in Hong Kong and the public sector for one third. Output is split roughly as follows:

PUBLIC AND PRIVATE SECTOR OUTPUT, HONG KONG

Type of work	Private %	Public %	Mixed %	Total %
Building	78	22	-	100
of which housing(1)	43	45	12	100
other construction	33	67	-	100
Total	67	33	-	100

(1)   Figures based on number of dwellings in 1988. The mixed are the Home Ownership Schemes built under the Private Sector Participation Schemes and the Middle Income Housing.

The Housing Authority is a statutory body established under the Housing Ordinance 1973. At first it was responsible for co-ordinating public housing but since April 1988 it has been responsible for nearly all public housing in Hong Kong including policy formulation. The Housing Authority is required to be self-financing on its current account. Over 40% of housing stock is in the Authority's control. The construction branch includes architectural engineering, planning and redevelopment, construction and maintenance divisions. The construction division has a quantity surveying and a building services section.

Most dwellings constructed by the Housing Authority are for public rental (41% of stock) but 6% of the stock are in the Home Ownership Scheme (HOS) under which flats were built by the government for purchase by families in the middle income bracket, and the Private Sector Participation Scheme (PSPS), under which sites are offered for sale to real estate developers on condition that flats produced are sold at a fixed price to purchasers nominated by the government. Finance for new public housing comes from the Housing Authority's own funds, from revenue account surplus, from rents from the commercial elements in the developments, and from sale of HOS flats and land for PSPS. The remainder comes from permanent capital injected by the government.

Private building work is financed by property developers and by big businesses such as Hutchinson Whampoa in the communications and property businesses, the Swire Group (which controls Cathay Pacific Airlines and has shipping, insurance and property interests), and Jardines (which controls the Hong Kong Land Company, a large property group which in turn controls the land in the central business district).

Another major source of funds for development is the Royal Hong Kong Jockey Club. Of the very large sums of money which accrues to the Club from racing and lotteries the majority is of course returned to the punters. However, 19% is retained, 13% going to government as betting tax and 6% to the Club. This latter sum is used for charities and financing community development projects at the discretion of the Stewards. For example, the University of Science and Technology, Kowloon Park, the Centre for the Performing Arts and the Ocean Park Oceanarium have all been partially or wholly funded by this body.

Selection of design consultants

No guidelines are published for selection of consultants and even the government will not comment on their selection criteria. They may be forced to make some statement on policy for work on the new airport. The comments below are therefore based on observations by local participants in the construction process.

Architects are usually appointed directly by the client without formal competition though competitions may be held in some cases. In the private sector track record is the most important criterion; personal contacts and recommendations play a part but price is less important. In the public sector architects are given jobs in rotation.

In the private sector engineers are sometimes appointed directly by the client and sometimes by the architect taking into account equally track record, recommendations and price. In the public sector selection is again on a rotation basis.

Surveying and cost consultants are mostly appointed by the client with some form of competition. Price is the dominant criterion in the private sector, usually a lump sum fee - with track record and recommendations important. In the public sector for surveyors, too, selection is on a rotation basis.

Other specialist consultants are appointed less formally usually on the basis of personal contact or recommendation.

All the main professional bodies publish non-mandatory fee scales and they are sometimes used for public work and for private work. However, it is not known how often they are used nor what discounts are negotiated.

Fees generally are being driven down by competition. Until now the lowest fee usually secured the appointment, at least of quantity surveyors, but it is now becoming common to be advised of the lowest fee and asked to match it. Some clients are becoming aware that low fees are reducing the levels of service provided and a few discard the lowest bid if a better quality firm quotes a reasonably competitive fee. Recently, government has been investigating the introduction of competitive fees for all consultants and negotiations on the basis for this are ongoing with the respective institutes.

Contractual arrangements

The scheme for registration of contractors has already been described under Characteristics and structure above. Since 1989 the Housing Authority has compiled its own list of contractors. From March 1993 only contractors who have been certified under the ISO 9000 quality management system will qualify to be on the Authority's list for its larger contracts.

For government work open tendering is the normal procedure. The British system of procurement is generally adopted and tenders are usually based on bills of quantities, drawings and specifications. Contracts let by the Housing Authority are based on the Government of Hong Kong General Conditions of Contracts for Building Works (1985 edition).

Contracts for site formation are usually let prior to the main contract. In the case of housing services contracts are tendered separately and then awarded as nominated subcontractors to the main contractors. Performance bonds are usually required.

Liability and insurance

Where a contract exists between the parties and one party breaches a term, whether expressly included in the contract or implied by law, the other party will have an action for damages to recover its loss. The amount of damages which will be recoverable will be the losses arising naturally from the breach and those losses in the reasonable contemplation of the parties as likely to result from the breach. For a contract executed under hand, claims may only be made within six years from the date of the breach. Where a contract is executed under seal, that period is extended to twelve years.

By contrast, liability in tort can arise between parties who have no direct contractual connection. The most frequently invoked tort, negligence, arises where one party owes a duty to take care in its dealings with another party and breaches that duty causing injury or damage. During the 1970s and 1980s the scope of claims allowed by the courts widened greatly, so that almost whenever a party suffered a loss by virtue of another's act, he would have a claim in tort.

The attitude of the courts in recent years has, however, been much more restrictive. Now, from the series of recent cases including, notably, *Murphy v Brentwood DC*, the position has been narrowed so that purely economic losses (such as loss of profit from being unable to use a building or the costs of rectifying a defective building) will generally not be recoverable from the contractor in tort. However, there are certain exceptional situations based on negligent mis-statements in which economic losses may still be recoverable. In general, despite this narrowing, negligence claims will still lie where the breach of duty causes personal injury or damage to property other than work carried out by the defendant. Claims in tort may be brought within six years from the cause of action arising which will be the first occurrence of the loss or, if later, three years from the date of knowledge of the loss, provided that this shall not extend beyond 15 years from the date of the act or omission causing the loss. This may be later than the time the defective work is actually performed and it is common for parties who are out of time for bringing a claim in contract to look to tort to obtain the benefit of a longer limitation period.

Accordingly, employers, contractors and consultants may still face claims in either, or both, contract and tort if they are at fault. There may also be criminal sanctions or claims for breach of statutory duties if the parties fail to comply with the local legislative framework in which they operate.

One point of interest in Hong Kong is that aside from particular requirements on very large projects, it remains relatively unusual for locally-based consultants to maintain professional indemnity insurance. There is no statutory necessity nor requirement of the professional bodies in Hong Kong to maintain such insurance and, so far at least, most employers have not insisted that consultants take out and maintain cover. This may change as a result of the increasing number of overseas consultants (who do hold insurance) coming to Hong Kong in search of work as a result of the Hong Kong Government's Port and Airport Development Strategy projects and the other opportunities in Hong Kong and the Region. One practical effect of the lack of professional indemnity insurance of consultants, however, is to decrease the risk of a claim being mounted against consultants, who are generally limited companies with few assets and could simply be wound up in the event of a claim. The fact that consultants are not insured operates to increase the risk allocation on the contractor and the employer.

Development control and standards

The government owns all land and allocates it as it wishes; planning laws are weak but are currently being tightened. The use of a site is designated and a plot ratio and height limit are set and then leases are auctioned. More than 70% of the cost of a city centre development is land and land auctions are an important source of revenue. The shortage of land has hitherto meant that if height or density limits are raised, buildings are demolished and new ones built. Because the terrain is mostly steep, there is a large component of civil engineering in the development process. Surplus excavated material and rock from the levelling process is deposited into the sea in designated areas thus creating more land for development. Up to 1984 33km^2 of land had been created through reclamation.

All projects have to comply with government regulations of which the main one is the Building Ordinance (Cap 123 of the Laws of Hong Kong). In the private sector, building control is exercised through the government which approves development and building plans. During construction the architect is directly responsible to the Building Ordinance Office and 'spot' inspections are carried out.

Geotechnical conditions in Hong Kong are a major factor in any development. Piling or other major foundation work together with ground stabilization is the 'norm'. To ensure high standards the Geotechnical Control Office provides an advisory service for projects. The Geotechnical Information Unit received more than 1,000 inquiries during 1990.

CONSTRUCTION COST DATA

Cost of labour

The figures below are typical of labour costs in Hong Kong as at the first quarter 1993. The wage rate is the basis of an employee's income, while the cost of labour indicates the cost to a contractor of employing that employee. The difference between the two covers a variety of mandatory and voluntary contributions - a list of items which could be included is given in section 2.

	Wage rate (per day) HK$	Cost of labour (per day) HK$	Number of hours worked per year
Site operatives			
Bricklayer	545	600	2,400
Mason	551	606	2,400
Carpenter	549	604	2,400
Plumber	529	582	2,400
Electrician	449	494	2,400
Structural steel erector	549	604	2,400
Semi-skilled worker	438	482	2,400
Unskilled labourer	375	413	2,400
Equipment operator	455	501	2,400
	(per month)	(per month)	
Watchman/security	5,500	6,600	2,400
Site supervision			
General foreman	17,000	20,400	2,400
Trades foreman	12,000	14,400	2,400
Clerk of works	15,000	18,000	2,400

	Wage rate (per month) HK$	Cost of labour (per month) HK$	Number of hours worked per year
Contractors' personnel			
Site manager	20,000	24,000	2,400
Resident engineer	17,000	20,400	2,400
Resident surveyor	17,000	20,400	2,400
Junior engineer	11,000	13,200	2,400
Junior surveyor	11,000	13,200	2,400
Planner	14,000	16,800	2,400
Consultants' personnel			
Senior architect	40,000	48,000	1,900
Senior engineer	40,000	48,000	1,900
Senior surveyor	40,000	48,000	1,900
Qualified architect	30,000	36,000	1,900
Qualified engineer	30,000	36,000	1,900
Qualified surveyor	30,000	36,000	1,900

Cost of materials

The figures that follow are the costs of main construction materials, delivered to site in the Hong Kong area, as incurred by contractors in the first quarter 1993. These assume that the materials would be in quantities as required for a medium sized construction project and that the location of the works would be neither constrained nor remote.

	Unit	Cost HK$
Cement and aggregate		
Ordinary portland cement in 50kg bags	tonne	525
Coarse aggregates for concrete	m^3	81
Fine aggregates for concrete	m^3	64
Ready mixed concrete (Grade 40)	m^3	380
Ready mixed concrete (Grade 10)	m^3	320
Steel		
Mild steel reinforcement	tonne	3,166
High tensile steel reinforcement	tonne	3,059
Structural steel sections	tonne	3,507
Bricks and blocks		
Common bricks (225 x 105 x 70mm)	1,000	671
Good quality facing bricks (225 x 105 x 70mm)	1,000	763
Hollow concrete blocks (300 x 150 x 75mm)	1,000	1,114
Solid concrete blocks (300 x 150 x 75mm)	1,000	1,212
Precast concrete cladding units with exposed aggregate finish	m^2	400

	Unit	Cost HK$
Timber and insulation		
Softwood sections for carpentry	m³	1,516
Softwood for joinery	m³	1,640
Hardwood for joinery	m³	1,874
Exterior quality plywood (19mm)	m²	74
Plywood for interior joinery (19mm)	m²	68
Softwood strip flooring (25mm)	m²	105
Chipboard sheet flooring (19mm)	m²	59
100mm thick quilt insulation	m²	40
100mm thick rigid slab insulation	m²	60
Softwood internal door complete with frames and ironmongery	each	2,000
Glass and ceramics		
Float glass (6mm)	m²	58
Sealed double glazing units (4 x 4mm)	m²	190
Plaster and paint		
Good quality ceramic wall tiles (150 x 75mm)	m²	120
Plasterboard (12mm thick)	m²	100
Emulsion paint in 5 litre tins	litre	20
Gloss oil paint in 5 litre tins	litre	28
Tiles and paviors		
Clay floor tiles (250 x 250 x 20mm)	m²	50
Vinyl floor tiles (300 x 300 x 2.3mm)	m²	50
Precast concrete paving slabs (250 x 250 x 25mm)	m²	100
Clay roof tiles	1,000	4,000
Precast concrete roof tiles (300 x 300 x 25mm)	1,000	5,000
Drainage		
WC suite complete	each	1,150
Lavatory basin complete	each	1,050
150mm diameter cast iron drain pipes	m	65

Unit rates

The descriptions below are generally shortened versions of standard descriptions listed in full in section 4. Where an item has a two digit reference number (e.g. 05 or 33), this relates to the full description against that number in section 4. Where an item has an alphabetic suffix (e.g. 12A or 34B) this indicates that the standard description has been modified. Where a modification is major the complete modified description is included here and the standard description should be ignored; where a modification is minor (e.g. the insertion of a named hardwood) the shortened description has been modified here but, in general, the full description in section 4 prevails.

The unit rates below are for main work items on a typical construction project in Hong Kong in the first quarter 1993. The rates include all necessary labour, materials and equipment. Allowances of 8 to 15% to cover preliminary and general items and 7.5% to cover contractors' overheads and profit should be added to the rates.

		Units	Rate HK$
Excavation			
01	Mechanical excavation of foundation trenches	m³	156
02	Hardcore filling making up levels	m²	42
03	Earthwork support	m²	44
Concrete work			
04	Plain insitu concrete in strip foundations in trenches	m³	450
05	Reinforced insitu concrete in beds	m³	500
06	Reinforced insitu concrete in walls	m³	500
07	Reinforced insitu concrete in suspended floor or roof slabs	m³	500
08	Reinforced insitu concrete in columns	m³	500
09	Reinforced insitu concrete in isolated beams	m³	500
10	Precast concrete slab	m²	330
Formwork			
11	Softwood formwork to concrete walls	m²	106
12	Softwood formwork to concrete columns	m²	128
13	Softwood formwork to horizontal soffits of slabs	m²	112
Reinforcement			
14	Reinforcement in concrete walls	tonne	4,500
15	Reinforcement in suspended concrete slabs	tonne	4,500
16	Fabric reinforcement in concrete beds	m²	40
Steelwork			
17	Fabricate, supply and erect steel framed structure	tonne	16,500
Brickwork and blockwork			
18	Precast lightweight aggregate hollow concrete block walls	m²	155
19	Solid (perforated) concrete blocks	m²	155
20	Sand lime bricks	m²	128
21	Facing bricks	m²	143
Roofing			
22	Concrete interlocking roof tiles 430 x 380mm	m²	403
23	Plain clay roof tiles 260 x 160mm	m²	358
25	Sawn softwood roof boarding	m²	240
26	Particle board roof coverings	m²	200
27	3 layers glass-fibre based bitumen felt roof covering	m²	168
28	Bitumen based mastic asphalt roof covering	m²	123
29	Glass-fibre mat roof insulation 160mm thick	m²	79

	Units	Rate HK$
30 Rigid sheet loadbearing roof insulation 75mm thick	m^2	112
31 Troughed galvanized steel roof cladding	m^2	280

Woodwork and metalwork

32 Preservative treated sawn softwood 50 x 100mm	m	55
33 Preservative treated sawn softwood 50 x 150mm	m	71
34 Single glazed casement window in hardwood, 650 x 900mm	each	1,200
35 Two panel glazed door in hardwood, size 850 x 2000mm	each	4,080
36 Solid core half hour fire resisting hardwood internal flush doors, size 800 x 2000mm	each	3,330
37 Aluminium double glazed window, size 1200 x 1200mm	each	2,240
38 Aluminium double glazed door, size 850 x 2100mm	each	5,040
39 Hardwood skirtings	m	60
40 Framed structural steelwork in universal joist sections	tonne	20,000
41 Structural steelwork lattice roof trusses	tonne	20,000

Plumbing

42 UPVC half round eaves gutter	m	114
43 UPVC rainwater pipes	m	171
44 Light gauge copper cold water tubing	m	103
45 High pressure plastic pipes for cold water supply	m	35
46 Low pressure plastic pipes for cold water distribution	m	80
47 UPVC soil and vent pipes	m	172
48 White vitreous china WC suite	each	1,590
49 White vitreous china lavatory basin	each	1,480
50 Glazed fireclay shower tray	each	1,480
51 Stainless steel single bowl sink and double drainer	each	1,700

Electrical work

52 PVC insulated and copper sheathed cable	m	28
53 13 amp unswitched socket outlet	each	156
54 Flush mounted 20 amp, 1 way light switch	each	268

Finishings

55 2 coats gypsum based plaster on brick walls	m^2	54
56 White glazed tiles on plaster walls	m^2	128
57 Red clay quarry tiles on concrete floor	m^2	203
58 Cement and sand screed to concrete floors	m^2	40
59 Thermoplastic floor tiles on screed	m^2	97
60 Mineral fibre tiles on concealed suspension system	m^2	213

Glazing

61 Glazing to wood	m^2	133

Painting

62 Emulsion on plaster walls	m^2	28
63 Oil paint on timber	m^2	38

Approximate estimating

The building costs per unit area given below are averages incurred by building clients for typical buildings in the Hong Kong area as at the first quarter 1993. They are based upon the total floor area of all storeys, measured between external walls and without deduction for internal walls.

Approximate estimating costs generally include mechanical and electrical installations but exclude furniture, loose or special equipment, and external works; they also exclude fees for professional services. The costs shown are for specifications and standards appropriate to Hong Kong and this should be borne in mind when attempting comparisons with similarly described building types in other countries. A discussion of this issue is included in section 2. Comparative data for countries covered in this publication, including construction cost data, is presented in Part Three.

Approximate estimating costs must be treated with caution; they cannot provide more than a rough guide to the probable cost of building.

	Cost m² HK$	Cost ft² HK$
Industrial buildings		
Factories for letting	3,250	302
Factories for owner occupation (light industrial use)	3,800	353
Factories for owner occupation (heavy industrial use)	4,300	400
Factory/office (high-tech) for letting (shell and core only)	4,200	390
Factory/office (high-tech) for letting (ground floor shell, first floor offices)	4,600	427
Factory/office (high tech) for owner occupation (controlled environment, fully finished)	5,100	474
High tech laboratory workshop centres (air conditioned)	6,650	618
Warehouses, low bay (6 to 8m high) for letting (no heating)	4,800	446
Warehouses, low bay for owner occupation	5,100	474
Warehouses, high bay for owner occupation	5,600	520
Cold stores/refrigerated stores	9,200	854
Administrative and commercial buildings		
Civic offices, fully air conditioned	6,700	622
Offices for letting, 5 to 10 storeys, air conditioned	6,900	641
Offices for letting, high rise, air conditioned	7,200	669
Offices for owner occupation high rise, air conditioned	8,200	762
Prestige/headquarters office, 5 to 10 storeys, air conditioned	8,700	808
Prestige/headquarters office, high rise, air conditioned	9,200	855
Health and education buildings		
General hospitals (1000 beds)	9,200	855
Private hospitals (500 beds)	10,300	957

	Cost m² HK$	Cost ft² HK$
Health centres	6,700	622
Nursery schools	6,150	571
Primary/junior schools	3,900	362
Secondary/middle schools	4,600	427
University (arts) buildings	6,650	618
University (science) buildings	7,000	650
Management training centres	7,700	715

Recreation and arts buildings

	Cost m² HK$	Cost ft² HK$
Theatres (over 500 seats) including seating and stage equipment	10,300	957
Theatres (less than 500 seats) including seating and stage equipment	11,300	1,050
Concert halls including seating and stage equipment	10,300	957
Swimming pools (international standard) including changing and social facilities	each 3,600,000	
Swimming pools (schools standard) including changing facilities	each 1,650,000	
National museums including full air conditioning and standby generator	10,300	957
Local museums including air conditioning	7,700	715
City centre/central libraries	8,200	762
Branch/local libraries	8,200	762

Residential buildings

	Cost m² HK$	Cost ft² HK$
Private/mass market single family housing 2 storey detached/semidetached (multiple units)	6,400	595
Purpose designed single family housing 2 storey detached (single unit)	8,700	808
Social/economic apartment housing, high rise (with lifts)	3,050	283
Private sector apartment building (standard specification)	4,300	400
Private sector apartment buildings (luxury)	6,400	595
Student/nurses halls of residence	4,500	418
Homes for the elderly (shared accommodation)	5,900	548
Homes for the elderly (self contained with shared communal facilities)	6,400	595
Hotel, 5 star, city centre	11,300	1,050
Hotel, 3 star, city/provincial	9,300	864

EXCHANGE RATES AND INFLATION

The combined effect of exchange rates and inflation on prices within a country and price comparisons between countries is discussed in section 2.

Exchange rates

The graph below plots the movement of the Hong Kong dollar against sterling, the US dollar and the Japanese yen since 1980. The figures used for the graph are quarterly and the method of calculating these and other related issues are discussed in section 2. The exchange rates at June 1993 were HK$11.48 to the pound sterling, HK$7.74 to the US dollar and HK$6.30 to 100 Japanese yen.

THE HONG KONG DOLLAR AGAINST STERLING, THE US DOLLAR
AND THE JAPANESE YEN

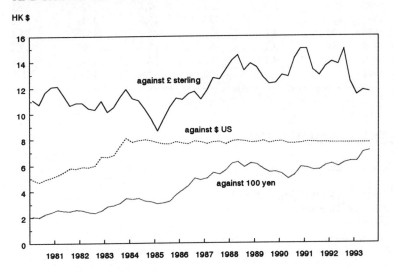

Price inflation

The table overleaf presents consumer price, building price and tender price inflation in Hong Kong since 1982. The year on year rate of increase in the consumer price index has been easing since April 1991 and this is expected to continue largely in line with expected world trends and to be helped by the easing of some previous capacity constraints in the economy. Building price and tender price inflation are similar to each other and significantly higher than that for consumer prices.

CONSUMER PRICE, BUILDING PRICE AND TENDER PRICE INFLATION

Year	Consumer price inflation		Building price index		Tender price index	
	average index	average change %	average index	average change %	average index	average change %
1982			99	-11.5	103	-8.4
1983			92	-7.0	91	-11.5
1984			99	7.2	97	6.5
1985	100		100	1.3	100	2.7
1986	105	5.0	107	7.1	112	12.1
1987	111	5.7	122	13.6	121	7.6
1988	120	8.1	152	24.8	151	25.4
1989	131	9.2	175	15.0	162	7.2
1990	144	9.9	182	4.2	171	5.1
1991			187	2.8	169	-1.0

USEFUL ADDRESSES

Public Organizations

Buildings and Land Department
    Murray Building
    Garden Road
    Hong Kong
    Tel: 848 2198

Architectural Services Department
    34/F and 35/F, Queensway
    Government Offices
    66 Queensway
    Hong Kong
    Tel: 867 3628

Civil Engineering Department
    101 Princess Margaret Road
    Kowloon
    Hong Kong
    Tel: 762 5111

Electrical and Mechanical Services Department
    98 Caroline Hill Road
    Hong Kong
    Tel: 895 8620/895 8817

Highways Department
    10/F Empire Centre
    Tsimshatsui, Kowloon
    Hong Kong
    Tel: 721 0564

Territory Development Department
    13/F Leighton Centre
    77 Leighton Road
    Hong Kong
    Tel: 882 7170

Environmental Protection Department
    24/F-28/F Southern Centre
    Hong Kong
    Tel: 835 1018

Water Supplies Department
    Wanchai Tower II
    7 Gloucester Road
    Wanchai
    Hong Kong
    Tel: 829 4500

Census and Statistics Department
    Wanchai Tower 1
    12 Harbour Road
    Wanchai
    Hong Kong
    Tel: 582 5073

Land Development Corporation
    Great Eagle Centre
    Wanchai
    Hong Kong
    Tel: 828 4900

Hong Kong Housing Authority
    9/F 33 Fat Kwong Street
    Block 2, Ho Man Tin
    Kowloon
    Hong Kong

Trade and Professional Associations

The Hong Kong Contractors' Association Ltd
    3/F, 182 Hennessy Road
    Wanchai
    Hong Kong
    Tel: 572 4414

The Society of Builders, HK
        Room 801/2, On Lok Yuen Bldg
        25 Des Voeux Road Central
        Hong Kong
        Tel: 523 2081/2

The Hong Kong Institute of Architects
        Success Commercial Building
        Wanchai
        Hong Kong
        Tel: 833 6323

The Hong Kong Institute of Engineers
        9th Floor, Island Centre
        Hong Kong
        Tel: 895 4446

The Hong Kong Institute of Surveyors
        1934 Swire House
        Chater Road
        Hong Kong
        Tel: 526 3679

Chambers of Commerce
        Trade Department
        Trade Department Tower
        700 Nathan Road
        Kowloon
        Hong Kong
        Tel: 398 5333

Construction Management and Economics

Editors: **Ranko Bon** and **Will Hughes**, University of Reading, UK. North American Editor: **David S Haviland**, Rensselaer Polytechnic Institute, New York, USA

Construction Management and Economics is a bimonthly international journal serving all practitioners in the construction industry and researchers in academic and research institutes. By bringing together new ideas and developments in construction management and economics from around the world, this Journal helps construction clients and owners find better ways of running and using their buildings and other constructed facilities. The Journal publishes research papers, original reviews of current knowledge, case studies and reports of innovative practice as well as short notes commenting on issues of current interest. In addition to forming original contributions, the shorter papers stimulate debate through comments on papers already published by this Journal and rejoinders by their authors. Special issues of the Journal cover important topics and are compiled under the guidance of invited guest editors.

Construction Management and Economics is encouraged by CIB.

A Selection of Papers

Economic comparison of an air conditioner and a desert cooler for residences in arid areas. **R Navon** and **H Arkin (Israel)**. Stereotypes and themes in building designs: insights for model buildings. **B Atkin (UK)**. Claim quantification using the differential method. **G F Jergeas** and **S O Revay (Canada)**. Modelling standard cost commitment curves for contractors' cash flow forecasting. **A P Kaka** and **A D F Price (UK)**. Forecasting methodology of national demand for construction labour. **Y Rosenfeld** and **A Warszawski (USA)**. The rationalization of quality in the construction industry: some empirical findings. **L S Pheng (Singapore)**.

Subscription Information

ISSN: 0144-6193
Published bimonthly
Volume 11 will be published in 1993
European Community: £185
USA/Canada: $342
Rest of World: £200

There are reduced rates for members of CIoB and ARCOM.

For a free sample copy, or to subscribe, please contact:
Journals Promotion Dept., Chapman & Hall,
2-6 Boundary Row, London SE1 8HN, UK
Tel: +44 (71) 865 0066 Fax: +44 (71) 522 9623 email: journal@chall.mhs.compuserve.com
or
Journals Promotion Dept., Chapman & Hall,
29 West 35th Street, New York, NY 10001-2299, USA
Tel: +1 (212) 244 3336 Fax: +1 (212) 563 2269 email: 71201.1651.@compuserve.com

In Indonesia.

DAVIS LANGDON & SEAH INDONESIA PT

The strategic and integrated management of cost, time and quality - the client "risk" areas of a contract - are essential functions, which are necessary to ensure the satisfactory planning, procurement, execution and operation of construction projects.

We specialise in the financial management of construction projects and their risk areas, from project inception to completion and we concentrate on:

* being positive and creative in our advice, rather than simply reactive;

* providing value for money via efficient management, rather than on superficial cost monitoring;

* giving advice that is matched to the Client's requirements, rather than imposing standard or traditional solutions;

* paying attention to the life-cycle costs of constructing and occupying a building, rather than to the initial capital cost only.

Our aim is to provide our clients with risk assurance, cost control and value for money, via effective advice, cost planning and management.

DAVIS LANGDON & SEAH INDONESIA PT
Wisma Metropolitan 1, Level 13
Jalan Jendral Sudirman Kav. 29
PO Box 3139/Jkt
Jakarta 10001, Indonesia
Tel : (010 6221) 514745
Fax : (010 6221) 514764

DAVIS LANGDON & SEAH INTERNATIONAL

MANAGE AND LIMIT CLIENT RISK - ADDING VALUE

Indonesia

KEY DATA

Population

Population (1991)	183m
Urban population	31%
Population under 15	35%
Population over 65	3%
Average annual growth rate (1980 to 1990)	1.8%

Geography

Land area (comprising more than 13,000 islands)	1,919,000 km²
Agricultural area	18%
Capital city	Jakarta (population 9.5m)

Economy

Monetary unit	Rupiah (Rp)
Exchange rate (average first quarter 1993) to:	
the pound sterling	Rp 3,066
the US dollar	Rp 2,069
the yen x 100	Rp 1,683
Average annual inflation (1980 to 1990)	8.4%
Annual inflation rate (1991)	9%
Gross Domestic Product (GDP)	Rp 197,700bn
GDP per capita	Rp 1,109,000
Real GDP growth (1980 to 1990)	5.5%
Private consumption as a proportion of GDP	54%
Public consumption as a proportion of GDP	9%
Investment as a proportion of GDP	36%
Central government expenditure as a proportion of Gross National Product	19%

Construction

Net value of construction output (1991)	Rp 12,856bn
Net value of construction output per capita (1991)	Rp 70,251
Net value of construction output as a proportion of GDP	5.5%

Note: All data relate to 1990 unless otherwise indicated.

THE CONSTRUCTION INDUSTRY

Construction output

The value of the net output of the construction industry in 1990 was 10,749 billion rupiahs equivalent to US$5.8 billion and 5.5% of GDP, and in 1991 was 12,856 billion rupiahs at current prices. In 1990 the value of completed construction work was recorded as being about 17,000 billion rupiahs but the official data is believed to represent only a part of total output.

The activity of the construction sector increased very substantially in the 1970s and early 1980s but the growth rate then slowed until 1988 and 1989 when there was a small boom. In this boom period about 70% of orders were from the public sector including many major infrastructure schemes.

There are still many large projects planned throughout Indonesia. Notable is a large port project - the Tanjung Priok Port valued at US$825 million for development from 1991 to 1995. The Sepinggan Airport is being expanded from 1991 to 1994 at a cost of US$171 million and the government has drawn up detailed plans to manage the environment. However, total public investment is unlikely to reach the levels of the 1970s boom.

The breakdown of output in 1990 was as follows:

CONSTRUCTION OUTPUT BY TYPE OF WORK,
INDONESIA, 1990

Type of work	Percentage of value of total output completed
Building	
Residential	5.9
Non residential	28.8
Mixed type of building	0.5
Specialist work related mainly to building	7.5
Civil Engineering	
Water supply	1.9
Electricity supply and network	3.5
Construction or improvement of roads/bridges	33.8
Irrigation/drainage	10.3
Airport, harbours, bus stations, etc.	2.4
Other	5.3
Total	100.0

The government finances a low cost housing programme through the national urban development corporation, *Perum Perumnas*. In 1989/90 about 4,500 units were built but this is down to a fraction of that built in the 1970s: in 1978/79 the total was 31,000 and even in 1988/89 it was 17,605. Private construction, however, is rising. Foreign and domestic investment applications have dramatically increased in the last five years and the number and value of commercial and industrial projects will rise. Housing, however, is likely to be constrained by high interest rates.

The distribution of construction work is very uneven but relates closely to population as is indicated below.

CONSTRUCTION OUTPUT BY REGIONS, INDONESIA

Province	Percentage of population 1989	Percentage of construction output 1990
D.I. Aceh	1.4	1.3
North Sumatera	2.9	2.9
West Sumatera	1.8	1.9
Riau (incl. Batam)	2.2	2.2
Jambi	0.9	1.2
South Sumatera	2.6	2.4
Bengkulu	1.8	1.1
Lampung	2.7	2.5
DKI Jakarta	34.6	33.7
West Java	14.1	13.8
Central Java	5.9	6.9
D.I. Yogyakarta	1.0	1.0
East Java	6.4	6.8
Bali	0.9	0.9
West Nusa Tenggara	1.3	0.9
East Nusa Tenggara	1.4	1.4
East Timor	0.9	0.9
West Kalimantan	1.5	1.5
Central Kalimantan	0.6	0.7
South Kalimantan	1.6	1.6
East Kalimantan	4.0	3.2
North Sulawesi	1.4	1.5
Central Sulawesi	1.3	1.4
South Sulawesi	2.0	2.3
South East Sulawesi	0.9	0.9
Maluku	1.1	1.2
Irian Jaya	3.1	2.3
Total	100	100

Source: Building/Construction Statistics - Central Bureau of Statistics

Characteristics and structure of the industry

As construction activity has increased so has the development of the domestic construction industry. It is estimated that there are now some 50,000 firms of all sizes. Large scale and aid-financed infrastructure projects continue to be carried out by international construction companies though usually with local participation. All government housing schemes and smaller projects are, however, undertaken by local contractors.

The construction process is managed in a number of ways. The traditional system with a main contractor is still the most usual but design and build, construction management, build, operate and transfer (BOT) and turnkey are also now important. Management contracting is not much used.

The top ten national contractors in Indonesia selected by *Konstruksi* magazine for 1990 are as follows:

TOP TEN NATIONAL CONTRACTORS IN INDONESIA, 1990

| | | Gross output (billion Rupiahs) | | |
| | | | | 1990 |
	Company	1988	1989	estimate
1.	P T Pembangunan Perumahan *	136	177	260
2.	P T Waskita Karya *	139	196	202
3.	P T Wijaya Karya *	121	149	180
4.	P T Total Bangun Persada	60	80	150
5.	P T Hutama Karya *	80	115	140
6.	P T Jaya Konstruksi MP	72	121	133
7.	P T Nindya Karya *	91	129	133
8.	P T Bangun Tjipta Sarana	90	129	125
9.	P T Murthy Kurnia Utama	40	60	70
10.	P T Dimensi Engineering Contractors	20	30	60

Source: Konstruksi magazine, November 1990 edition
* Government backed constructing organization (BUMN)

Quantity surveying practices have had a presence in Indonesia for more than fifteen years, primarily serving the private construction sector plus the oil and gas industries. Property and land surveyors are also present. They are of limited importance in the public sector. The traditional QS role is evolving into management, co-ordination, administration and general financial advice.

There are a number of substantial practices of architects and engineers, often in multidisciplinary practices, as shown in the table on the next page.

MAIN PROFESSIONAL PRACTICES IN INDONESIA, 1990

Name of company	Type	Number of employees	Gross income 1990 (est) Rp billion	1991 Rp billion
1. P T Atelier 6	A,E	292	10.6	12.7
2. P T Perentjana Djaja	A,E,S	341	5.5	7.5
3. P T Parama Loka Consultant	A,E	180	n.a.	n.a.
4. P T Airmas Asri	A,E	78	n.a.	n.a.
5. P T Wiratman and Associates	E	550	13.3	13.3
6. P T Desakota	E	115	4.7	4.8
7. P T Team 4	A,E	140	3.8	5.0
8. P T Arkonin	A,E	212	n.a.	n.a.
9. PRW Architects, P T	A,E	70	2.0	2.5
10. P T Ciriajasa	A,E	156	4.5	6.0

Source: Konstruksi magazine, November 1991 edition
Note: A : Architects
           E : Engineers
           S : Building Services
           n.a. not available

Clients and finance

The client for almost all public works is the government (central and regional), but in the last five years private companies have started to be involved to a limited extent in funding public works (toll roads, electricity generation).

Construction work in the private sector is dominated by government backed or national contractors: it is common for large projects to involve foreign joint venture partners or consortia.

Government obtains finance from various external sources as well as the national development budget, for example the Asian Development Bank, the World Bank and other multilateral and bilateral aid agencies. Private sector financing is obtained through local and foreign financial institutions including state and private banks, pension funds and private investors.

Selection of design consultants

A decree of the President (No. 29 of 1984) states that a pre-qualification system should be followed in tendering for consultancy work on government projects. The procedure is set out in the decree and a standard tender procedure has been added to the decree in a memorandum from the Minister of Public Works.

Competition is important, especially on very large projects. In the private sector, the procedure is more flexible, but still follows the basic government rules. In-house design organizations are uncommon in Indonesia.

Housing consultancy contracts are generally awarded directly by the owner or the owner's contractor without a formal bidding process, but other building projects generally follow standard construction procedures for bidding and appointment. Most civil engineering projects originate from government and they too are usually awarded following the same standard procedures. There are no known recommended or mandatory published fee scales.

Contractual arrangements

Tenderers are selected subject to a pre-qualification process both in the public and in the private sector. In the public sector the tender is usually on a lump sum basis but in the private sector a variety of methods are used. Bills of quantities, either firm or approximate, are usually provided and contracts are based on internationally recognized forms adapted for Indonesian conditions. Bank guarantees are normally required and cash retention is usually preferred to bonds. Advance payments are sometimes made. Variations are authorized through contract instructions and change orders with consequent adjustment in the contract sum.

Liability and insurance

Insurance is compulsory for all parties. The CAR (Contractor's All Risk and Public Liability) insurance is normally taken out by the owner or the contractor in joint names for the full project value and is valid until practical completion of the project (including the maintenance period). By law contractors must insure their workers. Insurance companies are common in Indonesia but risks are normally reinsured offshore. Insurance claims are usually settled satisfactorily.

Development control and standards

The Directorate of Regional and City Planning produces general Master Plans and regional government ensures implementation by the land user. Detailed Master Plans should normally be used as one of the references when seeking planning permission. If all other requirements are fulfilled, full or partial building permission takes about one month.

At the planning stage an architectural, structural and building services review is carried out by the appropriate authority to check the design for compliance with laws, rules and standing instructions relating to health and safety.

Before buildings can obtain an Occupation Permit, approval from the Fire Prevention Authority must be obtained.

The national standard for building materials/products is Standard Industrial Indonesia (SII) - Indonesian Standard for Industry. Foreign standards such as ASTM, BS, DIN, SISIR, and JIS are also used extensively.

CONSTRUCTION COST DATA

Cost of labour

The figures below are typical of labour costs in the Jakarta area as at the first quarter 1993. The wage rate is the basis of an employee's income, while the cost of labour indicates the cost to a contractor of employing that employee. The difference between the two covers a variety of mandatory and voluntary contributions - a list of items which could be included is given in section 2.

	Wage rate (per hour) Rp	Cost of labour (per day) Rp	Number of hours worked per year
Site operatives			
Mason/bricklayer	785	6,900	2,208
Carpenter	900	8,000	2,208
Plumber	930	8,200	2,208
Electrician	950	8,400	2,208
Structural steel erector	900	7,900	2,208
HVAC installer	950	8,400	2,208
Semi-skilled worker	625	5,500	2,208
Unskilled labourer	510	4,500	2,208
Equipment operator	850	7,500	2,208
Watchman/security	650	5,750	2,208
Site supervision			
General foreman	900	8,000	2,208
Trades foreman	850	7,500	2,208

Cost of materials

The figures that follow are the costs of main construction materials, delivered to site in the Jakarta area, as incurred by contractors in the first quarter 1993. These assume that the materials would be in quantities as required for a medium sized construction project and that the location of the works would be neither constrained nor remote.

All the costs in this section exclude value added tax (VAT - see below).

	Unit	Cost Rp
Cement and aggregate		
Ordinary portland cement in 40kg bags	tonne	135,000
Coarse aggregates for concrete	m^3	25,000
Fine aggregates for concrete	m^3	27,000
Ready mixed concrete (K-350) slump 10	m^3	120,000
Ready mixed concrete (K-225) slump 12	m^3	115,000

	Unit	Cost Rp
Steel		
Mild steel reinforcement	tonne	807,000
High tensile steel reinforcement	tonne	810,000
Structural steel sections	tonne	1,100,000
Bricks and blocks		
Common bricks (220 x 100 x 50mm)	1,000	70,000
Hollow concrete blocks (400 x 200 x 100mm)	1,000	350,000
Solid concrete blocks (380 x 180 x 100mm)	1,000	550,000
Precast concrete cladding units with exposed		
aggregate finish	m^2	120,000
Timber and insulation		
Softwood sections for carpentry	m^3	300,000
Softwood for joinery (Kamper)	m^3	600,000
Hardwood for joinery (Teak)	m^3	3,000,000
Exterior quality plywood (18mm)	m^2	21,000
Plywood for interior joinery (18mm)	m^2	19,000
100mm thick quilt insulation	m^2	18,000
100mm thick rigid slab insulation	m^2	20,000
Softwood internal door complete with frames and		
ironmongery	each	400,000
Glass and ceramics		
Float glass (8mm)	m^2	42,000
Good quality ceramic wall tiles (20 x 10mm)	m^2	24,000
Plaster and paint		
Plasterboard (9mm thick)	m^2	14,900
Emulsion paint in 5 litre tins	litre	7,000
Gloss oil paint in 5 litre tins	litre	9,100
Tiles and paviors		
Clay floor tiles (150 x 150 x 10mm)	m^2	7,500
Vinyl floor tiles (300 x 300 x 2mm)	m^2	10,000
Precast concrete paving slabs (600 x 600 x 50mm)	m^2	9,000
Clay roof tiles	1,000	400,000
Precast concrete roof tiles	1,000	2,500,000
Drainage		
WC suite complete	each	350,000
Lavatory basin complete	each	240,000
100mm diameter UPVC drain pipes	m	17,000

Unit rates

The descriptions below are generally shortened versions of standard descriptions listed in full in section 4.   Where an item has a two digit reference number (e.g. 05 or 33), this relates to the full description against that number in section 4. Where an item has an alphabetic suffix (e.g. 12A or 34B) this indicates that the standard description has been modified. Where a modification is major the complete modified description is included here and the standard description should be ignored; where a modification is minor (e.g. the insertion of a named hardwood) the shortened description has been modified here but, in general, the full description in section 4 prevails.

The unit rates below are for main work items on a typical construction project in the Jakarta area in the first quarter 1993. The rates include all necessary labour, materials and equipment. An allowance of 7 to 10% has been included to cover contractors' overheads and profit. A further 10 to 20% should be added to cover preliminary and general items.

All the rates in this section exclude value added tax (VAT - see below).

		Unit	Rate Rp
Excavation			
01	Mechanical excavation of foundation trenches	m³	4,200
02	Hardcore filling making up levels	m²	5,355
Concrete work			
04	Plain insitu concrete in strip foundations in trenches	m³	128,100
05	Reinforced insitu concrete in beds	m³	133,350
06	Reinforced insitu concrete in walls	m³	137,550
07	Reinforced insitu concrete in suspended floor or roof slabs	m³	135,450
08	Reinforced insitu concrete in columns	m³	136,500
09	Reinforced insitu concrete in isolated beams	m³	142,800
10	Precast concrete slab	m³	153,300
Formwork			
11	Softwood formwork to concrete walls	m²	10,605
12	Softwood or metal formwork to concrete columns	m²	14,700
13	Softwood or metal formwork to horizontal soffits of slabs	m²	21,210
Reinforcement			
14	Reinforcement in concrete walls	tonne	940,800
15	Reinforcement in suspended concrete slabs	tonne	940,800
16	Fabric reinforcement in concrete beds	m²	17,640
Steelwork			
17	Fabricate, supply and erect steel framed structure	tonne	2,709,000
Brickwork and blockwork			
19	Solid (perforated) concrete blocks	m²	9,408

		Unit	Rate Rp
Roofing			
22	Concrete interlocking roof tiles 430 x 380mm	m^2	35,280
23	Plain clay roof tiles 260 x 160mm	m^2	29,400
24	Fibre cement roof slates 600 x 300mm	m^2	52,920
31	Troughed galvanized steel roof cladding	m^2	32,970
Woodwork and metalwork			
32	Preservative treated sawn softwood 50 x 100mm	m	4,116
33	Preservative treated sawn softwood 50 x 150mm	m	5,292
34A	Single glazed casement window in Kamper hardwood, size 650 x 900mm	each	106,050
35A	Two panel glazed door in Kamper hardwood, size 850 x 2000mm	each	529,200
36	Solid core half hour fire resisting hardwood internal flush doors, size 800 x 2000mm	each	764,400
37	Aluminium double glazed window, size 1200 x 1200mm	each	470,400
38	Aluminium double glazed door, size 850 x 2100mm	each	705,600
39	Hardwood skirtings	m	2,940
40	Framed structural steelwork in universal joist sections	tonne	2,583,000
41	Structural steelwork lattice roof trusses	tonne	2,467,500
Plumbing			
42	UPVC half round eaves gutter	m	28,245
43	UPVC rainwater pipes	m	17,640
44	Light gauge copper cold water tubing	m	15,330
46	Low pressure plastic pipes for cold water distribution	m	4,704
47	UPVC soil and vent pipes	m	18,795
48	White vitreous china WC suite	each	499,800
49	White vitreous china lavatory basin	each	370,650
50	Glazed fireclay shower tray	each	382,200
51	Stainless steel single bowl sink and double drainer	each	235,200
Electrical work			
52	PVC insulated and copper sheathed cable	m	1,176
53	13 amp unswitched socket outlet	each	5,586
54	Flush mounted 20 amp, 1 way light switch	each	5,292
Finishings			
55A	2 coats gypsum based plaster on brick walls	m^2	3,413
56	White glazed tiles on plaster walls	m^2	22,365
57	Red clay quarry tiles on concrete floor	m^2	12,915
58	Cement and sand screed to concrete floors	m^2	5,880
59	Thermoplastic floor tiles on screed	m^2	5,586
60	Mineral fibre tiles on concealed suspension system	m^2	35,280
Glazing			
61	Glazing to wood	m^2	22,344

	Unit	Rate Rp
Painting		
62 Emulsion on plaster walls	m^2	3,297
63 Oil paint on timber	m^2	4,589

Approximate estimating

The building costs per unit area given below are expressed in US$ and are averages incurred by building clients for typical buildings in the Jakarta area as at the first quarter 1993. They are based upon the total floor area of all storeys, measured between external walls and without deduction for internal walls.

Approximate estimating costs generally include mechanical and electrical installations but exclude furniture, loose or special equipment, and external works; they also exclude fees for professional services. The costs shown are for specifications and standards appropriate to Indonesia and this should be borne in mind when attempting comparisons with similarly described building types in other countries. A discussion of this issue is included in section 2. Comparative data for countries covered in this publication including construction cost data is presented in Part Three.

Approximate estimating costs must be treated with caution; they cannot provide more than a rough guide to the probable cost of building.

All the rates in this section exclude value added tax (VAT - see below).

	Cost m^2 US$	Cost ft^2 U$
Industrial buildings		
Factories for letting	250	23
Factories for owner occupation (light industrial use)	280	26
Factories for owner occupation (heavy industrial use)	360	33
Factory/office (high-tech) for letting (shell and core only)	250	23
Factory/office (high-tech) for letting (ground floor shell, first floor offices)	320	29
Factory/office (high tech) for owner occupation (controlled environment, fully finished)	460	42
High tech laboratory workshop centres (air conditioned)	460	42
Warehouses, low bay (6 to 8m high) for letting (no AC)	250	23
Warehouses, low bay for owner occupation (including AC)	325	30
Warehouses, high bay for owner occupation (including AC)	405	37
Cold stores/refrigerated stores	380	35
Administrative and commercial buildings		
Civic offices, non air conditioned	360	33
Civic offices, fully air conditioned	450	41
Offices for letting, 5 to 10 storeys, air conditioned	550	51
Offices for letting, high rise, air conditioned	625	58
Offices for owner occupation high rise, air conditioned	700	64
Prestige/headquarters office, 5 to 10 storeys, air conditioned	650	60
Prestige/headquarters office, high rise, air conditioned	825	76

	Cost m² US$	Cost ft² U$
Residential buildings		
Purpose designed single family housing 2 storey detached (single unit)	325	30
Social/economic apartment housing, low rise (no lifts)	425	39
Social/economic apartment housing, high rise (with lifts)	525	49
Private sector apartment building (standard specification)	600	56
Private sector apartment buildings (luxury)	700	65
Hotel, 5 star, city centre	1,250	115
Hotel, 3 star, city/provincial	900	83
Motel	700	64
Golf courses	250,000 per hole	
Golf clubhouse	950	88

Regional variations

The approximate estimating costs are based on projects in Jakarta. Costs elsewhere can vary by up to plus or minus 20%.

Value added tax (VAT)

The standard rate of value added tax (VAT) is currently 10%, chargeable on general building work.

EXCHANGE RATES

The graph opposite plots the movement of the Indonesian rupiah against sterling, the US dollar and the Japanese yen since 1980. The figures used for the graph are quarterly and the method of caculating these and other related issues are discussed in section 2. The average exchange rate for the first quarter 1993 was Rp3,066 to the pound sterling, Rp2,069 to the US dollar and Rp16.83 to the Japanese yen.

THE INDONESIAN RUPIAH AGAINST STERLING, THE US DOLLAR
AND THE JAPANESE YEN

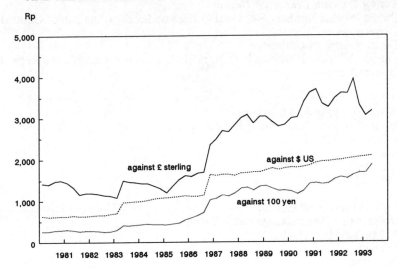

USEFUL ADDRESSES

Public Organizations

Ministry of Public Works
    Departemen Pekerjaan Umum
    Jl Pattimura 20,
    Jakarta
    Indonesia
    Tel: 021 7395588/710311

The Ministry of Public Works is subdivided into:

- *Direktorat Binamarga*   - a directorate covering roads and bridges construction works
- *Direktorat Cipta Karya*   - a directorate covering general building works
- *Direktorat Pengairan*   - a directorate covering hydrologic construction works
- *Direktorat Air Bersih*   - a directorate covering sanitation works.

Regional Goverment Construction Ministries:

- *Kantor Wilayah Pekerjaan Umum*
  Public Works; Ministry Regional Offices under coordination of Central Government
- *Dinas Pekerjaan Umum*
  Public Works Provincial Offices under coordination of Regional Government

State Ministry of Public Housing
Menteri Negara Perumahan Rakyat
Jl Kebon Sirih 31
Jakarta
Indonesia
Tel: 021 323235

Ministry of Mining and Energy
Departemen Pertambangan dan Energi
Jl. Medan Merdeka Selatan No. 18
Jakarta
Indonesia
Tel: 021 360232

Ministry of Industry
Departemen Perindustrian
Jl. Jendral Gatot Subroto Kav. 52-53
Jakarta
Indonesia
Tel: 021 515509

Ministry of Tourism, Post and Telecommunication
Departemen Pariwisata, Pos dan Telekomunikasi
Jl. Kebon Sirih 36
Jakarta
Indonesia
Tel: 021 366705

National Development Planning Agency
Badan Perencana Pembangunan Nasional (BAPPENAS)
Jl. Taman Suropati 2
Jakarta
Indonesia
Tel: 021 366207

The Investment Coordinating Board
Badan Koordinasi Penanaman Modal (BKPM)
Jl. Jendral Gatot Subroto 44
Jakarta
Indonesia
Tel: 021 512008

Direktorat Penyelidikan Masalah Bangunan
Direcktorat Jendral Cipta Karya
Departemen Pekerjaan Umum
Directorate for Investigation into Building Problems
Directorate General Cipta Karya
Ministry of Public Works
    Jl. Tamansari 84, P.O. Box 15, Bandung
    Jawa Barat
    Indonesia
    022 81082/81083

Agency of Assessment and Application of Technology
    Badan Pengkajian dan Penerapan Teknologi (BPPT)
    Jl. M.H. Thamrin 8
    Jakarta
    Indonesia
    Tel: 021 3904533/3904537 - 42

Indonesian Institute of Science
    Lembaga Ilmu Pengetahuan Indonesia (LIPI)
    Jl. Jendral Gatot Subroto 10
    Jakarta
    Indonesia
    Tel: 021 511542

Science and Technology Research Centre
    Pusat Penelitian Ilmu Pengetahuan dan Teknologi (PUSPITEK)
    Desa Setu Kecamatan Serpong, Tangerang
    Jawa Barat
    Indonesia
    Tel: 021 7560541/7560562

National Statistic Bureau
    Biro Pusat Statistik
    Jl. Dr. Sutomo 8
    Jakarta
    Indonesia
    Tel: 021 3810291/3810295

Trade and Professional Associations

National Contractors' Association of Indonesia
    Gabungan Pelaksana Konstruksi Nasional Indonesia (GAPENSI)
    Jl. Raya Pasar Minggu Km. 17 No. 11A
    Jakarta
    Indonesia
    Tel: 021 7981670

Indonesian Contractors' Association
  Asosiasi Kontraktor Indonesia
  Jl. Wijaya Grant Centre Blok D No. 1
  Jl. Darmawangsa III
  Jakarta
  Indonesia
  Tel: 021 7202997

Indonesian Architect Association
  Ikatan Arsitek Indonesia (IAI)
  Jakarta Design Centre 6th Floor
  Jl. Letjen S. Parman 53
  Jakarta
  Indonesia
  Tel: 021 5304711

Indonesian National Consultant Association
  Ikatan Konsultan Nasional Indonesia (INKINDO)
  Jakarta Design Centre 4th Floor
  Jl. Letjen S. Parman 53
  Jakarta
  Indonesia
  Tel: 021 5304639

Indonesian Construction Expert Association
  Himpunan Ahli Konstruksi Indonesia (HAKI)
  Jl. Tebet Barat Dalam X/5
  Jakarta
  Indonesia
  Tel: 021 8298518

Indonesian Engineers Association
  Persatuan Insinyur Indonesia
  Jl. Teuku Umar No. 23
  Jakarta
  Indonesia

City Development Coordinator
  Dinas Pengawasan Pembangunan Kota (P2K)
  Kantor Gubernur D.K.I. Jakarta
  Jl. Taman Jatibaru No. 1
  Jakarta
  Indonesia
  Tel: 352275

National Chamber of Trade and Industry
  Kamar Dagang dan Industri Nasional
  Jl. M.H. Thamrin 20
  Jakarta
  Indonesia
  Tel: 021 324064

Batam Industrial Estate Development Authority
Otorita Pengembangan Daerah Industri
Pulau Batam
Jl. M.H. Thamrin 20
Jakarta
Indonesia
Tel: 021 325828

Jakarta Design Centre
Jl. Letjen S. Parman 53
Jakarta
Indonesia

The National Centre for Research
Science and Technology
Jl. Raden Saleh 43
Jakarta
Indonesia
Tel: 021 323209

Japan

KEY DATA

Population
Population	123.5m
Urban population	77%
Population under 15	18%
Population over 65	12%
Average annual growth rate (1980 to 1990)	0.6%

Geography
Land area	378,000 km²
Agricultural area	14%
Capital city	Tokyo
	(population 11.9m)

Economy
Monetary unit	Yen (¥)
Exchange rate (average first quarter 1993) to:	
the pound sterling	¥ 182
the US dollar	¥ 123
Average annual inflation (1980 to 1990)	1.5%
Inflation rate (1991)	3.3%
Gross Domestic Product (GDP) (1991*) estimate	¥ 452,700bn
GDP per capita (1991*) (estimate)	¥ 3,665,587
Real GDP growth (1980 to 1990)	4.1%
Private consumption as a proportion of GDP	57%
Public consumption as a proportion of GDP	9%
Investment as a proportion of GDP	33%
Central government expenditure as a proportion of Gross National Product	17%

Construction
Gross value of construction output (1991*)	¥ 86,610bn
Net value of construction output (1991*) (estimate)	¥ 43,000bn
Net value of construction output per capita (1991*) estimate	¥ 348,000
Net value of construction output as a proportion of GDP (1991*) estimate	9.5%

Note: All data relate to 1990 unless otherwise indicated.
* fiscal year to 31 March 1992

THE CONSTRUCTION INDUSTRY

Construction output

During the 1980s domestic construction activity increased steadily and gross output of the Japanese construction industry in 1991 was ¥ 86.6 trillion, equivalent to US$636 billion or about 19% of fiscal year GDP. The table below shows the type of work undertaken. The Japanese economy is slowing down in 1992 and the construction industry is suffering in terms of new orders though not so much in the level of output. In these circumstances it is normally the policy of the government to increase public investment.

CONSTRUCTION COMPLETIONS BY TYPE OF WORK AND SECTOR, JAPAN (1991 estimates)

Sector/type of work	1991 ¥ billion	%
Residential building		
Private	26,549	30.3
Public	1,135	1.3
Total	27,684	31.6
Non-residential building		
Private	23,056	26.3
Public	4,551	5.2
Total	27,607	31.5
Civil engineering works		
Private	8,920	10.2
Public	23,501	26.8
Total	32,421	37.0
Total	87,712	100.0

Of the private non-residential building work 28% was in offices, 23% in factories and offices, and 10% in schools and hospitals.

These figures include extension, reconstruction and remodelling as well as routine repair and maintenance work. Recently the construction industry has enjoyed a boom in new buildings so that the proportion of reconstruction and remodelling is currently low but is expected to grow as the economy continues to slow. The proportion for routine repair and maintenance is also low, perhaps less than 10% of total output.

Over 50% of construction activity is concentrated in the Kanto and Kinki regions which encompass Tokyo and Osaka, Japan's two biggest conurbations.

The Housing Survey of 1988 shows that Japan has an adequate number of dwellings related to the number of households, but the average size is only 89 square metres (about half that of the USA). The government recognizes that the country's social capital stock lags behind that of other industrialized nations and therefore that the nation's economic strength is not reflected in its housing and other social capital. In 1990 a Public Investment Basic Plan was formulated to bring these facilities up to the level of other industrialized countries by the year 2000. In particular the average house floor area is planned to increase to 100 square metres by the year 2000.

Characteristics and structure of the industry

Construction companies in Japan usually carry out both design and construction, especially for private projects. Design departments of contractors may have as many as 1,000 professionals.

Most civil engineering work is publicly sponsored and the public sector offices either have their own design sections or hire specialized consultant firms to design their projects. It is quite usual for firms of consultant engineers to employ over 500 people. The largest architectural consultancy firm has over 1,000 employees and many have several hundred. There is co-operation as well as competition between consultants and contractors; contractors may be invited to participate in consultants' design work or vice versa.

In 1991 there were about 515,000 construction contractors licensed either by the Ministry of Construction or by the Governors of Prefectures. Most contractors are small but there are six large companies: Shimizu Corporation, Kajima Corporation, Taisei Corporation, Takenaka Corporation, Ohbayashi Corporation and Kumagai Gumi Company. They each have annual turnover of over ¥ 1,000 billion. They all provide a comprehensive range of construction services in building, civil and heavy engineering; they can find construction sites for clients, help finance and then design, construct and maintain high quality buildings and engineering projects. They all have head offices in Tokyo. Below these top few contractors there are many contractors who are much smaller with broadly similar capabilities.

For the last few decades local contractors have had an expanding domestic market because Japan lags behind western developed countries in the provision of infrastructure, most notably roads, sewerage, housing and the city environments. During the 1980s the economy expanded more or less continuously. Government policy is used to regulate the economy and this helps to give the construction industry a relatively even work flow.

The Contract Construction Business Law requires contractors to obtain a licence to start a construction business. Nearly all site work in Japan is undertaken by trade contractors who maintain a special relationship with a general contractor, known as a *zenecon*. Under this relationship the general contractor will endeavour to provide continuous employment for his subcontractors, in return for which each subcontractor will allow the general contractor to stipulate a contract price, and to monitor both his financial and project performance. The very large companies do not have a permanent workforce, but a family of subcontractors who are loosely connected to them.

MAJOR JAPANESE CONTRACTORS, 1991

Company	Place in ENR's Top 225 International Contractors 1991	Contracts 1991 US$ bn	Foreign contracts as a % of work obtained 1991	Work breakdown 1990
Kajima Corporation	34	17.7	6	Building 72% Civils 24% Real estate 4%
Taisei Corporation	70	17.7	2	Building 74% Civils 23% Real estate 3%
Takenaka Corporation	44	16.3	5	Building 97% Other 3%
Ohbayashi Corporation	26	14.6	9	Building 74% Civils 23% Real estate 4%
Shimizu Corporation	25	10.2	11	Building 80% Civils 15% Real estate 5%
Kumagai Gumi Company Ltd	95	9.1	2	Building 58% Civils 35% Real estate 7%

Sources: Various

Major Japanese construction firms are developing in a number of directions: internationally; diversifying into other businesses in some way linked to construction; strengthening the total engineering competence by research and development; and providing construction related finance. The Japanese have both the expertise and experience to compete with Western European and American contractors. During the 1980s Japanese international contractors have increasingly directed their efforts to the industrialized regions of the world. According to the *Engineering News Record*, 28 Japanese contractors in 1991 had 7.5% of the world construction export market of the top 225 contractors compared to 32 Japanese contractors in 1990 with 14% of the market of the top 250 contractors. There were 16 Japanese contractors in the top 100 of *Engineering News Record*'s international contractors in 1991 compared with 15 in 1990. Some of these are very specialized, for example in petrochemicals, but most have a broad range of operations.

One of the features of contracting organizations in Japan is that they undertake a considerable amount of research and development work. The range of research is very wide, from soil testing to air supported domes. Earthquake engineering is important and the Japanese are generally regarded as world leaders in both research on the use of robots in construction and the development of intelligent buildings. Direct expenditure on research and development by the large construction firms is about 1% of turnover, but they also fund a considerable amount of outside research.

The government is, however, concerned that a number of sub-standard unqualified construction companies have entered the market; the smaller companies tend to have less stable management and to be smaller due to the shortage of young Japanese workers.   In response, the Ministry of Construction has formulated the Structural Adjustment Promotion Program to run from fiscal year 1989 for three years to improve and upgrade industrial training and management.

Only recently have foreign contracting firms been allowed a licence to operate in Japan.   As a result of pressure from the USA in 1988 the first Japan-US Construction Agreement permitted registration of foreign firms. By May 1992 contractor permits had been issued to 27 foreign contractors: 13 from the USA, 10 from South Korea and one each from France, Australia, Switzerland and the Netherlands.

Architectural designers and construction supervisors in Japan must be licensed.   There are three types: first class architects, second class architects and wooden building architects.   First class architects must have passed an examination set by the Minister of Construction and be licensed. The other two categories are dealt with on a similar basis by prefectural governors.

Clients and finance

The table by type of work (page 128) shows that in 1991, 68% of all new construction work was funded privately, including over 96% of housing, 83% of non-housing and about 28% of civil engineering.   In 1990 the clients for new housing construction were as indicated in the table below:

OWNERSHIP OF NEW DWELLINGS 1990

Clients	No of dwelling units	%
National government	23.0	1.4
Prefectures	28.3	1.7
City wards, towns and villages	26.7	1.6
Companies and other corporations	648.2	38.9
Individuals	939.1	56.4
Total	1,665.4	100.0

It is noteworthy that of the private dwellings only 59% are owned by individuals and the remainder by companies and corporations. Contractors (*zenecons*) are increasingly moving into development projects, both in Japan and elsewhere.

Selection of design consultants

Architects, engineers and cost consultants are usually appointed by the client either directly or after some form of competition. Other consultants are chosen by one of the main consultants. The most important basis for selection is track record with price a secondary factor. Personal contacts and recommendations are sometimes relevant in the private sector but rarely in the public sector. The Ministry of Construction publication - Public Announcement No 1206 - includes guidelines for the appointment of consultants. The professional associations publish recommended - but not mandatory - fee scales.

Contractual arrangements

In the public sector, construction companies of the appropriate category and experience are invited to bid. In selecting those invited, central and local governments rank construction firms according to past orders obtained, sales, financial status and technological capabilities. The contract is then awarded to the lowest bidder. In the private sector the client may appoint a specific contractor or invite selected contractors to bid - the latter is the more common system. Many projects are also undertaken on a design and build basis where the architect is employed by the contractor.

The Japanese contractual system is based on trust and mutual understanding. It is very important for both parties to maintain a good and long-term relationship. The Japanese rarely bring a lawyer into negotiations - that implies mistrust - and litigation is only undertaken as a last resort. Clients tend to work regularly with a contracting firm, and will often have in-house staff with knowledge of building design and construction who will have prepared outline drawings of the proposed works. The contractor generally prepares the working drawings, except for building services, which are prepared by the specialist contractor.

The two contract forms in most common use are the Standard Form of Agreement and General Conditions of Government Contract for Works of Building and Civil Engineering, prepared and recommended by the Construction Industry Council of Japan, and the General Conditions of Construction Contracts (GCCC) approved by a number of architects' and contractors' associations. Contract documents, which are relatively short, normally consist of the written contract, general conditions, the design drawings and the specification. There is no bill of quantities but the contractor submits an itemized list of prices (including quantities). Liquidated damages are payable if a project is delayed, and there is a guarantee period of two years for brick or concrete buildings and one year for timber structures. The employer is given express rights to vary the work and negotiations take place on dates and costs. Claims are rare.

Liability and insurance

The Registration Organization for Warrantied Houses, administered by the Construction Ministry, provides a warranty scheme. This gives a ten year guarantee on the durability of structural components, including foundations, floors, walls and roofs plus a five year warranty on the weather resistance of roofs.   The scheme is available to single unit housebuilders using traditional Japanese housebuilding techniques. Prefabricated house builders, who compete with the single unit home builders, also provide a ten year protection on structural components. Some condominium builders have recently started a similar ten year guarantee.   In response, the Housing and Urban Development Corporation, the government-managed house supplier, has, since 1983, developed a long-term warranty programme for some condominiums with warranties of ten years for structural elements, including the roof, and five to ten years for other elements.

Before this long-term warranty of houses and buildings can apply to all builders, a number of problems must be solved regarding such issues as design responsibilities, insurance systems, business profitability and so on.   The principle behind long-term warranty is not to guarantee free repair services for ten years, but to build structures in which defects will not occur for at least ten years.   Since this puts greater importance on quality, a long-term warranty is a necessity for all construction companies and an inevitable outcome in today's quality-conscious market. Those companies unable to offer such a warranty will eventually lose out in a competitive market.

Materials and construction methods

Although the basic materials and methods of construction used in Japan are similar to those of other developed countries, there are considerable differences in detail.   Generally, structures are heavy reinforced concrete, steel framed reinforced concrete, or steel frame with spray applied fireproofing for large buildings, whereas for housing, timber frame is predominant.   Although some prefabrication of components for smaller elements is used, a considerably greater amount of skilled trade work, for example cutting, fitting and welding of steelwork, cutting and threading of steel pipes, and the preparation of natural stone cladding, takes place on site.   The use of tower cranes is unusual; instead materials are either distributed by hoists at the perimeter of buildings, or by small cranes mounted on the top construction level through holes left in the floors.

CONSTRUCTION COST DATA

Cost of labour

The figures below are typical of labour costs in the Tokyo area as at the first quarter 1993. The wage rate is the basis of an employee's income.

	Wage rate (per day) ¥
Site operatives	
Mason/bricklayer	15,000
Carpenter	25,824
Plumber	20,165
Electrician	20,645
Structural steel erector	21,332
HVAC installer	15,008
Semi-skilled worker	15,375
Unskilled labourer	13,026
Equipment operator	21,492
Watchman/security	18,500
Site supervision	
General foreman	26,000
Trades foreman	24,000
Contractors' personnel	
Site manager	39,500
Resident engineer	31,000
Resident surveyor	31,000
Junior engineer	12,500
Junior surveyor	12,500
Planner	12,500
Consultants' personnel	
Senior architect	47,000
Senior engineer	47,000
Senior surveyor	47,000
Qualified architect	39,500
Qualified engineer	39,500
Qualified surveyor	39,500

Cost of materials

The figures that follow are the costs of main construction materials, delivered to site in the Tokyo area, as incurred by contractors in the first quarter 1993. These assume that the materials would be in quantities as required for a medium sized construction project and that the location of the works would be neither constrained nor remote.

	Unit	Cost ¥
Cement and aggregates		
Ordinary portland cement in 40kg bags	tonne	16,000
Coarse aggregates for concrete	m³	4,600
Fine aggregates for concrete	m³	4,400
Ready mixed concrete (210kg cement/cm²)	m³	11,700
Steel		
Mild steel reinforcement	tonne	51,000
High tensile steel reinforcement	tonne	58,800
Precompressing tendon	tonne	45,000
Structural steel sections	tonne	50,000
Bricks and blocks		
Common bricks (210 x 100 x 60mm)	1,000	80,000
Good quality facing bricks (210 x 100 x 60mm)	each	180
Hollow concrete blocks (190 x 190 x 390mm)	each	213
Solid concrete blocks (190 x 190 x 200mm)	each	800
Precast concrete cladding units with exposed aggregate finish	m²	11,900
Timber and insulation		
Softwood sections for carpentry	m³	61,000
Softwood for joinery	m³	127,000
Hardwood for joinery	m³	160,000
Exterior quality plywood (12mm)	m²	970
Plywood for interior joinery (5mm)	m²	730
Softwood strip flooring (15mm)	m²	10,500
Chipboard sheet flooring (15mm)	m²	3,000
Softwood internal door complete with frames and ironmongery	each	79,100
Glass and ceramics		
Float glass (5 mm)	m²	4,030
Sealed double glazing units (FL3+A6+FL3) 12mm thick	m²	8,910
Good quality ceramic wall tiles	m²	3,550
Plaster and paint		
Plaster in 25 kg bags	tonne	45,000
Plasterboard (9mm thick)	m²	170
Emulsion paint in 5 litre tins	kg	350
Gloss oil paint in 5 litre tins	kg	410

	Unit	Cost ¥
Tiles and paviors		
Clay floor tiles (200 x 200mm)	m²	6,000
Vinyl floor tiles (2 x 300 x 300mm)	m²	10,930
Precast concrete paving slabs (300 x 300 x 60mm)	m²	4,780
Clay roof tiles	1,000	126,000
Precast concrete roof tiles	1,000	104,000
Drainage		
WC suite complete	each	43,500
Lavatory basin complete	each	53,900
100mm diameter clay drain pipes	m	2,270
150mm diameter stainless steel drain pipes	m	7,900

Unit rates

The descriptions below are generally shortened versions of standard descriptions listed in full in section 4. Where an item has a two digit reference number (e.g. 05 or 33), this relates to the full description against that number in section 4. Where an item has an alphabetic suffix (e.g. 12A or 34B) this indicates that the standard description has been modified. Where a modification is major the complete modified description is included here and the standard description should be ignored; where a modification is minor (e.g. the insertion of a named hardwood) the shortened description has been modified here but, in general, the full description in section 4 prevails.

The unit rates below are for main work items on a typical construction project in the Tokyo area in the first quarter 1993. The rates include all necessary labour, materials and equipment. Allowances of 7% to cover preliminary and general items and 10% to cover contractors' overheads and profit should be added to the rates.

		Unit	Rate ¥
Excavation			
01	Mechanical excavation of foundation trenches	m³	5,370
02	Hardcore filling making up levels	m²	1,370
03	Earthwork support	m²	15,800
Concrete work			
04	Plain insitu concrete in strip foundations in trenches	m³	13,650
05	Reinforced insitu concrete in beds	m³	13,600
06	Reinforced insitu concrete in walls	m³	13,650
07	Reinforced insitu concrete in suspended floor or roof slabs	m³	13,650
08	Reinforced insitu concrete in columns	m³	13,650
09	Reinforced insitu concrete in isolated beams	m³	13,650
10	Precast concrete slab	m²	10,900

	Unit	Rate ¥
Formwork		
11A Softwood formwork to concrete walls	m²	6,090
12A Softwood formwork to concrete columns	m²	6,090
13 Softwood or metal formwork to horizontal soffits		
of slabs	m²	6,090
Reinforcement		
14 Reinforcement in concrete walls	tonne	126,000
15 Reinforcement in suspended concrete slabs	tonne	126,000
Steelwork		
17 Fabricate, supply and erect steel framed		
structure	tonne	293,400
Brickwork and blockwork		
18 Precast lightweight aggregate hollow concrete		
block walls	m²	5,300
19A Solid (perforated) common bricks	m²	17,500
Roofing		
22 Concrete interlocking roof tiles 430 x 380mm	m²	7,120
23 Plain clay roof tiles 260 x 160mm	m²	8,520
24 Fibre cement roof slates 600 x 300mm	m²	3,700
25 Sawn softwood roof boarding	m²	1,800
26 Particle board roof coverings	m²	2,780
27 3 layers glass-fibre based bitumen felt		
roof covering	m²	7,620
28 Bitumen based mastic asphalt roof covering	m²	5,450
29 Glass-fibre mat roof insulation 160mm thick	m²	1,600
31 Troughed galvanized steel roof cladding	m²	4,400
Woodwork and metalwork		
32 Preservative treated sawn softwood 50 x 100mm	m	4,400
35 Two panel glazed door in hardwood		
size 850 x 2000mm	each	198,000
36 Solid core half hour fire resisting hardwood		
internal flush doors, size 800 x 2000mm	each	50,400
37 Aluminium double glazed window,		
size 1200 x 1200mm	each	97,000
38 Aluminium double glazed door, size 850 x 2100mm	each	107,000
39 Hardwood skirtings	m	2,050
40 Framed structural steelwork in universal		
joist sections	tonne	166,000
41 Structural steelwork lattice roof trusses	tonne	185,000
Plumbing		
42 UPVC half round eaves gutter	m	1,600
43 UPVC rainwater pipes	m	3,700
44 Light gauge copper cold water tubing	m	2,320
45 High pressure plastic pipes for cold water supply	m	1,400

		Unit	Rate ¥
46	Low pressure plastic pipes for cold water distribution	m	1,690
47	UPVC soil and vent pipes	m	6,070
48	White vitreous china WC suite	each	73,600
49	White vitreous china lavatory basin	each	67,200
51	Stainless steel single bowl sink and double drainer	each	80,200

Electrical work

		Unit	Rate ¥
52	PVC insulated and copper sheathed cable	m	330
53	13 amp unswitched socket outlet	each	4,580
54	Flush mounted 20 amp, 1 way light switch	each	4,680

Finishings

		Unit	Rate ¥
55A	2 coats gypsum based plaster on concrete walls 20mm thick	m²	5,000
56	White glazed tiles on plaster walls	m²	10,700
57	Red clay quarry tiles on concrete floor	m²	10,800
58A	Cement and sand screed to concrete floors 30mm thick	m²	2,200
59	Thermoplastic floor tiles on screed	m²	2,000
60	Mineral fibre tiles on concealed suspension system	m²	4,050

Glazing

		Unit	Rate ¥
61	Glazing to wood	m²	5,880

Painting

		Unit	Rate ¥
62	Emulsion on plaster walls	m²	850
63	Oil paint on timber	m²	1,200

Approximate estimating

The building costs per unit area given below are averages incurred by building clients for typical buildings in the Tokyo area as at the first quarter 1993. They are based upon the total floor area of all storeys, measured between external walls and without deduction for internal walls. Approximate estimating costs generally include mechanical and electrical installations but exclude furniture, loose or special equipment, and external works; they also exclude fees for professional services. The costs shown are for specifications and standards appropriate to Japan and this should be borne in mind when attempting comparisons with similarly described building types in other countries. A discussion of this issue is included in section 2. Comparative data for countries covered in this publication including construction cost data are presented in Part Three.

Approximate estimating costs must be treated with reserve; they cannot provide more than a rough guide to the probable cost of building.

	Cost m^2 ¥	Cost ft^2 ¥
Industrial buildings		
Factories for letting	270,000	25,000
Warehouses, low bay (6 to 8m high) for letting (no heating)	200,000	18,500
Administrative and commercial buildings		
Civic offices, fully air conditioned	355,000	33,000
Offices for letting, high rise, air conditioned	405,000	37,500
Prestige/headquarters office, high rise, air conditioned	450,000	42,000
Health and education buildings		
General hospitals (300 beds)	550,000	51,000
Secondary/middle schools	420,000	39,000
Recreation and arts buildings		
Theatres (over 500 seats) including seating and stage equipment	610,000	56,500
Residential buildings		
Social/economic apartment housing, high rise (with lifts)	300,000	28,000
Private sector apartment buildings (luxury)	390,000	36,000
Hotel, 5 star, city centre	500,000	46,000
Hotel, 3 star, city/provincial	400,000	37,000

Regional variations

The approximate estimating costs are based on projects in Tokyo. These costs should be adjusted by the following factors to take account of regional variations:

Nagoya	: -7%	Fukuoka:	-11%
Osaka	: -3%	Sapporo:	-6%
Hiroshima:	-7%		

EXCHANGE RATES AND INFLATION

The combined effect of exchange rates and inflation on prices within a country and price comparisons between countries is discussed in section 2.

Exchange rates

The graph overleaf plots the movement of the Japanese yen against sterling and the US dollar since 1980. The figures used for the graph are quarterly and the method of calculating these and other related issues are discussed in section 2. The exchange rate at the first quarter 1993 was yen 182 to the pound sterling and yen 123 to the US dollar.

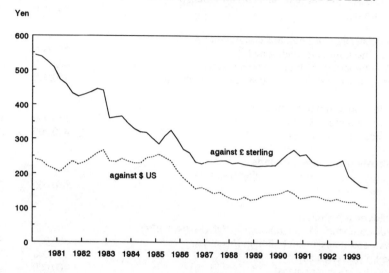

THE JAPANESE YEN AGAINST STERLING AND THE US DOLLAR

Price inflation

The table opposite presents consumer price and building cost inflation in Japan since 1980.

CONSUMER PRICE AND BUILDING COST INFLATION

Year	Consumer price inflation average index	average change %	Building cost index average index	average change %
1980	100		100	
1981	105	5.0	103	3.0
1982	108	2.9	104	1.0
1983	110	1.9	103	-1.0
1984	112	1.8	103	0.0
1985	115	2.7	103	0.0
1986	115	0.0	102	-1.0
1987	115	0.0	104	2.0
1988	116	0.9	111	6.7
1989	119	2.6	118	6.3
1990	122	2.5	127	7.6
1991	126	3.3	135	6.3

USEFUL ADDRESSES

Public Organizations

Ministry of Construction, 1 - 3 Kasumigaseki
2 - chome, Chiyoda-ku
Tokyo 100
Tel: 03 3580 4311
Fax: 03 5251 1926

Contractors' Registration Board

Prefectural Office of the Ministry of Construction

Kanto Regional Construction Bureau (6 other locations)
1 - 3 1 Otemachi, Chiyoda-ku
Tokyo 100
Tel: 03 3211 6261
Fax: 03 3285 0287

National Land Agency,
1 - 2 - 1 Kasumigaseki, Chiyoda-ku
Tokyo 100
Tel: 03 3593 3311
Fax: 03 3501 5349

Ministry of Transport
          2 - 1 - 3 Kasumigaseki, Chiyoda-ku
          Tokyo 100
          Tel: 03 3580 3111
          Fax: 03 3593 0474

Housing and Urban Development
          1 - 14 - 6 Kudankita, Chiyoda-ku
          Tokyo 100
          Tel: 03 3263 8111
          Fax: 03 3263 8177

Japanese Industrial Standards
          4 - 1 - 24, Akasaka, Minato- ku
          Tokyo 107
          Tel: 03 3583 8005
          Fax: 03 3586 2014

Management and Coordination Agency
          The Statistics Bureau
          19 - 1 Wakamatsu - cho, Shinjuku - ku
          Tokyo
          Tel: 03 3202 1111
          Fax: 03 5273 1180

Trade and Professional Associations

Japan Federation of Construction Contractors, Inc.
          Tokyo Kensetsu Bldg., 2 - 5 - 1 Hacchobori
          Chuo-ku
          Tokyo 104
          Tel: 03 3553 0701
          Fax: 03 3552 2360

The Associated General Contractors of Japan Inc
          2 - 5 - 1 Hacchobori
          Chuo-ku
          Tokyo
          Tel: 03 3551 9396
          Fax: 03 3555 3218

Japan Civil Engineering Contractors' Association Inc
          Tokyo Kensetsu Bldg., 5 - 1 Hacchobori
          2 - chome, Chuo-ku, Tokyo 104
          Tel: 03 3553 3201
          Fax: 03 3552 3206

Japan Construction Consultants Association
    Shin Kudan Bldg., 2 - 4 Kudan Minami
    2 - chome, Chiyoda-ku, Tokyo 102
    Tel: 03 3239 7992

The Japan Chamber of Commerce and Industry
    3 - 2 - 2 Marunouchi
    Chiyoda - ku, Tokyo 100
    Tel: 03 3283 7823
    Fax: 03 3211 4859

Japan Institute of Architects
    2 - 3 - 16 Jingumae
    Shibuya - ku, Tokyo 150
    Tel: 03 3408 8291
    Fax: 03 3408 8294

Japan Structural Consultants Association
    Ohasgi Bldg., 1 - 3 - 2 Kudan Kita
    Chiyoda-ku, Tokyo
    Tel: 03 3262 8498
    Fax: 03 3262 8486

The Building Surveyors' Institute of Japan
    2 - 26 - 20 Shiba, Minato - ku
    Tokyo 108
    Tel: 03 3453 9591
    Fax: 03 3453 9597

Management Research Society (Construction Industry)
    11 - 8 Nihonbashi - Odenmachon
    Chuo-ku, Tokyo
    Tel: 03 3663 2411
    Fax: 03 3663 2417

The Building Centre of Japan
    No. 30 Mori Bldg, 3 - 2 - 2 Toranomon
    Minato - ku, Tokyo
    Tel: 03 3434 7161
    Fax: 03 3431 3301

In Malaysia:

DAVIS LANGDON & SEAH MALAYSIA

The strategic and integrated management of cost, time and quality - the client "risk" areas of a contract - are essential functions, which are necessary to ensure the satisfactory planning, procurement, execution and operation of construction projects.

We specialise in the financial management of construction projects and their risk areas, from project inception to completion and we concentrate on:

* being positive and creative in our advice, rather than simply reactive;

* providing value for money via efficient management, rather than on superficial cost monitoring;

* giving advice that is matched to the Client's requirements, rather than imposing standard or traditional solutions;

* paying attention to the life-cycle costs of constructing and occupying a building, rather than to the initial capital cost only.

Our aim is to provide our clients with risk assurance, cost control and value for money, via effective advice, cost planning and management.

Kuala Lumpur, Johor Bahru,
Kota Kinabalu, Kuching, Penang

DAVIS LANGDON & SEAH INTERNATIONAL

MANAGE AND LIMIT CLIENT RISK - ADDING VALUE

Malaysia

KEY DATA

Population

Population (1991)	17.6m
Urban population	38%
Population under 15	38%
Population over 65	4%
Average annual growth rate (1980 to 1990)	2.6%

Geography

Land area comprising more than 13,000 islands	329,758 km²
Agricultural area	13%
Capital city	Kuala Lumpur (population 1.1m)

Economy

Monetary unit	Malaysian dollar (M$) (or Ringgit)
Exchange rate (average first quarter 1993) to:	
the pound sterling	M$ 3.88
the US dollar	M$ 2.62
the yen x 100	M$ 2.13
Inflation rate (1991)	4.4%
Average annual inflation (1980 to 1990)	1.6%
Gross Domestic Product (GDP) (1991)	M$ 129.5bn
GDP per capita (1991)	M$ 7,360
Real GDP growth (1980 to 1990)	5.2%
Private consumption as a proportion of GDP	54%
Public consumption as a proportion of GDP	13%
Investment as a proportion of GDP	34%
Central government expenditure as a proportion of Gross National Product	31%

Construction

Net value of construction output (1991)	M$ 4.9 bn
Net value of construction per capita (1991)	M$ 277
Net value of construction output as a proportion of GDP (1991)	3.8%

Note: All data relate to 1990 unless otherwise indicated.

THE CONSTRUCTION INDUSTRY

Construction output

The net value of construction output - output excluding materials - in 1991 was M$4.9 billion, equivalent to US$2.2 billion. This represents an increase of 14.6% over 1990 and is nearly 4% of GDP. The construction sector has experienced growth of over 10% per annum since 1989 after recovering from a slump (1984 to 1987) accompanying the nation's recession of 1984 and 1985. The sector is expected to expand by over 13% in 1992, and has been showing double digit growth for four consecutive years.

Investment in the provision of new sports and ancillary facilities for the 1998 Commonwealth Games and the proposed new M$20 billion Kuala Lumpur International Airport offer the possibility of extending the current buoyant construction activities still further.

It is expected that a total of 25,500 new jobs will be created in the industry in 1992 increasing the total number employed to 481,400. This represents about 6.8% of the total Malaysian workforce. However, with accelerated growth, the sector is currently experiencing a labour shortage particularly of skilled and semi-professional workers. At present, a large number of workers in the industry are immigrants from Indonesia and Thailand. To ease the labour shortage, illegal foreign workers have been given to 30 June 1992 to register with the authorities.

An indication of the split of building output into types of work is that residential construction starts in square metres in 13 major towns represented over 70% of total building starts in 1990 and over 77% in 1991 though completions were only around 50% of the total. In each case the remainder is non-residential building projects. There was a great deal of activity in housing in 1991 related to a steady increase in disposable income, the availability of loans, the increased supply of affordable houses and the relaxation of eligibility conditions for government housing loans. However, the current demand for houses, is expected to moderate.

In line with strong economic growth, demand for office space has continued to expand. During the first half of 1992, the demand for office space in and around Kuala Lumpur persisted with an average occupancy rate of 97%.

In parallel with the government's commitment to boost the tourist industry, development of projects in this sector has been rapid with the construction of golf courses, tourist resorts (generally incorporating golf courses, hotels, villas and theme parks) and hotels. At the end of 1991, more than ten tourist resorts with theme parks were at various stages of planning or construction. The hotel occupancy rate is expected to pick up in 1993 to 1994 following a slight drop of 2.8% to 62.6% during the first seven months of 1992 from the corresponding period in 1991.

Civil engineering construction has continued to focus on the provision and improvement of infrastructure related to social development, public works and transport; implementation of several large projects, including the North-South Highway Project, the Peninsular Gas Utilization Project II and the Antah Biwater Project (National Rural Water Supply). It is expected that this sector will continue to provide significant stimulus to the growth of construction activity over the medium term.

Characteristics and structure of the industry

In 1989 there were some 5,000 large contracting companies in Malaysia. Large contracting companies are those reporting M$100,000 and over value of work per annum. These firms, though only one-tenth of the total number of companies in the construction sector, undertake about 97% (amounting to M$8,289 million in 1989) of the total value of work done. The breakdown by numbers for large firms, according to type of construction undertaken, is 1,244 (residential), 917 (non-residential), 1,719 (civil engineering) and 1,586 (special trade). There is a contractors' registration board.

The professions are regulated by the appropriate professional bodies - *Pertubuhan Akitek Malaysia* (PAM), Institution of Engineers Malaysia and the Association of Consulting Engineers Malaysia, and the Institution of Surveyors Malaysia. Individual professional consultants have to be registered with their respective professional boards: the Board of Architects, the Board of Engineers and the Board of Quantity Surveyors. In addition, all firms of quantity surveyors must be registered with the Board. The latest figures show the numbers of professional consulting firms to be as follows:

PROFESSIONAL CONSULTING FIRMS IN MALAYSIA

Location	Architectural firms	Engineering firms	Surveying firms
Peninsular Malaysia	280	312	286
Sabah	25	24	41
Sarawak	35	40	34
Total	340	376	361*

* 79 of these are quantity surveying firms

Architects and engineers are equally important in the development process. Generally, projects involving building works will have the architect as the supervising officer; in civil works, the engineer is the supervising officer.

Clients and finance

In total construction investment about one third is by the public sector and the balance by the private sector. The government has a positive policy towards foreign investment and foreign capital accounts for the majority of investment funds. Taiwan and Japan are the dominant investors followed by Singapore, the United Kingdom, the United States, Indonesia and Hong Kong.

Selection of design consultants

Professional consultants are normally appointed by the client and whether the project is residential, non-residential building, or civil engineering the method used in selecting consultants is broadly the same. In public works the main selection criteria used are quota, track record, contacts and price. (Consultants cannot exceed their allocated quota of appointments in the public sector.) In the private sector a firm's track record and personal relationships are important, weighing almost as heavily as cost considerations.

The guidelines which professional bodies produce on the procurement of their members' services or for the appointment of consultants are listed in their respective fee scales and conditions of engagement - Board of Architects Scale of Fees and Conditions of Engagement and Board of Quantity Surveyors Scale of Fees and Conditions of Engagement. Though these fee scales are theoretically mandatory, they are rarely used, mainly due to modifications to the actual service required. In the private sector discounts are negotiated.

Contractual arrangements

A general contractor is usually appointed by competitive tender. Bills of quantities are normally used. Specialist contractors are usually employed for mechanical and electrical installations and, for major or prestige projects, international contractors are often appointed.

Two main forms of building contract are used. The JKR (*Jabatan Kerja Raya* or Public Works Department) form of contract is used for all government works; and the PAM (produced by *Pertubuhan Akitek Malaysia*) is currently in use in Malaysia for most private sector projects and is accepted and understood by the local building industry.

Development control and standards

The land administration in Malaysia is based on the Torren System. Provisions for the disposal of land, land use, subdivision, partition and amalgamation etc. are provided under the National Land Code (Act 56 of 1965). The rights and powers are vested solely in the state authority (the State Government). Basically there are three categories of land use: agriculture, building and industry. The National Land Code provides uniformity in law and policy pertaining to land throughout Peninsular Malaysia, including land tenure, registration of titles to land, transfer of land, leases and charges, easements and other rights and interests in land.

The promulgation of a separate Act of Parliament governing town planning countrywide is proposed. Currently there are three pieces of planning legislation that are wholly or partly enforced. These are:

- City of Kuala Lumpur (Planning) Act No. 107, 1973
- Town and Country Planning Act No. 172, 1976
- Federal Territory (Planning) Act No. 267, 1982

Planning permission is required for all types of development as defined in the Town and Country Planning Act 1976. Procedures for obtaining planning approval vary, depending on the various local authorities in Peninsular Malaysia. The granting of approval can take between three months and twelve months.

Buildings are required to comply with the Uniform Building By Laws and Street, Drainage & Building Act 1974 (Act 133). Local authorities and statutory bodies are responsible for ensuring compliance with standards.

Research

There is presently no established organization conducting research in construction. Efforts are being made by government institutions to establish a construction industry development board to undertake research, development and training and manpower in the industry. The following institutions are undertaking some research on industry related subjects:

- Statistical Department of Malaysia : Building Cost Index

- Public Works Department of Malaysia : Tender Price Index
  Schedule of Rates

- Institution of Surveyors (Malaysia) : Cost Analysis
  Basic Material Prices

CONSTRUCTION COST DATA

Cost of labour

The figures below are typical of labour costs in Kuala Lumpur as at the first quarter 1993. Cost of labour indicates the cost to a contractor of employing that employee.

	Labour rate (per day = 8 hr) *M$*
Site operatives	
Mason/bricklayer	60
Carpenter	60
Plumber	60
Electrician	60
Structural steel erector	60

	Labour rate (per day = 8 hr) M$
HVAC installer	60
Semi-skilled worker	45
Unskilled labourer	28
Equipment operator	60
Watchman/security	20

	(per month)
Site supervision	
General foreman	1,800
Trades foreman	1,500
Clerk of works	1,200
Contractors' personnel	
Site manager	5,000
Resident engineer	4,500
Resident surveyor	3,000
Junior engineer	1,500
Junior surveyor	1,500
Consultants' personnel	
Senior architect	5,000
Senior engineer	5,000
Senior surveyor	3,000
Qualified architect	3,000
Qualified engineer	3,000
Qualified surveyor	3,000

Cost of materials

The figures that follow are the costs of main construction materials, delivered to site in the capital area, as incurred by contractors in the first quarter 1993. These assume that the materials would be in quantities as required for a medium sized construction project and that the location of the works would be neither constrained nor remote.

	Unit	Cost M$
Cement and aggregate		
Ordinary portland cement in 50kg bags	tonne	184.00
Coarse aggregates for concrete in 20mm granite	m^3	43.50
Fine aggregates for concrete	m^3	12.00
Ready mixed concrete (mix 1:2:4)	m^3	128.00
Ready mixed concrete (mix 1:1:2)	m^3	141.00
Steel		
Mild steel reinforcement 10mm - 40mm diameter	tonne	1,200.00
High tensile steel reinforcement 10mm - 40mm diameter	tonne	1,240.00

	Unit	Cost M$
Structural steel sections	tonne	1,800.00
Bricks and blocks		
Common bricks (215 x 102 x 65mm)	1,000	250.00
Good quality facing bricks (210 x 100 x 70mm)	1,000	550.00
Hollow concrete blocks (200 x 400 x 190mm)	1,000	1,300.00
Solid concrete blocks (200 x 400 x 190mm)	1,000	1,700.00
Timber and insulation		
Softwood sections for carpentry	m^3	350.00
Softwood for joinery	m^3	450.00
Hardwood for joinery	m^3	600.00
Exterior quality plywood	m^2	12.00
Plywood for interior joinery	m^2	10.00
Softwood strip flooring	m^2	120.00
100mm thick quilt insulation	m^2	9.00
100mm thick rigid slab insulation	m^2	16.00
Softwood internal door complete with frames and		
ironmongery	each	200.00
Glass and ceramics		
Float glass (5 mm)	m^2	41.00
Good quality ceramic wall tiles (150 x 150mm)	m^2	31.00
Plaster and paint		
Plasterboard (5mm thick)	m^2	9.00
Emulsion paint in 5 litre tins	litre	9.85
Gloss oil paint in 5 litre tins	litre	14.00
Tiles and paviors		
Clay floor tiles (3 x 200 x 200mm)	m^2	32.50
Vinyl floor tiles (2 x 300 x 300mm)	m^2	26.00
Precast concrete paving slabs (300 x 300 x 60mm)	m^2	35.00
Clay roof tiles	1,000	3,800.00
Precast concrete roof tiles	1,000	1,050.00
Drainage		
WC suite complete	each	435.00
Lavatory basin complete	each	200.00
100mm diameter clay drain pipes	m	22.00
150mm diameter stainless steel drain pipes	m	28.00

Unit rates

The descriptions below are generally shortened versions of standard
descriptions listed in full in section 4.   Where an item has a two digit
reference number (e.g. 05 or 33), this relates to the full description
against that number in section 4. Where an item has an alphabetic suffix

(e.g. 12A or 34B) this indicates that the standard description has been modified. Where a modification is major the complete modified description is included here and the standard description should be ignored; where a modification is minor (e.g. the insertion of a named hardwood) the shortened description has been modified here but, in general, the full description in section 4 prevails.

The unit rates below are for main work items in a typical construction project in the Kuala Lumpur area in the first quarter 1993. The rates include all necessary labour, materials and equipment. Allowances of 6 to 8% to cover preliminary and general items and 15% to cover contractors' overheads and profit have been included in the rates.

		Unit	Rate M$
Excavation			
01	Mechanical excavation of foundation trenches	m^3	7.00
02	Hardcore filling making up levels	m^2	6.00
Concrete work			
04	Plain insitu concrete in strip foundations in trenches	m^3	178.00
05	Reinforced insitu concrete in beds	m^3	178.00
06	Reinforced insitu concrete in walls	m^3	178.00
07	Reinforced insitu concrete in suspended floor or roof slabs	m^3	178.00
08	Reinforced insitu concrete in columns	m^3	191.00
09	Reinforced insitu concrete in isolated beams	m^3	178.00
Formwork			
11A	Softwood formwork to concrete walls	m^2	22.00
12A	Softwood formwork to concrete columns	m^2	25.00
13	Softwood or metal formwork to horizontal soffits of slabs	m^2	22.00
Reinforcement			
14	Reinforcement in concrete walls	tonne	2,460.00
15	Reinforcement in suspended concrete slabs	tonne	2,460.00
16	Fabric reinforcement in concrete beds	m^2	11.00
Steelwork			
17	Fabricate, supply and erect steel framed structure	tonne	3,690.00
Brickwork and blockwork			
18	Precast lightweight aggregate hollow concrete block walls	m^2	20.00
19A	Solid (perforated) common bricks	m^2	34.00
20A	Sand lime bricks	m^2	32.00
21A	Facing bricks	m^2	74.00
Roofing			
22	Concrete interlocking roof tiles 430 x 380mm	m^2	25.00
23	Plain clay roof tiles 260 x 160mm	m^2	74.00

		Unit	*Rate M$*
24	Fibre cement roof slates 600 x 300mm	m²	22.00
25	Sawn softwood roof boarding	m²	30.00
26	Particle board roof coverings	m²	25.00
27	3 layers glass-fibre based bitumen felt roof covering	m²	31.00
28	Bitumen based mastic asphalt roof covering	m²	25.00
29	Glass-fibre mat roof insulation 160mm thick	m²	6.00
31	Troughed galvanized steel roof cladding	m²	33.00

Woodwork and metalwork

32	Preservative treated sawn softwood 50 x 100mm	m³	1,050.00
33	Preservative treated sawn softwood 50 x 150mm	m³	1,050.00
34	Single glazed casement window in hardwood, size 650 x 900mm	each	98.00
35	Two panel glazed door in hardwood size 850 x 2000mm	each	492.00
36	Solid core half hour fire resisting hardwood internal flush doors, size 800 x 2000mm	each	431.00
37	Aluminium double glazed window, size 1200 x 1200mm	each	677.00
38	Aluminium double glazed door, size 850 x 2100mm	each	677.00
39	Hardwood skirtings	m	7.00
40	Framed structural steelwork in universal joist sections	tonne	3,380.00
41	Structural steelwork lattice roof trusses	tonne	3,940.00

Plumbing

42	UPVC half round eaves gutter	m	25.00
43	UPVC rainwater pipes	m	20.00
44	Light gauge copper cold water tubing	m	31.00
45	High pressure plastic pipes for cold water supply	m	10.00
46	Low pressure plastic pipes for cold water distribution	m	9.00
47	UPVC soil and vent pipes	m	20.00
48	White vitreous china WC suite	each	615.00
49	White vitreous china lavatory basin	each	431.00
51	Stainless steel single bowl sink and double drainer	each	738.00

Electrical Work

52	PVC insulated and copper sheathed cable	m	6.00
53	13 amp unswitched socket outlet	each	79.00
54	Flush mounted 20 amp, 1 way light switch	each	102.00

Finishings

55A	2 coats gypsum based plaster on concrete walls 20mm thick	m²	22.00
56	White glazed tiles on plaster walls	m²	37.00
57	Red clay quarry tiles on concrete floor	m²	55.00
58A	Cement and sand screed to concrete floors 30mm thick	m²	9.00

		Unit	Rate M$
59	Thermoplastic floor tiles on screed	m²	25.00
60	Mineral fibre tiles on concealed suspension system	m²	55.00

Glazing

61	Glazing to wood	m²	55.00

Painting

62	Emulsion on plaster walls	m²	4.00
63	Oil paint on timber	m²	6.00

Approximate estimating

The building costs per unit area given below are averages incurred by building clients for typical buildings in the capital area as at the first quarter 1993. They are based upon the total floor area of all storeys, measured between external walls and without deduction for internal walls.

Approximate estimating costs generally include mechanical and electrical installations but exclude furniture, loose or special equipment, and external works; they also exclude fees for professional services. The costs shown are for specifications and standards appropriate to Malaysia and this should be borne in mind when attempting comparisons with similarly described building types in other countries. A discussion of this issue is included in section 2. Comparative data for countries covered in this publication, including construction cost data, are presented in Part Three.

Approximate estimating costs must be treated with reserve; they cannot provide more than a rough guide to the probable cost of building.

	Cost m² M$	Cost ft² M$
Industrial buildings		
Factories for letting	480	45.00
Factories for owner occupation (light industrial use)	650	60.00
Factories for owner occupation (heavy industrial use)	970	90.00
Factory/office (high-tech) for letting (shell and core only)	860	80.00
Factory/office (high-tech) for letting (ground floor shell, first floor offices)	1,080	100.00
Factory/office (high tech) for owner occupation (controlled environment, fully finished)	1,940	180.00
High tech laboratory workshop centres (air conditioned)	430	40.00
Administrative and commercial buildings		
Civic offices, non air conditioned	750	70.00
Civic offices, fully air conditioned	1,020	95.00
Offices for letting, 5 to 10 storeys, non air conditioned	860	80.00
Offices for letting, 5 to 10 storeys, air conditioned	1,130	105.00

	Cost m² M$	Cost ft² M$
Offices for letting, high rise, air conditioned	1,610	150.00
Offices for owner occupation, 5 to 10 storeys, non air conditioned	1,080	100.00
Offices for owner occupation, 5 to 10 storeys, air conditioned	1,290	120.00
Offices for owner occupation, high rise, air conditioned	1,830	170.00
Prestige/headquarters office, 5 to 10 storeys, air conditioned	1,510	140.00
Prestige/headquarters office, high rise, air conditioned	2,040	190.00

Health and education buildings

General hospitals	bed	30,000
Private hospitals (181 beds)	900	83.50
Primary/junior schools (m²)	440	41.00
Secondary/middle schools (m²)	490	46.00

Recreation and arts buildings

Theatres (over 500 seats) including seating and stage equipment	seat	3,500
Theatres (less than 500 seats) including seating and stage equipment	seat	4,000
Concert halls including seating	1,250	116.00
Sports hall including changing and social facilities	910	85.00
Swimming pools (international standard) including changing and social facilities	each	350,000
Swimming pools (schools standard) including changing facilities	each	250,000
National museums including full air conditioning and standby generator	1,020	95.00
Local museums including air conditioning	970	90.00

Residential buildings

Social/economic single family housing (multiple units)	480	45.00
Private/mass market single family housing 2 storey detached/semidetached (multiple units)	590	55.00
Purpose designed single family housing 2 storey detached (single unit)	750	70.00
Social/economic apartment housing, low rise (no lifts)	380	35.00
Social/economic apartment housing, high rise (with lifts)	700	65.00
Private sector apartment building (standard specification)	810	75.00
Private sector apartment buildings (luxury)	970	90.00
Student/nurses halls of residence	590	55.00
Homes for the elderly (shared accommodation)	480	45.00
Homes for the elderly (self contained with shared communal facilities)	590	55.00
Hotel, 5 star, city centre	3,010	280.00
Hotel, 3 star, city/provincial	2,040	190.00
Motel	1,180	110.00

Regional variations

The approximate estimating costs are based on projects in the capital. Adjust these costs by the following factors to take account of regional variations:

Selangor	0%
Penang	+5%
Johore	+15%
Kota Kinabalu	+20%
Kuching	+15%

EXCHANGE RATES AND INFLATION

The combined effect of exchange rates and inflation on prices within a country and price comparisons between countries is discussed in section 2.

Exchange rates

The graph below plots the movement of the Malaysian dollar (ringgit) against sterling, the US dollar and the Japanese yen since 1980. The figures used for the graph are quarterly and the method of calculating these and other related issues are discussed in section 2. The exchange rates at the first quarter 1993 were M$3.88 to the pound sterling, M$2.62 to the US dollar and M$2.13 to 100 Japanese yen.

THE MALAYSIAN DOLLAR (RINGGIT) AGAINST STERLING, THE US DOLLAR AND THE JAPANESE YEN

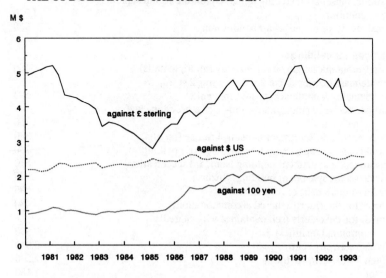

Price inflation

The table below presents consumer price and building price inflation in Malaysia since 1980.

CONSUMER PRICE AND BUILDING PRICE INFLATION

Year	Consumer price inflation average index	average change %	Building price index average index	average change %
1980	100		100	
1981	109	9.0	114	14.0
1982	116	6.4	123	7.9
1983	122	5.2	125	1.6
1984	125	2.5	124	-0.8
1985	126	0.8	125	0.8
1986	126	0.0	124	-0.8
1987	128	1.6	123	-0.8
1988	131	2.3	126	2.4
1989	135	3.1	131	4.0
1990	140	3.7	140	6.7

USEFUL ADDRESSES

Public Organizations

The Ministry of Works
 Kementerian Kerjaraya Malaysia
 Jalan Sultan Salahuddin
 50580 Kuala Lumpur
 Tel: (03) 2919011
 Fax: (03) 2936954
 Cable: MINWORK, KUALA LUMPUR
 Telex: KRT MA 30415

Department of National Housing
 Jabatan Perumahan Negara
 Tel: (03) 2540222

The Public Works Department
 Jabatan Kerja Awam
 (in every state there is a State Public Works Department)

The Ministry of Housing and Local Government
Kementerian Perumahan dan Kerajaan Tempatan
Paras 4 & 5 Block K
Pusat Bandar Damansara
50644 Kuala Lumpur
Tel: (03) 2547470/7332/7033
Fax: (03) 2554066

Urban Development Authority (UDA)
Perbadanan Pembangunan Bandar
Perbadanan Pembangunan Bandar ibu Pejabat
Menara Bukit Bintang
Lot 111 Jalan Bukit Bintang
55100 Kuala Lumpur
Tel: (03) 2428022

The Ministry of Land and Regional Development
Kementerian Kemajuan Tanah dan Kemajuan Wilayah
T.4 Bangunan Sri MARA
Jalan Raja Laut
50574 Kuala Lumpur
Tel: (03) 2921566

The Ministry of Public Enterprises
Kementerian Perusahaan Awam
Tingkat 3 Wisma P.K.N.S
Jalan Raja Laut
50625 Kuala Lumpur
Tel: (03) 2985022

The Ministry of Science, Technology and the Environment
Kementerian Sains, Teknologi dan Alam Sekitar Malaysia
Tingkat 14 Wisma Sime Darby
Jalan Raja Laut
50662 Kuala Lumpur
Tel: (03) 2938955

The Malaysian Highway Authority
Lembaga Lebuhraya Malaysia
Bangunan Yayasan Syed Kechik
Jalan Pantai Baru
59100 Kuala Lumpur
Tel: (03) 2545566

Town and Country Planning Department
Jabatan Perancang Bandar dan Desa
Tel: (03) 2989211

Board of Architects Malaysia
Lembaga Akitek Malaysia
2nd Floor Block C
Cawangan Bangunan, ibu Pejabat JKR
Jalan Tun Ismail, P O Box 12695
50786 Kuala Lumpur
Tel: (03) 2982978
Fax: (03) 2936881

Board of Engineers Malaysia
Lembaga Jurutera Malaysia
c/o Kementerian Kerja Raya Malaysia
Jalan Sultan Salahuddin
50580 Kuala Lumpur
Tel: (03) 2912090
Fax: (03) 2925017

Board of Quantity Surveyors Malaysia
Lambaga Jurukur Bahan Malaysia
Tingkat 9 ibupejatbat JKR
Jalan Sultan Salahuddin
50582 Kuala Lumpur

Board of Land Surveyors Malaysia
Lembaga Jurukur Tanah Malaysia
2735 Tingkat 1 Jalan Permata 4
Taman Pertama Ulu Kelang
Tel: (03) 4085191
Fax: (03) 4085178

Standards and Industrial Research Institute (SIRIM)
Persiaran Dato' Menteri, Seksyen 2 P O Box 7035
40911 Shah Alam
Tel: (03) 5592601, 5591630
Fax: (03) 5508095
Telex: SIRIM MA 38672
Hotline: (03) 5503535

Department of Statistics
Jabatan Perangkaan
Jalan Cenderasari, 50514 Kuala Lumpur

Trade and Professional Associations

Master Builders Association Malaysia
13C Jalan Gereja (3rd Floor)
50100 Kuala Lumpur
Tel: (03) 2321636, 2382433
Fax: (03) 2383228

Association of Malaysian Architects
Pertubuhan Akitek Malaysia (PAM)
4 & 6 Jalan Tangsi
P O Box 10855
50726 Kuala Lumpur
Tel: (03) 2984136, 2928733, 2918605
Fax: (03) 2928782

Association of Consulting Engineers Malaysia
63 & 65-2 Medan Setia 1
Damansara Heights
50490 Kuala Lumpur
Tel: (03) 2550031, 2550079, 2550158
Fax: (03) 24553499

The Institution of Engineers Malaysia
Bangunan Ingenieur
Lots 60 & 62 Jalan 52/4
P O Box 223, Jalan Sultan
46720 Petaling Jaya
Tel: (03) 7569173, 7569575
Fax: (03) 7577678

Institution of Surveyors Malaysia
Penthouse Bangunan Jurukur
Lots 64 & 66 Jalan 52/4
P O Box 171, 46720 Petaling Jaya
Tel: (03) 7569728, 7551773, 7550253
Fax: (03) 7550253

Malaysian Institute of Planners
51B Jalan SS 21/56B
Damansara Utama
47400 Petaling Jaya
Tel: (03) 7187272

Malaysian Professional Centre
51B Jalan SS 21/56B
Damansara Utama
47400 Petaling Jaya
Tel: (03) 7187171, 7189894
Fax: (03) 7177354

Housing Developers' Association Malaysia
1606 16th Floor Wisma Lim Foo Yong
Jalan Raja Chulan
50200 Kuala Lumpur
Tel: (03) 2442057
Fax: (03) 2445461

Malaysian Timber Industry Board
    5th & 6th Floor Wisma DNP
    Jalan Ampang P O Box 10887
    50728 Kuala Lumpur
    Tel: (03) 2486233
    Fax: (03) 2413416

The Malaysian Timber Industry Development Council
    9B 9th Floor Bangunan Arab-Malaysian
    55 Jalan Raja Chulan
    50200 Kuala Lumpur
    Tel: (03) 2323999
    Fax: (03) 2386376

Malaysian International Chamber of Commerce and Industry
    10th Floor, Wisma Damansara
    Jalan Semantan
    50490 Kuala Lumpur
    Tel: (03) 2542677 (Hunting Line)/ (03) 2542117
    Fax: (03) 2554946, 2561929

The National Chamber of Commerce and Industry of Malaysia
    17th Floor Plaza Pekeliling
    Jalan Tun Pazak
    50400 Kuala Lumpur
    Tel: (03) 4429871
    Fax: (03) 4416043

Malaysian Industrial Development Authority (M.I.D.A)
    G, 3rd-6th and 9th Floor, Wisma Damansara
    Jalan Semantan P O Box 10618
    50720 Kuala Lumpur
    Tel: (03) 2553633
    Fax: (03) 2557970
    Telex: MIDA MA 30752

OUR EXPERIENCE

MAKES A WORLD OF DIFFERENCE

Fletcher is an international constructor with more than half its business won in tough offshore markets. Fletcher companies are constructing projects in North America, Hong Kong, Hawaii, South East Asia, Australia, New Zealand and the Pacific.

Fletcher delivers three key advantages to our clients.

- *Superior quality without a cost or time premium.*

- *Accountability for delivering solutions.*

- *Early certainty of completion cost and time.*

Around the Pacific Rim, Fletcher provides a full range of construction services, in every facet of commercial, residential and institutional building and civil, marine and industrial engineering construction.

 FLETCHER CONSTRUCTION GROUP

Fletcher Construction New Zealand and South Pacific
Private Bag 92060, Auckland
NEW ZEALAND
Phone: 00−64−9−579 9979
Fax: 00−64−9−579 8578

Fletcher Construction Australia
40 City Road, South Melbourne
Victoria 3205
AUSTRALIA
Phone: 00−61−3−274 8400
Fax: 00−61−3−274 8484

Fletcher Construction USA
Box 3784, Seattle, WA 98124−2264
UNITED STATES OF AMERICA
Phone: 00−1−206−447 7545
Fax: 00−1−206−447 7533

Fletcher Construction Asia
4th floor, East Block
Wisma Selangor Dredging
142−B Jalan Ampang 50450
Kuala Lumpur
MALAYSIA
Phone: 00−60−3−263 3148
Fax: 00−60−3−263 3153

Fletcher Construction Group
Level 11, AMP Centre
50 Bridge Street, Sydney, NSW 2000
AUSTRALIA
Phone: 00−61−2−239 2000
Fax: 00−61−2−223 3477

New Zealand

KEY DATA

Population

Population (1992)	3.4m
Urban population (1991)	76%
Population under 15 (1991)	23%
Population over 65	12%
Average annual growth rate (1981 to 1991)	0.8%

Geography

Land area	269,000 km²
Agricultural area	53.3%
Capital city	Wellington
	(population 0.3m)
Largest city	Auckland
	(population 0.9m)

Economy

Monetary unit	New Zealand dollar (NZ$)
Exchange rate (average first quarter 1993) to:	
the pound sterling	2.87
the US dollar	1.94
the yen x 100	1.58
Average annual inflation (1980 to 1990)	10.5%
Inflation rate (1992)	1%
Gross Domestic Product (GDP) (1991/92)*	NZ$ 74.1bn
GDP per capita (1991/92)*	NZ$ 21,585
GDP growth (real) (1982 to 1992)	1.1%
Private consumption as a proportion of GDP (1991)	62%
Public consumption as a proportion of GDP (1991)	17%
Investment as a proportion of GDP (1991)	22%
Central government expenditure as a proportion of Gross National Product (1991)	41%

Construction

Net value of construction output (1990/91)*	NZ$ 3.1bn
Net value of construction output per capita (1990/91)*	NZ$ 911
Net value of construction output as a proportion of GDP (1990/91)*	4.2%

Note: All data relate to 1990 unless otherwise indicated.
* year ending 31st March

THE CONSTRUCTION INDUSTRY

Construction output

The value of construction-related gross fixed capital formation in 1990/91 was NZ$7,304 million equivalent to US$4,956 million. This is not total construction output because it does not include repair and maintenance. Of this investment 48% was in residential building, 29% non-residential and 23% other construction and land improvements.

The construction industry in New Zealand is in a state of depression with the level of commercial building activity in the year ending 31 March 1992 being the lowest since 1960. The table below shows the value of building work put in place in 1991/92 prices.

VALUE OF BUILDING WORK PUT IN PLACE
(NZ$ million; years ending Mar 31; 1991/92 prices)

	1987/88	1988/89	1989/90	1990/91	1991/92
New dwellings	1,476	1,577	1,914	2,089	1,708
Alterations and additions	449	503	531	488	462
Total dwellings	1,924	2,080	2,445	2,576	2,171
Commercial buildings	1,630	1,432	1,208	965	565
Factories	401	336	303	354	172
Hotels and boarding houses	199	197	196	127	32
Schools	116	111	110	98	128
Hospitals	87	132	115	95	91
Other	260	225	279	218	215
Total non-residential buildings	2,652	2,412	2,197	1,854	1,203
Total all buildings	4,577	4,492	4,643	4,431	3,374

Source: Department of Statistics, Key Statistics.

While the table shows a clear downward trend in levels of activity since 1987/88, it must be noted that 1987/88 itself was a year of record levels of activity fuelled by deregulation of financial markets and a share market boom. The latter provided the means to finance a significant amount of, often speculative, commercial building activity. Consequently, the share market crash in October 1987 led to a sharp drop in commercial and factory building activity, subsequently reinforced by a prolonged recession. However, an export-led recovery emerged in the New Zealand economy in 1992 and the first signs of positive growth in levels of building activity are apparent. The volume of residential construction is expected to increase. Non-residential construction is also expected to show positive growth in the year ending March 1993, although the recovery of commercial building activity is expected to remain modest.

Characteristics and structure of the industry

Major legislative reforms have occurred in 1991/92 which are having a significant impact on the characteristics and structure of the industry. The former Ministry of Works has been privatized along with many other government departments.

The industry is just beginning to feel the impact of several other reforms: the Resource Management Act 1991 (which replaces all land, water and air legislation and subsumes the Town & Country Planning Act 1977); the Employment Contracts Act 1992 (which allows individual bargaining rather than national awards); and more generally the requirement for all public and private sector dealings to uphold the principles of the Treaty of Waitangi in recognizing the Maori people of New Zealand.

The principles of the Resource Management Act are 'sustainable development and minimal adverse environmental effects' but the definitions and implications are unclear and there is expected to be considerable litigation.

Because of the serious falls in building output since 1987/88 contractors have cut staff to minimal levels. The number of persons employed in the industry has fallen dramatically since early 1990. Between June quarter 1990 and June quarter 1991 the construction industry lost around 22% of its workers. Presumably some of these emigrated to Australia and may return if business picks up. However, even with the modest increases in activity some developers have suggested that there are already some capacity constraints with contractors reporting they are too busy even to price jobs.

The Fletcher Construction Company Ltd is number 20 in the 1991 *Engineering News Record* with contracts of nearly US$2 billion of which over 90% were abroad.

Development control and standards

In December 1991, the new Building Act reformed the building control system, generally in line with the 1990 recommendations of the NZ Building Industry Commission. There is now a national performance-based New Zealand Building Code (NZBC) replacing all local building bylaws and including energy efficiency requirements. The Building Industry Authority (BIA), established under the new Act, now monitors NZBC administration by Territorial Authorities (amalgamated from 231 local councils in 1989 to 81 local and 14 district councils) that issue determinations, grant national accreditation of products and systems, and approve private certifiers. The Act also limits latent defects liability to 10 years from contract completion and introduces durability requirements. Approved documents issued by the BIA contain non-mandatory examples of compliance. The transition period from the old control system ended on 31 December 1992.

CONSTRUCTION COST DATA

Cost of labour

The figures below are typical of labour costs in Auckland as at the first quarter 1993. The wage rate is the basis of an employee's income.

	Wage rate (per hour) NZ$	Number of hours worked per year
Site operatives		
Mason/bricklayer	21.00	1,980
Carpenter	16.00	1,980
Plumber	27.00	1,980
Electrician	24.00	1,980
Structural steel erector	22.00	1,980
HVAC installer	19.00	1,980
Semi-skilled worker	18.00	1,980
Unskilled labourer	16.00	1,980
Equipment operator	19.00	1,980
Watchman/security	16.00	1,980
Site supervision		
General foreman	26.00	1,800
Trades foreman	24.00	1,800
Clerk of works	27.00	1,800
Contractors' personnel		
Site manager	32.00	1,800
Resident engineer	45.00	1,800
Resident surveyor	45.00	1,800
Junior engineer	10.00	1,800
Junior surveyor	14.00	1,800
Planner	14.00	1,800
Consultants' personnel		
Senior architect	50.00	1,800
Senior engineer	45.00	1,800
Senior surveyor	48.00	1,800
Qualified architect	48.00	1,800
Qualified engineer	48.00	1,800
Qualified surveyor	48.00	1,800

Cost of materials

The figures that follow are the costs of main construction materials, delivered to site in the Auckland area, as incurred by contractors in the first quarter 1993.   These assume that the materials would be in quantities as required for a medium sized construction project and that the location of the works would be neither constrained nor remote.

All the costs in this section exclude general sales tax (GST - see below).

	Unit	Cost NZ$
Cement and aggregate		
Ordinary portland cement in 40kg bags	tonne	270.00
Coarse aggregates for concrete	m^3	67.60
Fine aggregates for concrete	m^3	64.00
Ready mixed concrete (17.5 MPa)	m^3	142.00
Ready mixed concrete (30.0 MPa)	m^3	159.00
Steel		
Mild steel reinforcement (16mm)	tonne	1,200.00
High tensile steel reinforcement (16mm)	tonne	1,255.00
Structural steel sections	tonne	1,200.00
Bricks and blocks		
Common bricks (190 x 90 x 90mm)	1,000	850.00
Good quality facing bricks (190 x 90 x 90mm)	1,000	920.00
Hollow concrete blocks	100	205.00
Solid concrete blocks	m^2	232.00
Precast concrete cladding units with exposed aggregate finish (200mm thick)	m^2	190.00
Timber and insulation		
Softwood sections for carpentry	m^3	400.00
Softwood for joinery	m^3	500.00
Hardwood for joinery	m^3	980.00
Exterior quality plywood (9mm)	m^2	24.00
Plywood for interior joinery (9mm)	m^2	27.00
Softwood strip flooring (50mm)	m	1.10
Chipboard sheet flooring (20mm)	m^2	21.00
100mm thick quilt insulation	m^2	12.00
100mm thick rigid slab insulation	m^2	28.00
Softwood internal door complete with frames and ironmongery	each	290.00
Glass and ceramics		
Float glass (6mm)	m^2	98.00
Sealed double glazing units	m^2	340.00
Plaster and paint		
Good quality ceramic wall tiles (150 x 150mm)	m^2	108.00

	Unit	Cost NZ$
Plaster in 50kg bags	tonne	302.00
Plasterboard (12.5mm thick)	m²	16.00
Emulsion paint in 5 litre tins	m²	6.80
Gloss oil paint in 5 litre tins	m²	9.80
Tiles and paviors		
Clay floor tiles (200 x 200mm)	m²	90.00
Vinyl floor tiles (2mm thick)	m²	22.00
Precast concrete paving slabs (100mm)	m²	60.00
Precast concrete roof tiles	m²	26.50
Drainage		
WC suite complete	each	680.00
Lavatory basin complete	each	265.00
100mm diameter clay drain pipes	m	25.00

Unit rates

The descriptions below are generally shortened versions of standard descriptions listed in full in section 4. Where an item has a two digit reference number (e.g. 05 or 33), this relates to the full description against that number in section 4. Where an item has an alphabetic suffix (e.g. 12A or 34B) this indicates that the standard description has been modified. Where a modification is major the complete modified description is included here and the standard description should be ignored; where a modification is minor (e.g. the insertion of a named hardwood) the shortened description has been modified here but, in general, the full description in section 4 prevails.

The unit rates below are for main work items on a typical construction project in the Auckland area in the first quarter 1993. The rates include all necessary labour, materials and equipment. Allowances of 10% to cover preliminary and general items and 6% to cover contractors' overheads and profit should be added to these rates. All the rates in this section exclude general sales tax (GST - see below).

		Unit	Rate NZ$
Excavation			
01	Mechanical excavation of foundation trenches	m³	26.80
02	Hardcore filling making up levels	m²	7.00
03	Earthwork support	m²	40.80
Concrete work			
04	Plain insitu concrete in strip foundations in trenches	m³	204.00
05	Reinforced insitu concrete in beds	m³	239.00
06	Reinforced insitu concrete in walls	m³	216.00

		Unit	Rate NZ$
07	Reinforced insitu concrete in suspended floor or roof slabs	m³	198.00
08	Reinforced insitu concrete in columns	m³	210.00
09	Reinforced insitu concrete in isolated beams	m³	204.00
10	Precast concrete slab	m²	97.00

Formwork

11	Softwood or metal formwork to concrete walls	m²	79.00
12	Softwood or metal formwork to concrete columns	m²	82.00
13	Softwood or metal formwork to horizontal soffits of slabs	m²	94.00

Reinforcement

14	Reinforcement in concrete walls	tonne	2,100.00
15	Reinforcement in suspended concrete slabs	tonne	2,050.00
16	Fabric reinforcement in concrete beds	m²	12.90

Steelwork

17	Fabricate, supply and erect steel framed structure	tonne	3,380.00

Brickwork and blockwork

18	Precast lightweight aggregate hollow concrete block walls	m²	70.00
19	Solid (perforated) concrete blocks	m²	111.00
21	Facing bricks	m²	128.00

Roofing

22	Concrete interlocking roof tiles 430 x 380mm	m²	45.50
24	Fibre cement roof slates 600 x 300mm	m²	117.00
25	Sawn softwood roof boarding	m²	134.00
27	3 layers glass-fibre based bitumen felt roof covering	m²	105.00
28	Bitumen based mastic asphalt roof covering	m²	64.70
29	Glass-fibre mat roof insulation 160mm thick	m²	35.00
31	Troughed galvanized steel roof cladding	m²	58.50

Woodwork and metalwork

32	Preservative treated sawn softwood 50 x 100mm	m	2.16
33	Preservative treated sawn softwood 50 x 150mm	m	3.85
34	Single glazed casement window in hardwood, 650 x 900mm	m²	735.00
35	Two panel glazed door in hardwood, 850 x 2000mm	each	303.00
36	Solid core half hour fire resisting hardwood internal flush doors, size 800 x 2000mm	each	250.00
37	Aluminium double glazed window, size 1200 x 1200mm	m²	403.00
38	Aluminium double glazed door, size 850 x 2100mm	each	1,920.00
39	Hardwood skirtings	m	19.80
40	Framed structural steelwork in universal joist sections	tonne	1,690.00
41	Structural steelwork lattice roof trusses	tonne	3,600.00

		Unit	*Rate NZ$*
Plumbing			
42	UPVC half round eaves gutter	m	23.30
43	UPVC rainwater pipes	m	21.60
44	Light gauge copper cold water tubing	m	18.40
45	High pressure plastic pipes for cold water supply	m	8.20
46	Low pressure plastic pipes for cold water distribution	m	9.90
47	UPVC soil and vent pipes	m	37.80
48	White vitreous china WC suite	each	793.00
49	White vitreous china lavatory basin	each	466.00
51	Stainless steel single bowl sink and double drainer	each	567.00
Electrical work			
52	PVC insulated and copper sheathed cable	m	4.90
53	13 amp unswitched socket outlet	each	13.40
54	Flush mounted 20 amp, 1 way light switch	each	13.40
Finishings			
55	2 coats gypsum based plaster on brick walls	m^2	39.60
56	White glazed tiles on plaster walls	m^2	126.00
57	Red clay quarry tiles on concrete floor	m^2	105.00
58	Cement and sand screed to concrete floors	m^2	46.60
60	Mineral fibre tiles on concealed suspension system	m^2	52.50
Glazing			
61	Glazing to wood	m^2	65.30
Painting			
62	Emulsion on plaster walls	m^2	8.40
63	Oil paint on timber	m^2	10.40

Approximate estimating

The building costs per unit area given below are averages incurred by building clients for typical buildings in the Auckland area as at the first quarter 1993. They are based upon the total floor area of all storeys, measured between external walls and without deduction for internal walls.

Approximate estimating costs generally include mechanical and electrical installations but exclude furniture, loose or special equipment, and external works; they also exclude fees for professional services. The costs shown are for specifications and standards appropriate to New Zealand and this should be borne in mind when attempting comparisons with similarly described building types in other countries. A discussion of this issue is included in section 2. Comparative data for countries covered in this publication including construction cost data is presented in Part Three.

Approximate estimating costs must be treated with caution; they cannot provide more than a rough guide to the probable cost of building. All the rates in this section exclude general sales tax (GST - see below).

	Cost m² NZ$	Cost ft² NZ$
Industrial buildings		
Factories for letting	375	35
Factories for owner occupation (light industrial use)	400	37
Factories for owner occupation (heavy industrial use)	450	42
Factory/office (high-tech) for letting (shell and core only)	550	51
Factory/office (high-tech) for letting (ground floor shell, first floor offices)	600	56
Factory/office (high tech) for owner occupation (controlled environment, fully finished)	750	70
High tech laboratory workshop centres (air conditioned)	1,400	131
Warehouses, low bay (6 to 8m high) for letting (no heating)	400	37
Warehouses, low bay for owner occupation (including heating)	600	56
Warehouses, high bay for owner occupation (including heating)	750	70
Administrative and commercial buildings		
Civic offices, non air conditioned	1,400	131
Civic offices, fully air conditioned	1,520	141
Offices for letting, 5 to 10 storeys, non air conditioned	1,500	139
Offices for letting, 5 to 10 storeys, air conditioned	1,750	162
Offices for letting, high rise, air conditioned	2,000	186
Offices for owner occupation 5 to 10 storeys, non air conditioned	1,700	158
Offices for owner occupation high rise, air conditioned	2,000	186
Prestige/headquarters office, 5 to 10 storeys, air conditioned	2,000	186
Prestige/headquarters office, high rise, air conditioned	2,300+	213+
Health and education buildings		
General hospitals (100 beds)	2,200	204
Teaching hospitals (100 beds)	2,200	204
Private hospitals (100 beds) aged persons	1,400	131
Health centres	1,400	131
Nursery schools	950	88
Primary/junior schools	950	88
Secondary/middle schools	1,000	93
University (arts) buildings	1,400	131
University (science) buildings	1,650	153
Management training centres	1,450	135
Recreation and arts buildings		
Theatres (over 500 seats) including seating and stage equipment	1,500	139
Theatres (less than 500 seats) including seating and stage equipment	1,700	158
Concert halls including seating and stage equipment	1,600	149
Sports halls including changing and social facilities	1,300	121

	Cost m² NZ$	Cost ft² NZ$
Swimming pools (international standard) including changing and social facilities	1,700	158
Swimming pools (schools standard) including changing facilities	1,600	149
National museums including full air conditioning and standby generator	2,500+	232+
Local museums including air conditioning	2,100	195

Residential buildings

Social/economic single family housing (multiple units)	780	72
Private/mass market single family housing 2 storey detached/semidetached (multiple units)	800	74
Purpose designed single family housing 2 storey detached (single unit)	1,050	98
Social/economic apartment housing, low rise (no lifts)	1,600	149
Private sector apartment building (standard specification)	1,700	158
Private sector apartment buildings (luxury)	2,000	186
Student/nurses halls of residence	1,500	121
Homes for the elderly (shared accommodation)	1,200	111
Homes for the elderly (self contained with shared communal facilities)	1,200	111
Hotel, 5 star, city centre	2,400	223
Hotel, 3 star, city/provincial	2,000	186
Motel	1,500	139

General sales tax (GST)

The standard rate of general sales tax (GST) is currently 12.5%, chargeable on building work.

EXCHANGE RATES AND INFLATION

The combined effect of exchange rates and inflation on prices within a country and price comparisons between countries is discussed in section 2.

Exchange rates

The graph on the next page plots the movement of the New Zealand Dollar against sterling, the US dollar and Japanese yen since 1980. The figures used for the graph are quarterly and the method of calculating these and other related issues are discussed in section 2. The exchange rate at the first quarter 1993 was NZ$2.87 to the pound sterling, NZ$1.94 to the US dollar and NZ$1.58 to 100 Japanese yen.

THE NEW ZEALAND DOLLAR AGAINST STERLING, THE US DOLLAR
AND THE JAPANESE YEN

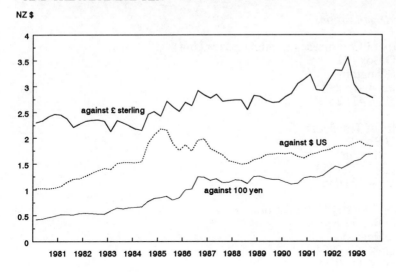

Price inflation

The table below presents consumer price, house price and construction
price inflation in New Zealand since 1980.

CONSUMER PRICE, HOUSE PRICE AND CONSTRUCTION COST INFLATION

Year	Consumer price index average index	average change %	House price index average index	average change %	Construction cost index average index	average change %
1980	100		100		100	
1981	116	16.0	110	10.0	130	30.0
1982	134	15.5	143	30.0	156	20.0
1983	157	17.2	176	23.1	179	14.7
1984	165	5.1	191	8.5	181	1.1
1985	177	7.3	216	13.1	195	7.7
1986	205	15.8	247	14.4	215	10.3
1987	228	11.2	265	7.3	237	10.2
1988	267	17.1	323	21.9	257	8.4
1989	282	5.6	346	7.1	273	6.2
1990	302	7.1	372	7.5	285	4.4
1991	317	5.0	400	7.5	296	3.9
1992	324	2.2	393	-1.8	302	2.0

USEFUL ADDRESSES

Public Organizations

Ministry of Commerce (Building Issues Unit)
    PO Box 173
    Wellington
    Tel: 4 474 2921
    Fax: 4 471 2658

Ministry of Transport
    PO Box 3175
    Wellington
    Tel: 4 472 1253
    Fax: 4 495 0565

Building Industry Commission
    PO Box 11-846
    Wellington
    Tel: 4 471 0794
    Fax: 4 471 0798

Housing Corporation of New Zealand
    PO Box 5009
    Wellington
    Tel: 4 472 1293
    Fax: 4 472 3152

Standards Association of New Zealand
    Executive Director
    Private Bag
    Wellington
    Tel: 4 384 2108
    Fax: 4 384 3936

Department of Statistics
    Marketing Manager
    PO Box 2822
    Wellington
    Tel: 4 472 9119
    Fax: 4 472 9135

Department of Scientific and Industrial Research
    Director General
    PO Box 1378
    Wellington
    Tel: 4 472 9979
    Fax: 4 472 4025

Trade and Professional Associations

National Contractors' Association
  Chief Executive
  New Zealand Contractors Federation
  PO Box 12-013
  Wellington
  Tel: 4 473 6514
  Fax: 4 473 2730

New Zealand Institute of Architects
  Secretary
  PO Box 483
  Wellington
  Tel: 4 473 53476
  Fax: 4 472 0182

Institute of Professional Engineers
  Chief Executive Director
  PO Box 12-241
  Wellington
  Tel: 4 473 9444
  Fax: 4 473 3011

New Zealand Institute of Surveyors
  Secretary
  PO Box 831
  Wellington
  Tel: 4 471 1774
  Fax: 4 471 1907

New Zealand Institute of Quantity Surveyors
  Executive Director
  PO Box 3635
  Wellington
  Tel: 4 473 5521
  Fax: 4 473 2918

Building Industry Authority
  PO Box 11-846
  Wellington
  Tel: 4 471 0794
  Fax: 4 471 0798

Building Research Association of New Zealand
  PO Box 50908
  Porirua
  Tel: 4 235 7600
  Fax: 4 235 8070

Cement and Concrete Association of New Zealand
　　Private Bag 50902
　　Porirua
　　Tel:　4 232 8379
　　Fax: 4 235 4393

New Zealand Heavy Engineering Research Association
　　Director
　　PO Box 76-134
　　Manukau City
　　Tel:　9 262 2885
　　Fax: 9 262 2858

Auckland Building Exhibition Centre
　　Centre Manager
　　Downtown Centre
　　Auckland
　　Tel:　9 309 0976
　　Fax: 9 379 2988

Architectural Aluminium Association of New Zealand
　　Director General
　　PO Box 11-543
　　Wellington
　　Tel:　4 473 3000
　　Fax: 4 473 3004

Designers Institute of New Zealand
　　Administrator
　　PO Box 5521
　　Auckland
　　Tel:　9 377 6012
　　Fax: 9 388 4713

Electrical Contractors Association of New Zealand Inc.
　　Secretary
　　PO Box 6372
　　Wellington
　　Tel:　4 385 9657
　　Fax: 4 385 4645

In the Phillipines:

DAVIS LANGDON & SEAH PHILLIPINES INC

The strategic and integrated management of cost, time and quality - the client "risk" areas of a contract - are essential functions, which are necessary to ensure the satisfactory planning, procurement, execution and operation of construction projects.

We specialise in the financial management of construction projects and their risk areas, from project inception to completion and we concentrate on:

* being positive and creative in our advice, rather than simply reactive;

* providing value for money via efficient management, rather than on superficial cost monitoring;

* giving advice that is matched to the Client's requirements, rather than imposing standard or traditional solutions;

* paying attention to the life-cycle costs of constructing and occupying a building, rather than to the initial capital cost only.

Our aim is to provide our clients with risk assurance, cost control and value for money, via effective advice, cost planning and management.

DAVIS LANGDON & SEAH PHILIPPINES INC
7th Floor, Electra House
Esteban Street
Legaspi Village, Makati
Metro Manila, Philippines
Tel : (010 632) 812 2679
Fax : (010 632) 815 6460

DAVIS LANGDON & SEAH INTERNATIONAL

MANAGE AND LIMIT CLIENT RISK - ADDING VALUE

Philippines

KEY DATA

Population

Population (1991)	64.6m
Urban population (1991)	44%
Population under 15	40%
Population over 65	3%
Average annual growth rate (1980 to 1990)	2.4%

Geography

Land area	300,000 km²
Agricultural area	31%
Capital city	Manila
(population Metropolitan Manila 8.4m)	
(population Manila 1.6m)	

Economy

Monetary unit	Peso (P)
Exchange rate (average first quarter 1993) to:	
the pound sterling	P 36.66
the US dollar	P 24.73
the yen x 100	P 20.12
Average annual inflation (1980 to 1990)	14.9%
Inflation rate (1991)	18%
Gross Domestic Product (GDP)	P 1,066.3bn
GDP per capita	P 17,338
Real GDP growth (1980 to 1990)	0.9%
Private consumption as a proportion of GDP	75%
Public consumption as a proportion of GDP	9%
Investment as a proportion of GDP	22%
Central government expenditure as a proportion of Gross National Product	20%

Construction

Gross value of construction output (1991)	P 114.4bn
Net value of construction output	P 50.1bn
Net value of construction output per capita	P 776
Net value of construction output as a proportion of GDP	4.7%

Note: All data relate to 1990 unless otherwise indicated.

THE CONSTRUCTION INDUSTRY

Construction output

The gross value of construction output in the Philippines in 1991 was 114.34 billion pesos, equivalent to US$4.5 billion representing about 10% of gross domestic product.   The level of construction output has been declining rapidly but it showed a slight recovery in the second quarter of 1992 resulting in a 1% decline compared to the 29% decline registered in the first quarter of 1991.

The exact breakdown of work by type is difficult to determine. However, in 1989, of total building output in the private sector, residential buildings represented 67%, commercial 23%, industrial 4%, educational 3% and other 3%. Civil engineering is also important and over US$1 billion or 28 billion pesos were spent in 1991/92 on roads, bridges, airports, harbours, etc.   This accounts for much of the public sector expenditure on construction.   The regional distribution of net value of construction in 1990 in relation to the distribution of population is shown in the table below:

REGIONAL DISTRIBUTION OF CONSTRUCTION,
PHILIPPINES, 1990

Region		Population %	Construction %
National Capital Region (NCR) Metro Manila		13.0	39.0
I	Ilocos Region	7.0	4.6
II	Cagayan Valley	4.6	3.9
III	Central Luzon	10.0	9.5
IV	Southern Tagalog	13.2	13.7
V	Bicol Region	7.1	4.1
VI	Western Visayas	9.2	3.7
VII	Central Visayas	7.5	5.3
VIII	Eastern Visayas	5.5	2.2
IX	Western Mindanoa	5.2	2.5
X	Northern Mindanoa	5.9	2.9
XI	Southern Mindanoa	7.0	4.7
XII	Central Mindanoa	4.8	4.0
Total		100	100

Source: Economic and Social Statistics Office
           National Statistical Co-ordination Board and 1980 Census

The importance of the National Capital Region of Metropolitan Manila as the location for the country's construction output has increased in recent years but is now declining slightly.

Characteristics and structure of the industry

The majority of owners commission their own design with a separate planning or architectural firm and invite contractors to bid for its construction. Design and build is used only for small-scale projects such as low cost housing projects. In recent years, management contracting has developed considerably in the Philippines especially for large projects.

Two Philippines firms are in the *Engineering News Record*'s 1991 list of 225 international contractors.

MAJOR FILIPINO INTERNATIONAL CONTRACTORS

Contractor	Place in ENR list	Contracts obtained 1991 M$	Percentage of foreign
Engineering Equipment Inc	142	91	76
Atlantic, Gulf and Pacific Co of Manila Inc	218	22	7

Clients and finance

Just over half of construction output is financed by the private sector and private projects have dropped substantially starting from the early part of 1990. However, this drop in private construction has been offset by a surge in government construction activity which picked up during the first quarter of 1991, as the government intensified the rehabilitation programmes for disaster stricken areas and expanded transport-related infrastructure projects in the metropolis.

Selection of design consultants

Generally professional consultants are appointed directly by the client though sometimes another consultant will make the appointment and occasionally some form of competition is held. Both for private and public work price is the most important criterion followed by track record, personal contacts and recommendations. There are no recommended fee scales.

Contractual arrangements

In almost all cases building work is undertaken by general contractors. Selection is by competitive tender and the contract is awarded to the contractor who submits the lowest and most comprehensive bid. The principal contract documents comprise conditions of contract, general agreement, schedule of works and bills of quantities.

The selected contractor normally provides all construction materials, manpower, and other inputs. However, in some cases the owner supplies certain materials. Some major contracting companies nominate subcontractors to undertake specialized works such as prestressed concrete, plumbing, electrical, mechanical and drainage.

Development control and standards

The National Housing and Land Use Regulatory Board is responsible for controlling land use and building operations in the industry. The board is responsible for issuing development permits and for ensuring that developers comply with the required standards. Guidelines and procedures for obtaining permits are enumerated in their handbooks, PD 957 for high cost housing and BP 225 for low cost housing. The request for a permit is processed only after all requirements are met. It takes about one to three months before a certificate of registration and licence to sell is issued.

All new construction in the Philippines has to comply with the provisions set out in the 3rd edition of the National Structural Code of the Philippines or NSCP, the ACI-1989 edition, the 1985 edition of the Uniform Building Code and the 1985 edition of the AISC Steel Manual. Deviation from the codes may be allowed by the building official, provided it is shown and verified by test that such deviation is within the scope of the code. The ACI-1989 edition covers the proper design and construction of reinforced concrete buildings. It covers subjects such as permits, inspection, specifications, materials, concrete quality, mixing, formwork, embedded pipes, strength and serviceability, loads, specifications and provisions for seismic design. The quality and testing of materials used in construction are covered by the American ASTM standard specification and the welding of reinforcement by the American AWS standard.

Liability

The contractor, according to the contract, guarantees the materials and workmanship for a minimum period of one year and is therefore responsible for making good any defects in construction. This is usually supported by a Guarantee Bond to the value of 30% of the value of the contract. Main contractors, where relevant, will obtain guarantees from subcontractors. All disputes, claims or questions are settled according to the provisions of the Philippine Institute of Architects. The demand for arbitration must be made not later than the time of final payment.

CONSTRUCTION COST DATA

Cost of labour

The figures below are typical of labour costs in Metro Manila as at the first quarter 1993. The wage rate is the basis of an employee's income, while the cost of labour indicates the cost to a contractor of employing that employee. The difference between the two covers a variety of mandatory and voluntary contributions - a list of items which could be included is given in section 2.

	Wage rate (per hour) P	Cost of labour (per hour) P	Number of hours worked per year
Site operatives			
Mason/bricklayer	150	170	1,680
Carpenter	180	200	2,168
Plumber	150	170	2,168
Electrician	150	170	2,168
Structural steel erector	156	165	2,168
HVAC installer	250	290	2,168
Semi-skilled worker	125	145	2,168
Unskilled labourer	118	135	2,168
Equipment operator	160	185	2,168
Watchman/security	118	135	2,920
Site supervision			
General foreman	250	290	2,168
Trades foreman	235	275	2,168
Clerk of works	194	235	2,168
Contractors' personnel			
Site manager	480	520	2,168
Resident engineer	353	393	2,168
Resident surveyor	333	373	2,168
Junior engineer	250	290	2,168
Junior surveyor	265	305	2,168
Planner	250	290	2,168
Consultants' personnel			
Senior architect	480	520	1,752
Senior engineer	500	540	1,752
Senior surveyor	400	440	1,752
Qualified architect	350	390	1,752
Qualified engineer	350	390	1,752
Qualified surveyor	330	370	1,752

Cost of materials

The figures that follow are the costs of main construction materials, delivered to site in the Metro Manila area, as incurred by contractors in the first quarter 1993. These assume that the materials would be in quantities as required for a medium sized construction project and that the location of the works would be neither constrained nor remote. All the costs in this section exclude value added tax (VAT - see below).

	Unit	Cost P
Cement and aggregate		
Ordinary portland cement in 40kg bags	bag	106
Coarse aggregates for concrete	m^3	445
Fine aggregates for concrete	m^3	265
Ready mixed concrete (A: 34 MPa)	m^3	2,750
Ready mixed concrete (B: 27 MPa)	m^3	2,140
Steel		
Mild steel reinforcement	tonne	11,900
High tensile steel reinforcement	tonne	13,000
Structural steel sections	tonne	27,600
Bricks and blocks		
Common bricks (2" x 4" x 8")	1,000	4,250
Good quality facing bricks (2" x 4" x 8")	1,000	4,450
Hollow concrete blocks (6" x 8" x 16")	1,000	7,200
Solid concrete blocks (6" x 8" x 16")	1,000	7,650
Precast concrete cladding units with exposed aggregate finish	m^2	4,550
Timber and insulation		
Softwood sections for carpentry	m^3	9,000
Softwood for joinery	m^3	10,100
Hardwood for joinery	m^3	12,900
Exterior quality plywood (10mm)	m^2	260
Plywood for interior joinery (10mm)	m^2	305
Softwood strip flooring (10mm)	m^2	420
Chipboard sheet flooring (25mm)	m^2	1,260
100mm thick quilt insulation	m^2	1,010
100mm thick rigid slab insulation	m^2	785
Softwood internal door complete with frames and ironmongery	each	4,770
Plaster and paint		
Good quality ceramic wall tiles (108 x 108mm)	m^2	300
Plaster in 50 kg bags	tonne	2,010
Plasterboard (13mm thick)	m^2	630
Emulsion paint	gallon	230

	Unit	Cost P
Tiles and paviors		
Clay floor tiles (4.25" x 4.25" x 0.125")	m²	300
Vinyl floor tiles (300 x 300 x 3mm)	m²	380
Precast concrete paving slabs (400 x 185 x 50mm)	m²	1,580
Drainage		
WC suite complete	each	4,450
Lavatory basin complete	each	2,650
150mm diameter cast iron drain pipes	m	2,220

Unit rates

The descriptions below are generally shortened versions of standard descriptions listed in full in section 4. Where an item has a two digit reference number (e.g. 05 or 33), this relates to the full description against that number in section 4. Where an item has an alphabetic suffix (e.g. 12A or 34B) this indicates that the standard description has been modified. Where a modification is major the complete modified description is included here and the standard description should be ignored; where a modification is minor (e.g. the insertion of a named hardwood) the shortened description has been modified here but, in general, the full description in section 4 prevails.

The unit rates below are for main work items on a typical construction project in the Metro Manila area in the first quarter 1993. The rates include all necessary labour, materials and equipment. Allowances of 5 to 10% to cover preliminary and general items and 3 to 5% to cover contractors' overheads and profit have been included in the rates. All the rates in this section exclude value added tax (VAT - see below).

		Unit	Rate P
Excavation			
01	Mechanical excavation of foundation trenches	m³	253
02	Hardcore filling making up levels	m²	78
03	Earthwork support	m²	78
Concrete work			
04	Plain insitu concrete in strip foundations in trenches	m³	1,420
05	Reinforced insitu concrete in beds	m³	2,940
06	Reinforced insitu concrete in walls	m³	2,920
07	Reinforced insitu concrete in suspended floor or roof slabs	m³	2,960
08	Reinforced insitu concrete in columns	m³	2,920
09	Reinforced insitu concrete in isolated beams	m³	2,920
10	Precast concrete slab	each	8,060

		Unit	*Rate P*
Formwork			
11	Softwood or metal formwork to concrete walls	m²	339
12	Softwood or metal formwork to concrete columns	m²	332
13	Softwood or metal formwork to horizontal soffits of slabs	m²	361
Reinforcement			
14	Reinforcement in concrete walls	kg	19
15	Reinforcement in suspended concrete slabs	kg	19
16	Fabric reinforcement in concrete beds	m²	53
Steelwork			
17	Fabricate, supply and erect steel framed structure	tonne	57,000
Brickwork and blockwork			
18	Precast lightweight aggregate hollow concrete block walls	m²	485
19	Solid (perforated) concrete blocks	m²	374
20	Sand lime bricks	m²	52
Roofing			
22	Concrete interlocking roof tiles 430 x 380mm	m²	1,640
23	Plain clay roof tiles 260 x 160mm	m²	1,040
26	Particle board roof coverings	m²	858
27	3 layers glass-fibre based bitumen felt roof covering	m²	512
28	Bitumen based mastic asphalt roof covering	m²	556
29	Glass-fibre mat roof insulation 160mm thick	m²	512
30	Rigid sheet loadbearing roof insulation 75mm thick	m²	470
31	Troughed galvanized steel roof cladding	m²	3,160
Woodwork and metalwork			
32	Preservative treated sawn softwood 50 x 100mm	m	154
33	Preservative treated sawn softwood 50 x 150mm	m	154
34A	Single glazed casement window in hardwood, size 650 x 900mm	each	780
35A	Two panel glazed door in hardwood, size 850 x 2000mm	each	1,560
36	Solid core half hour fire resisting hardwood internal flush doors, size 800 x 2000mm	each	2,750
37	Aluminium double glazed window, size 1200 x 1200mm	each	23,200
38	Aluminium double glazed door, size 850 x 2100mm	each	41,700
39	Hardwood skirtings	m	190
40	Framed structural steelwork in universal joist sections	tonne	78,000
41	Structural steelwork lattice roof trusses	tonne	62,500
Plumbing			
42	UPVC half round eaves gutter	m	243
43	UPVC rainwater pipes	m	390

		Unit	Rate P
44	Light gauge copper cold water tubing	m	227
45	High pressure plastic pipes for cold water supply	m	260
46	Low pressure plastic pipes for cold water distribution	m	42
47	UPVC soil and vent pipes	m	243
48	White vitreous china WC suite	each	5,600

Electrical work

52	PVC insulated and copper sheathed cable	m	544
53	13 amp unswitched socket outlet	each	213
54	Flush mounted 20 amp, 1 way light switch	each	178

Finishings

55	2 coats gypsum based plaster on brick walls	m²	505
56	White glazed tiles on plaster walls	m²	700
57	Red clay quarry tiles on concrete floor	m²	390
58	Cement and sand screed to concrete floors	m²	282
59	Thermoplastic floor tiles on screed	m²	478
60	Mineral fibre tiles on concealed suspension system	m²	1,280

Glazing

61	Glazing to wood	m²	417

Painting

62	Emulsion on plaster walls	m²	203
63	Oil paint on timber	m²	130

Approximate estimating

The building costs per unit area given below are averages incurred by building clients for typical buildings in the Metro Manila area as at the first quarter 1993. They are based upon the total floor area of all storeys, measured between external walls and without deduction for internal walls.

Approximate estimating costs generally include mechanical and electrical installations but exclude furniture, loose or special equipment, and external works; they also exclude fees for professional services. The costs shown are for specifications and standards appropriate to the Philippines and this should be borne in mind when attempting comparisons with similarly described building types in other countries. A discussion of this issue is included in section 2. Comparative data for countries covered in this publication, including construction cost data, is presented in Part Three.

Approximate estimating costs must be treated with caution; they cannot provide more than a rough guide to the probable cost of building. All the rates in this section exclude value added tax (VAT - see below).

	Cost m² P	Cost ft² P
Industrial buildings		
Factories for letting	8,250	765
Factories for owner occupation (light industrial use)	10,400	965
Factories for owner occupation (heavy industrial use)	13,100	1,220
Factory/office (high-tech) for letting (shell and core only)	12,600	1,170
Factory/office (high-tech) for letting (ground floor shell, first floor offices)	10,200	950
Factory/office (high tech) for owner occupation (controlled environment, fully finished)	12,700	1,180
High tech laboratory workshop centres (air conditioned)	16,300	1,510
Warehouses, low bay (6 to 8m high) for letting (no heating)	6,500	605
Warehouses, low bay for owner occupation	7,550	705
Warehouses, high bay for owner occupation	8,650	805
Cold stores/refrigerated stores	13,000	1,210
Administrative and commercial buildings		
Civic offices, non air conditioned	15,100	1,410
Civic offices, fully air conditioned	18,400	1,710
Offices for letting, 5 to 10 storeys, non air conditioned	16,300	1,510
Offices for letting, 5 to 10 storeys, air conditioned	21,600	2,010
Offices for letting, high rise, air conditioned	26,000	2,410
Offices for owner occupation 5 to 10 storeys, non air conditioned	21,600	2,010
Offices for owner occupation 5 to 10 storeys, air conditioned	28,100	2,610
Offices for owner occupation high rise, air conditioned	29,300	2,720
Prestige/headquarters office, 5 to 10 storeys, air conditioned	31,400	2,920
Prestige/headquarters office, high rise, air conditioned	32,400	3,010
Health and education buildings		
General hospitals (230 beds)	29,300	2,720
Teaching hospitals (100 beds)	34,600	3,220
Private hospitals (100 beds)	32,400	3,010
Health centres	10,800	1,000
Nursery schools	10,800	1,000
Primary/junior schools	11,900	1,110
Secondary/middle schools	13,000	1,210
University (arts) buildings	14,100	1,310
University (science) buildings	16,300	1,510
Management training centres	16,300	1,510
Recreation and arts buildings		
Theatres (over 500 seats) including seating and stage equipment	24,900	2,320
Theatres (less than 500 seats) including seating and stage equipment	26,000	2,410
Concert halls including seating and stage equipment	26,000	2,410

	Cost m² P	Cost ft² P
Sports halls including changing and social facilities	16,300	1,510
National museums including full air conditioning and standby generator	23,800	2,210
Local museums including air conditioning	19,500	1,810
City centre/central libraries	16,300	1,510
Branch/local libraries	15,100	1,410

Residential buildings

	Cost m² P	Cost ft² P
Social/economic single family housing (multiple units)	5,410	502
Private/mass market single family housing 2 storey detached/semidetached (multiple units)	6,490	603
Purpose designed single family housing 2 storey detached (single unit)	8,650	804
Social/economic apartment housing, low rise (no lifts)	10,800	1,000
Social/economic apartment housing, high rise (with lifts)	13,000	1,210
Private sector apartment building (standard specification)	21,600	2,010
Private sector apartment buildings (luxury)	23,800	2,210
Student/nurses halls of residence	16,300	1,510
Homes for the elderly (shared accommodation)	16,300	1,510
Hotel, 5 star, city centre	32,400	3,010
Hotel, 3 star, city/provincial	28,100	2,610
Motel	18,400	1,710

Regional variations

The approximate estimating costs are based on projects in Metro Manila. For other parts of the Philippines, multiply these costs by the following factors:

Ilocos regions	1.41
Cagayan Valley	0.86
Central Luzon	1.47
Southern Tagalog	1.08
Bicol region	0
Western Visayas	1.82
Central Visayas	1.14
Eastern Visayas	1.29
Western Mindanao	1.28
Northern Mindanao	1.52

Value added tax (VAT)

The standard rate of value added tax (VAT) is currently 10%, chargeable on general building work.

EXCHANGE RATES AND INFLATION

The combined effect of exchange rates and inflation on prices within a country and price comparisons between countries is discussed in section 2.

Exchange rates

The graph below plots the movement of the Filipino peso against sterling, the US dollar and the Japanese yen since 1980. The figures used for the graph are quarterly and the method of calculating these and other related issues are discussed in section 2. The exchange rate at the first quarter 1993 was P36.7 to the pound sterling, P24.7 to the US dollar and P20.1 to 100 Japanese yen.

THE FILIPINO PESO AGAINST STERLING, THE US DOLLAR
AND THE JAPANESE YEN

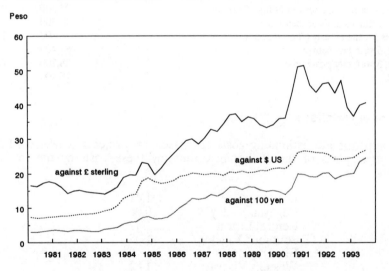

Consumer price inflation

The table on the next page presents general inflation in Philippines since 1984.

CONSUMER PRICE INFLATION

| | Consumer price inflation | |
Year	average index	average change %
1983	100	
1984	150	50.3
1985	185	23.1
1986	187	0.8
1987	194	3.8
1988	207	8.8
1989	236	14.1
1990	269	14.2
1991	314	16.6
1992	342	8.9

USEFUL ADDRESSES

Public Organizations

Department of Public Works and Highways (DPWH)
    Bonifacio Drive, Port Area
    Tel: 472663

National Housing Authority
    Elliptical Road, Q.C.
    Tel: 994561

Professional Regulation Commission (PRC)
    P Paredes St, Sampaloo, M.M.
    Tel: 7416061

Construction Industry Authority of the Philippines (CIAP)
    Finman Bldg, Pasong Tamo
    Makati, M.M.
    Tel: 8171230

National Statistics Office
    D&E Bldg, Quezon Ave
    Quezon City
    Tel: 971360

Department of Trade and Industry (DTI)
    361 Buendia Avenue, Makati
    Tel: 8185701

Construction Industry Arbitration Commission
    Finman Bldg, Makati, M.M.
    Tel: 8150709

Trade and Professional Associations

Philippine Contractors Association (PCA)
    INC The Padilla Building, Pasig
    Tel: 6313135

Philippine Contractors Accreditation Board (PCAB)
    DTI Building, Buendis Ave,
    Makati, M.M.
    Tel: 8150705

United Architects of the Philippines (UAP)
    CCP Complex, Roxas Blvd, M.M.
    Tel: 8323711

Philippine Institute of Civil Engineers (PICE)
    3rd Floor, Florentel Building
    800 EDSA, Q.C.
    Tel: 9242426

Association of Structural Engineers of the Philippines (ASEP)
    305 Quezon Avenue, Quezon City

Philippine Chamber of Commerce and Industry
    ODC Bldg, Makati, M.M.
    Tel: 8176981

The Multilingual Dictionary of Real Estate

A guide for the property professional in the Single European Market

L van Breugel, Gooch and Wagstaff, UK, **B Wood**, and **R H Williams**, both of University of Newcastle upon Tyne, UK

* Dutch *

* English *

* French *

* German *

* Italian *

* Spanish *

The Multilingual Dictionary of Real Estate is *more than* merely a word-for-word dictionary of specialist and technical terminology; it offers explanations of terms which cannot be translated exactly or are liable to cause confusion. A supplementary section of the dictionary provides detailed notes as well as translations of particularly tricky terms. There are also invaluable sections outlining the real estate and planning hierarchies and real estate associations throughout Europe.

March 1993: 234x170: 414pp
Hardback: 0-419-18020-6

Here's what is included in *The Multilingual Dictionary of Real Estate* in all 6 languages
* how to use this dictionary * objectives * word index * translations * explanations * key questions * government and planning hierarchies

For further information on this and other property related titles, please contact:
The Promotion Dept., E & F N Spon,
2-6 Boundary Row, London SE1 8HN
Tel 071 865 0066 Fax 071 522 9623

In Singapore:

DAVIS LANGDON & SEAH

The strategic and integrated management of cost, time and quality - the client "risk" areas of a contract - are essential functions, which are necessary to ensure the satisfactory planning, procurement, execution and operation of construction projects.

We specialise in the financial management of construction projects and their risk areas, from project inception to completion and we concentrate on:

*   being positive and creative in our advice, rather than simply reactive;

*   providing value for money via efficient management, rather than on superficial cost monitoring;

*   giving advice that is matched to the Client's requirements, rather than imposing standard or traditional solutions;

*   paying attention to the life-cycle costs of constructing and occupying a building, rather than to the initial capital cost only.

Our aim is to provide our clients with risk assurance, cost control and value for money, via effective advice, cost planning and management.

DAVIS LANGDON & SEAH
135 Cecil Street # 12 - 00
LKN Building
Singapore 0106
Tel : (010 65) 2223888
Fax : (010 65) 2247089

DAVIS LANGDON & SEAH INTERNATIONAL

MANAGE AND LIMIT CLIENT RISK - ADDING VALUE

Singapore

KEY DATA

Population
Population	2.8m
Urban population	100%
Population under 15	23%
Population over 65	6%
Average annual growth rate (1980 to 1990)	2.2%

Geography
Land area	639 km²
Agricultural area	2%
Capital city	Singapore

Economy
Monetary unit	Singapore dollar (S$)
Exchange rate (average first quarter 1993) to:	
the pound sterling	S$ 2.45
the US dollar	S$ 1.65
the yen x 100	S$ 1.34
Average annual inflation (1980 to 1990)	3.5%
Inflation rate 1991	3.5%
Gross Domestic Product (GDP) (1991)	S$ 69.1bn
GDP per capita	S$ 24,679
Real GDP growth (1980 to 1990)	6.8%
Private consumption as a proportion of GDP (1991)	43%
Public consumption as a proportion of GDP (1991)	11%
Investment as a proportion of GDP (1991)	40%
Central government expenditure as a proportion of Gross National Product	23%

Construction
Gross value of construction output (1991)	S$ 11bn
Net value of construction output (1991)	S$ 4.7bn
Net value of construction output per capita (1991)	S$ 1,679
Net value of construction output as a proportion of GDP (1991)	6.8%

THE CONSTRUCTION INDUSTRY

Construction output

The value of construction contracts awarded in 1991 was S$8.4 billion but the total value of construction output is probably nearer to S$10.0 billion equivalent to US$5.8 billion. Output is expected to have risen in 1992. The 1991 contracts figure is about 14% of GDP; value added is about 6.8% of GDP.

The value of expected 1992 contracts is apportioned as follows:

EXPECTED CONTRACTS IN SINGAPORE BY TYPE OF WORK 1992

Type of work	1992 Estimate (S$ million)	%
Private sector building works		
Residential	960	9.4
Commercial	2,500	24.5
Industrial	810	7.9
Institutional and others	130	1.3
	4,400	43.1
Public sector building works		
Residential	2,800	27.4
Commercial	170	1.7
Industrial	270	2.6
Institutional and others	870	8.5
	4,110	40.2
Public sector infrastructure works		
Utilities	170	1.7
Roads and bridges	390	3.8
Communications *	470	4.6
Sewerage and drainage	330	3.2
Others	350	3.4
	1,710	16.7
Total	10,220	100.0

* *includes Mass Transport System, port and airport*

Thirty-seven per cent of contracts are for residential building mainly in the public sector with the Housing Development Board as the major client. Other building was 46%, mainly in the private sector, and infrastructure works 17%, all in the public sector.

According to a report by David Wills, University of Greenwich, *Construction Opportunities in the Asia Pacific Rim*, major infrastructure projects over the next five years amount to about US$6 billion. Power generation plant to the value of US$2.6 billion will be constructed by 1995. Other planned projects include extensions to the Mass Transport System to the value of US$600 million by 1995, an expressway costing US$1.5 million by 2003, a third container terminal for US$1.2 billion starting in 1996 and an extension to the Changi Airport from 1991 to 1994 at a cost of US$470 million.

Characteristics and structure of the industry

The industry in Singapore is supported by the Construction Industry Development Board (CIDB). It is concerned with all aspects of the industry: business management, technology, training and quality.

In 1984, the CIDB established a Contractors' Registry to register contractors under various categories and grades for public sector procurement. Only CIDB registered contractors are permitted to tender for public sector construction projects. Contractors intending to be registered under the CIDB Contractors' Registry must have relevant experience. In addition, they are required to prove their financial, technical and management capability in executing construction projects. (This includes the employment of technically qualified personnel.) In September 1992, the Contractors' Registry covered more than 3,150 contractors and construction related specialist firms and is used not only by government agencies but also by private sector clients. Of registered contractors:

- 60% were building and civil engineering contractors
- 63 construction firms were registered in the top grade (G8)
- foreign firms accounted for 12% of the total.

It is government policy to favour local contractors and to encourage foreign contractors to form joint ventures with local firms. In the event that expatriate contractors are lowest bidders, contractors with more than 51% local ownership are given a preference expressed as a percentage of their tender prices. However, when the contract is signed, the contract price is the contractor's original tender price.

A panel of contractors credited with consistently good performance and quality workmanship has been established to encourage high standards. These contractors are given premiums to secure public sector tenders. The maximum premium is 5% or S$5 million, whichever is lower. The scheme began in January 1990 and in September 1992, there were a total of 52 contractors on the list.

The ten largest local construction firms ranked by turnover are as follows:

TOP TEN CONSTRUCTION FIRMS IN SINGAPORE

Rank	Name of company	Total turnover 1991 S$m
1	Lum Chang Building Contractors Pte Ltd	220.99
2	Low Keng Huat (Singapore) Ltd	67.13
3	L&M Group Investments Pte Ltd	160.20
4	Woh Hup (Pte) Ltd	63.26
5	Four Seas Construction Co Pte Ltd	36.06
6	Sembawang Construction Pte Ltd	64.55
7	CDC-Construction and Development	103.64
8	Jurong Engineering Ltd	213.18
9	Lee Kim Tah Pte Ltd	57.31
10	Singapore Piling and Civil Engineering Pte Ltd	62.42

Source: *Newsletter of the Construction Industry in Singapore Vol 4 No 9, Sept. 1992.*

Jurong Engineering Ltd was ranked 156 in the *Engineering News Record* list of top ten international construction firms. Its overseas contracts were around S$100 million - more than double its local contracts. The IPCO Group is listed also in the *Engineering News Record* at number 134. The L&M Group Investments Ltd, not included in the *Engineering News Record*, had overseas contracts in excess of S$250 million according to the *Newsletter of the Construction Industry in Singapore.*

Construction design work is undertaken mainly by architects and professional engineers. It is necessary to be registered with the Board of Architects, Singapore (a statutory board governing the practice of architects) before being allowed to practise in Singapore as an architect or use the designation 'architect'. There are currently about 850 registered architects. The Singapore Institute of Architects (SIA) is the only body representing professional architects in Singapore. It serves as a link between the profession and the government and technical authorities on matters affecting the profession.

The designation 'professional engineer' is registered and protected by the Professional Engineers Board (a statutory board governing the practice of engineers) and no one is allowed to practise in Singapore as a professional engineer unless registered with the Board. There are currently about 1,900 registered professional engineers of various disciplines in Singapore. There are also two bodies representing professional engineers: the Institution of Engineers Singapore (IES) and the Association of Consulting Engineers Singapore (ACES). The IES has about 4,500 members all of whom are registered engineers of various disciplines. Membership of ACES is only open to consulting engineers in private practice and the current membership figure stands at about 80.

The Singapore Institute of Surveyors and Valuers (SISV) is the only body representing surveyors and valuers in Singapore with a membership of slightly over 1,000. The main disciplines covered are quantity, valuation and land surveying.

Clients and finance

The principal bodies in the award of public sector contracts are the Housing and Development Board (HDB) and the Public Works Department (PWD) of the Ministry of National Development. HDB was established as a statutory board in 1960. Its main activity is the provision of suitable housing for sale (and to a lesser extent for rent) to lower and middle income groups. As of 1992, the HDB stock of flats housed 90% of the population in Singapore (up from 88% in 1990). It is the intention of the HDB to upgrade old HDB flats over a 15 year period costing about S$20 billion.

Government policy has been to encourage home ownership in Singapore. The key to this has been the availability of savings to purchase housing through compulsory contributions to the Central Provident Fund (CPF) by employers and employees. The current rates of contribution are 40% of wages, of which 18% is contributed by employers and 22% by employees. Members are permitted to draw on their CPF funds to purchase housing. The result is that, in 1990, 87% of HDB flats were owner-occupied.

The sources of finance for the HDB for capital expenditure are mainly government financed loans drawn from the Development Fund, though it is permitted to raise private loans. The Building and Development Division is responsible for the planning, design and construction of public housing; it has departments covering all the construction professions and, at March 1990, had a total staff of over 2,700.

Selection of design consultants

There are no prescribed criteria or specific tender or selection procedures for the choice of design consultants in Singapore. In the public sector, a pre-qualification exercise through the submission of credentials, including relevant experience, followed by interviews is usually adopted. In some instances a design competition is held. In the private sector, the design competition method of selection is rarely adopted. Clients may select the design consultants known to them or those who have a reputation for a specific type of building. Price is less important than in the public sector.

There are no published guidelines on the selection of consultants. All the professional bodies publish fee scales though these are not mandatory and are rarely used.

Contractual arrangements

Both HDB and the PWD have their own standard forms of contract. Most public contracts are awarded on the basis of the lowest tenders submitted by contractors registered with the CIDB. It is intended, in the long run, that there should only be a single standard form of contract to be used on all public sector projects.

Most private projects use the Singapore Institute of Architects' (SIA) forms of contract: a Measurement Contract (for use with bills of quantities); a Lump Sum Contract (where quantities are not part of contract); and a Minor Works Contract.

Liability and insurance

Professional indemnity insurance is compulsory for architectural and engineering firms practising as limited companies. In the case of partnerships, it is not compulsory, but most big practices do hold professional indemnity insurance.

Development control and standards

The Urban Redevelopment Authority (URA) is the National Planning and Conservation Authority regulating and facilitating the physical development of Singapore. Most types of development require written planning permission but certain types are not considered material or are specifically exempted and thus do not require planning permission. The URA published a series of development control handbooks to guide and inform applicants of the procedures to be observed in submitting development applications. They are:

- Change of Use
- Conservation
- Subdivision
- Additions and Alterations to Conventional Houses
- Erection of Buildings
- Development Control Parameters.

The Building Control Division (BCD) of the Public Works Department (PWD) of the Ministry of National Development is responsible for setting and monitoring building regulations which cover, for example, structural integrity, lighting, ventilation and thermal transmission. In 1989, a new regulation came into effect requiring all structural designs to be checked and endorsed by accredited checkers who are independent registered professional engineers approved by BCD, before such structural designs are lodged for planning approval.

The Singapore Institute of Standards and Industrial Research (SISIR) draws up and promulgates the Singapore Standards (SS), the standard specifications for products, and it is usual for manufacturers to comply with these. Architects and other building professionals generally follow the recommendations of the SS when specifying building products.

Research and development

The main organisations engaged in construction research are the Construction Industry Development Board and the Singapore Institute of Standards and Industrial Research.

CONSTRUCTION COST DATA

Cost of labour

The figures below are typical of labour costs in Singapore as at the first quarter 1993. The wage rate is the basis of an employee's income, while the cost of labour indicates the cost to a contractor of employing that employee. The difference between the two covers a variety of mandatory and voluntary contributions - a list of items which could be included is given in section 2.

	Wage rate (per day) S$	Cost of labour (per day) S$	Number of hours worked per year
Site operatives			
Mason/bricklayer	47.50	57.20	2,288
Carpenter	46.70	56.30	2,288
Plumber	48.70	58.70	2,288
Electrician	49.40	59.50	2,288
Structural steel erector	51.80	62.40	2,288
HVAC installer	47.90	57.70	2,288
Semi-skilled worker	35.20	52.90	2,288
Unskilled labourer	27.20	44.70	2,288
Equipment operator	52.80	63.60	2,288
Watchman/security	40.00	52.10	2,288
Site supervision	*(per month)*	*(per month)*	
General foreman	2,000	2,805	2,288
Trades foreman	1,500	2,100	2,288
Clerk of works	2,700	3,785	2,288
Contractors' personnel			
Site manager	3,800	5,825	2,280
Resident engineer	3,200	4,985	2,280
Resident surveyor	2,750	4,355	2,280
Junior engineer	2,500	3,505	2,280
Junior surveyor	2,300	3,225	2,280
Planner	2,500	3,505	2,280
Consultants' personnel			
Senior architect	6,000	8,410	2,080
Senior engineer	4,500	6,305	2,080
Senior surveyor	4,500	6,305	2,080
Qualified architect	4,000	5,605	2,080
Qualified engineer	3,500	4,905	2,080
Qualified surveyor	3,500	4,905	2,080

Cost of materials

The figures that follow are the costs of main construction materials, delivered to site in Singapore, as incurred by contractors in the first quarter 1993. These assume that the materials would be in quantities as required for a medium sized construction project and that the location of the works would be neither constrained nor remote.

	Units	Cost S$
Cement and aggregate		
Ordinary portland cement in 50kg bags	tonne	155.00
Coarse aggregates for concrete	tonne	18.00
Fine aggregates for concrete	m³	26.00
Ready mixed concrete (Grade 30)	m³	97.00
Ready mixed concrete (Grade 20)	m³	91.00
Steel		
Mild steel reinforcement	tonne	660.00
High tensile steel reinforcement	tonne	632.00
Structural steel sections	tonne	730.00
Bricks and blocks		
Common bricks (215 x 102.5 x 65mm)	1,000	250.00
Good quality facing bricks (215 x 102.5 x 65mm)	1,000	350.00
Hollow concrete blocks (390 x 190 x 100mm)	1,000	750.00
Timber and insulation		
Hardwood for joinery	m³	690.00
Exterior quality plywood (12mm)	m²	9.00
Plywood for interior joinery (12mm)	m²	8.00
50mm thick quilt insulation (16kg/m³)	m²	2.80
50mm thick rigid slab insulation (60kg/m³)	m²	7.00
Hardwood internal door complete with frames and ironmongery	each	700.00
Glass and ceramics		
Float glass (10mm)	m²	86.00
Sealed double glazing units (6/12/6)	m²	250.00
Plaster and paint		
Good quality ceramic wall tiles (300 x 300 x 8mm)	m²	45.00
Plasterboard (13mm thick) - Gypsum	m²	4.00
Emulsion paint in 5 litre tins	litre	3.50
Gloss oil paint in 5 litre tins	litre	6.00
Tiles and paviors		
Clay floor tiles (100 x 200 x 8mm)	m²	13.00
Vinyl floor tiles (300 x 300 x 2mm)	m²	6.00
Clay roof tiles	1,000	2,400.00
Precast concrete roof tiles	1,000	1,000.00

	Units	Cost S$
Drainage		
WC suite complete	each	200.00
Lavatory basin complete	each	88.00
100mm diameter clay drain pipes	m	16.00
150mm diameter cast iron drain pipes (medium grade)	m	17.00

Unit rates

The descriptions below are generally shortened versions of standard descriptions listed in full in section 4. Where an item has a two digit reference number (e.g. 05 or 33), this relates to the full description against that number in section 4. Where an item has an alphabetic suffix (e.g. 12A or 34B) this indicates that the standard description has been modified. Where a modification is major the complete modified description is included here and the standard description should be ignored; where a modification is minor (e.g. the insertion of a named hardwood) the shortened description has been modified here but, in general, the full description in section 4 prevails.

The unit rates below are for main work items on a typical construction project in Singapore in the first quarter 1993. The rates include all necessary labour, materials and equipment. Allowances of 7% for easily accessible sites to 9% for restricted or isolated sites should be added to the rates to cover preliminary and general items.

		Unit	Rate S$
Excavation			
01	Mechanical excavation of foundation trenches	m^3	15.00
02	Hardcore filling making up levels	m^2	10.00
Concrete work			
04	Plain insitu concrete in strip foundations in trenches	m^3	98.00
05	Reinforced insitu concrete in beds	m^3	138.00
06	Reinforced insitu concrete in walls	m^3	138.00
07	Reinforced insitu concrete in suspended floor or roof slabs	m^3	138.00
08	Reinforced insitu concrete in columns	m^3	138.00
09	Reinforced insitu concrete in isolated beams	m^3	138.00
Formwork			
11A	Hardwood and waterproof plywood formwork to concrete walls	m^2	28.00
12A	Hardwood and waterproof plywood formwork to concrete columns	m^2	28.00
13A	Hardwood and waterproof plywood formwork to horizontal soffits of slabs	m^2	28.00

		Unit	Rate S$
Reinforcement			
14	Reinforcement in concrete walls	tonne	1,150.00
15	Reinforcement in suspended concrete slabs	tonne	1,150.00
16	Fabric reinforcement in concrete beds	m^2	10.00
Steelwork			
17	Fabricate, supply and erect steel framed structure	tonne	3,200.00
Brickwork and blockwork			
18	Precast lightweight aggregate hollow concrete block walls	m^2	17.50
19	Solid (perforated) concrete blocks	m^2	47.00
21	Facing bricks	m^2	86.00
Roofing			
22	Concrete interlocking roof tiles 430 x 380mm	m^2	20.00
23	Plain clay roof tiles 260 x 160mm	m^2	50.00
27	3 layers glass-fibre based bitumen felt roof covering	m^2	28.00
31	Troughed galvanized steel roof cladding	m^2	30.00
Woodwork and metalwork			
32	Preservative treated sawn hardwood 50 x 100mm	m	8.10
33	Preservative treated sawn hardwood 50 x 150mm	m	12.20
35A	Two panel glazed door in Kapur hardwood, size 850 x 2000mm	each	550.00
36	Solid core half hour fire resisting hardwood internal flush doors, size 800 x 2000mm	each	750.00
37	Aluminium double glazed window, size 1200 x 1200mm	each	750.00
39	Hardwood skirtings	m	7.00
40	Framed structural steelwork in universal joist sections	tonne	2,500.00
41	Structural steelwork lattice roof trusses	tonne	2,700.00
Plumbing			
42	UPVC half round eaves gutter	m	22.00
43	UPVC rainwater pipes	m	17.00
44	Light gauge copper cold water tubing	m	18.00
45	High pressure plastic pipes for cold water supply	m	16.00
47	UPVC soil and vent pipes	m	24.00
48	White vitreous china WC suite	each	420.00
49	White vitreous china lavatory basin	each	150.00
51A	Stainless steel double bowl sink and double drainer	each	350.00
Electrical work			
52	PVC insulated and copper sheathed cable	m	2.00
53	13 amp unswitched socket outlet	each	38.00
54	Flush mounted 20 amp, 1 way light switch	each	112.00

	Unit	Rate S$
Finishings		
55A 2 coats cement and sand (1:4) plaster on brick walls	m²	11.00
56 White glazed tiles on plaster walls	m²	37.00
57 Red clay quarry tiles on concrete floor	m²	36.00
58 Cement and sand screed to concrete floors	m²	10.00
59 Thermoplastic floor tiles on screed	m²	15.00
60 Mineral fibre tiles on concealed suspension system	m²	35.00
Glazing		
61 Glazing to wood	m²	36.00
Painting		
62 Emulsion on plaster walls	m²	3.00
63 Oil paint on timber	m²	6.00

Approximate estimating

The building costs per unit area given below are averages incurred by building clients for typical buildings in Singapore as at the first quarter 1993. They are based upon the total floor area of all storeys, measured between external walls and without deduction for internal walls.

Approximate estimating costs generally include mechanical and electrical installations but exclude furniture, loose or special equipment, and external works; they also exclude fees for professional services. The costs shown are for specifications and standards appropriate to Singapore and this should be borne in mind when attempting comparisons with similarly described building types in other countries. A discussion of this issue is included in section 2. Comparative data for countries covered in this publication, including construction cost data, is presented in Part Three.

Approximate estimating costs must be treated with caution; they cannot provide more than a rough guide to the probable cost of building.

	Cost m² S$	Cost ft² S$
Industrial buildings		
Factories for letting	900	84
Factories for owner occupation (light industrial use)	950	88
Factories for owner occupation (heavy industrial use)	1,150	107
Factory/office (high-tech) for letting (shell and core only)	1,200	111
Factory/office (high-tech) for letting (ground floor shell, first floor offices)	1,300	121
Factory/office (high tech) for owner occupation (controlled environment, fully finished)	1,400	130
High tech laboratory workshop centres (air conditioned)	1,200	111
Warehouses, low bay (6 to 8m high) for letting (no heating)	750	70
Warehouses, low bay for owner occupation	800	74
Warehouses, high bay for owner occupation	850	79

	Cost m² S$	Cost ft² S$
Administrative and commercial buildings		
Offices for letting, 5 to 10 storeys, non air conditioned	1,200	111
Offices for letting, 5 to 10 storeys, air conditioned	1,500	139
Offices for letting, high rise, air conditioned	1,800	167
Offices for owner occupation high rise, air conditioned	1,900	177
Prestige/headquarters office, 5 to 10 storeys, air conditioned	2,200	204
Prestige/headquarters office, high rise, air conditioned	2,500	232
Health and education buildings		
General hospitals (100 beds)	1,700	158
Private hospitals (100 beds)	1,900	177
Health centres	1,100	102
Primary/junior schools	800	74
Secondary/middle schools	1,100	102
University (arts) buildings	1,400	130
University (science) buildings	1,400	130
Recreation and arts buildings		
Theatres (less than 500 seats)	1,800	167
Sports halls including changing and social facilities	1,200	111
Swimming pools (international standard) (Olympic size)	each 1,500,000	
Swimming pools (schools standard) including changing facilities	each 1,300,000	
City centre/central libraries	1,300	121
Branch/local libraries	1,100	102
Residential buildings		
Private/mass market single family housing 2 storey detached/semi detached (multiple units)	1,400	130
Purpose designed single family housing 2 storey detached (single unit)	1,700	158
Social/economic apartment housing, high rise (with lifts)	900	84
Private sector apartment building (standard specification)	1,200	111
Private sector apartment buildings (luxury)	1,600	149
Student/nurses halls of residence	1,100	102
Homes for the elderly (shared accommodation)	900	84
Hotel, 5 star, city centre	2,800	260
Hotel, 3 star, city/provincial	2,100	195

EXCHANGE RATES AND INFLATION

The combined effect of exchange rates and inflation on prices within a country and price comparisons between countries is discussed in section 2.

Exchange rates

The graph below plots the movement of the Singaporean dollar against sterling, the US dollar and the Japanese yen since 1980. The figures used for the graph are quarterly and the method of calculating these and other related issues are discussed in section 2. The exchange rates at the first quarter 1993 was S$2.45 to the pound sterling, S$1.65 to the US dollar and S$1.34 to 100 Japanese yen.

THE SINGAPOREAN DOLLAR AGAINST STERLING, THE US DOLLAR AND THE JAPANESE YEN

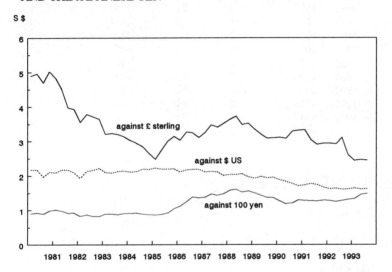

Price inflation

The table on the next page presents building cost and building material price inflation in Singapore since 1980.

BUILDING COSTS AND BUILDING MATERIAL
PRICE INFLATION

Year	Building costs average index	average change %	Building material prices index average index	average change %
1980	100		100	
1981	147	47.0	104	4.0
1982	149	1.4	99	-4.8
1983	142	-4.7	96	-3.0
1984	123	-13.4	74	-22.9
1985	111	-9.8	63	-14.9
1986	103	-7.2	56	-11.1
1987	107	3.9	55	-1.8
1988	112	4.7	57	3.6
1989	119	6.3	80	40.4
1990	134	12.6	98	22.5
1991	137	2.2	104	6.1
1992	143	4.4	104	-

USEFUL ADDRESSES

Public Organizations

Ministry of National Development
    5 Maxwell Road #21/22-00
    Tower Block
    MND Complex
    Singapore 0106
    Tel: 222 1211

Ministry of Environment
    40 Scotts Road
    Singapore 0922
    Tel: 732 7733

Urban Redevelopment Authority
    URA Building
    45 Maxwell Road
    Singapore 0106
    Tel: 221 6666

Construction Industry Development Board
    National Development Building #03-00
    Singapore 0106
    Tel: 225 6711

Board of Architects, Singapore
    1st Storey, National Development Building
    Singapore 0106
    Tel: 222 5295
    Fax: 222 4452

Professional Engineers Board
    c/o Public Works Department
    1st Storey, National Development Building
    Singapore 0106
    Tel: 222 9293
    Fax: 222 9471

Singapore Institute of Standards and Industrial Research
    SISIR Building
    1 Science Park Drive
    Singapore 0501
    Tel: 778 7777

Urban Development Authority
    URA Building
    45 Maxwell Road
    Singapore 0106
    Tel: 221 6666

Department of Statistics
    Ministry of Trade and Industry
    8 Shenton Way #10-01
    Treasury Building
    Singapore 0106
    Tel: 320 9686
    Fax: 320 9689
    Telex: RS 63001 STAT
    Cable: STATISTICS

Trade and Professional Associations

Singapore Contractors' Association Ltd
    Construction House
    1 Bukit Merah Lane 1
    Singapore 0315
    Tel: 278 9577
    Fax: 273 3977
    Telex: RS 22406 SCAL

Singapore Institute of Architects
  20 Orchard Road #02-00
  SMA House
  Singapore 0923
  Tel: 338 8977
  Fax: 336 8708
  Telex: RS 22652 SINARC
  Cable: INSTOFARCH

Institution of Engineers Singapore
  70 Bukit Tinggi Road
  Singapore 1128
  Tel: 469 5000
  Fax: 467 1108
  Telex: RS 2292 IESIN

Association of Consulting Engineers Singapore
  50 Jalan Sultan #07-08
  Jalan Sultan Centre
  Singapore 0719
  Tel: 292 4660
  Fax: 292 4628

Singapore Institute of Surveyors and Valuers
  20 Maxwell Road #10-09B
  Maxwell House
  Singapore 0106
  Tel: 222 3030
  Fax: 225 2453

Singapore Concrete Institute
  845 Concrete Centre #03-00
  Yishun Street 81
  Singapore 2778
  Tel: 754 5386
  Fax: 753 5896

Singapore Institute of Building Ltd
  10B Murray Street
  Singapore 0207
  Tel: 223 0258
  Fax: 224 4249

Singapore Institute of Landscape Architects
  617 Bukit Timah Road
  Singapore 1026
  Tel: 466 9211
  Telex: GARCEN RS 35451

Singapore Institute of Planners
   11 Penang Lane #05-02
   Singapore 0923
   Tel: 339 6577/339 2401
   Fax: 336 3056

Real Estate Developers' Association of Singapore (REDAS)
   190 Clemenceau Avenue #07-01
   Singapore Shopping Centre
   Singapore 0923
   Tel: 336 6655
   Fax: 337 2217

Singapore Federation Chamber of Commerce and Industry
   47 Hill Street #03-01
   Chinese Chamber of Commerce and Industry Building
   Singapore 0617
   Tel: 338 9761
   Fax: 339 5630

South Korea

KEY DATA

Population
Population	42.8m
Urban population	72%
Population under 15	25%
Population over 65	6%
Average annual growth rate (1980 to 1990)	1.1%

Geography
Land area	99,000 km²
Agricultural area	23%
Capital city	Seoul
	(population 9.6m) (1985)

Economy
Monetary unit	Won
Exchange rate (average first quarter 1993) to:	
the pound sterling	Won 1,176
the US dollar	Won 794
the yen x 100	Won 646
Average annual inflation (1980 to 1990)	5.1%
Inflation rate 1991	about 20% (estimate)
Gross Domestic Product (GDP) (1991)	Won 207,450bn
GDP per capita	Won 4,846,963
Real GDP growth (1980 to 1990)	9.7%
Private consumption as a proportion of GDP	63%
Public consumption as a proportion of GDP	63%
Investment as a proportion of GDP	37%
Central government expenditure as a proportion of Gross National Product	16%

Construction
Gross value of construction output (1991)	Won 60,000bn
Net value of construction output (1991)	Won 32,056bn
Net value of construction output per capita (1991)	Won 748,972
Net value of construction output as a proportion of GDP (1991)	15.5%

Notes: All data relate to 1990 unless otherwise indicated.
Also known as the Republic of Korea.

THE CONSTRUCTION INDUSTRY

Construction output

In 1991 the value of the gross domestic fixed capital formation in construction was about 50,000 billion Won but this is thought to be an understatement of total construction output which is estimated at about 60,000 billion Won equivalent to US$76 billion or about 29% of GDP. The net output is 15.5% of GDP. However, the reason why the percentage is so high is that construction prices have risen more than most prices.

Of the total construction output rather less than 70% is building construction; 30% is civil engineering with a relatively small amount of special construction.

South Korea has experienced a long construction boom since the mid 1960s. However, it is possible that the rate of growth may falter in the next year or so. This is because of the very high rate of construction and general inflation - the latter running in 1991 and 1992 at perhaps around 20% and in construction even higher. In 1990 and 1991 orders for manufacturing industry turned down in current prices and therefore very sharply in real terms. In addition, permits issued for building have fallen considerably since 1990 to the first quarter 1992. the figures for 1990 and 1991 are as follows:

INDICATORS OF CONSTRUCTION ACTIVITY, SOUTH KOREA, 1990 AND 1991

Indicators	1990	1991	Percentage of total 1991	% change
Permits issued, million m²				
- Dwellings	70.9	59.1	56	-16.7
- Factories	10.6	11.3	11	+6.7
- Commercial	26.4	25.6	24	-3.0
- Other	8.5	9.5	9	+8.2
- Total	116.4	105.2	100	-9.7
Domestic orders, billion Won				
- Manufacturers private	2,753	2,529	10	-8.1
- Non-manufacturers private	9,600	11,482	45	+19.6
- Public	8,603	11,546	45	+34.2
- Other	8	12	neg	+50.0
- Total	20,964	25,569	100	+22.0

Note: neg - negligible
Source: Bank of Korea Monthly Statistical Bulletin

Spending on infrastructure over the next five years is intended to be US$100 billion. About US$26 billion is to be spent from 1991 to 2000 on power generation plants. For transport projects US$5.2 billion will be spent on the Seoul subway project, US$30 billion on traffic alleviation schemes for six cities and US$6.82 billion on Asan and Kwanguang Bay Ports.   Seoul Airport near Inchon is to be upgraded at a cost of US$5 billion.

Overseas work has been very important but with the decline in the Middle East markets it has fallen.   However, in 1991, it was still over 10% of the work of the large contractors.

Characteristics and structure of the industry

The top ten contracting companies in South Korea account for around 20% of the work done in the country.   The principal companies, the largest having a turnover of nearly US$4 billion, are as follows:

MAJOR SOUTH KOREAN CONSTRUCTION
CONTRACTORS, 1991

Company	Employees	Work abroad %
Hyundai	4,802	17
Dae Woo	2,816	36
Dong A	2,893	neg
Sam Sung	2,123	4
Dae Lim	3,016	10
Hyundai Industries	1,429	-
Lucky	1,318	1
Kwangju	983	-
SunKyung	1,590	8
WooSung	1,167	-
Total	22,137	11

Source: Korean Construction Association and Korean
        Abroad Construction Association
neg - negligible

The Dae Woo Corporation is number 29, and the Hyundai Engineering and Construction Company is number 50, in the *Engineering News Record*'s 1991 list of top 225 international contractors and two others feature in the list.   The largest firms often have their own design, surveying and planning departments.

Clients and finance

Of the work undertaken by the top 10 contractors about half is for private sector clients and about half for public sector clients.   Private work is increasing rapidly.   Loans for housing are given by the Korea Housing Bank.

Selection of design consultants

In the public sector consultants are selected in competition. In the private sector the client usually chooses the designer but for large projects a competition may be held which may include foreign consultants.

Design is generally separated from construction but housing is normally carried out on a design and construct basis.

Contractual arrangements

There are three methods of selecting contractors. Selective tendering is most usual and contractors are short-listed according to their record and financial ratings. If, however, a special technology or construction method is needed, a limited competition of those contractors qualified for the project is held.

At the pre-tender stage contractors must submit a number of documents certifying their *bona fides* including, for example, certificates of tax paid, technical expert log book and state of the business. At the tendering stage after public notice of the tender, detailed information on the project is given. The contract documents include specifications, tax certificates, written guarantees etc. and the contract itself covers the normal contractual arrangements including provisions for delay and defects.

Liability and insurance

Various insurances are compulsory: those relating to performance in bidding, carrying out the work, maintenance, and also for protection against dumping. There is also obligatory insurance for workers' compensation and fire. Some contractors make other additional insurance arrangements.

Development control and standards

In each town planning area zoning is compulsory. While alterations to the plans are possible they are very unusual and difficult to achieve.

Each project is assessed in terms of its traffic impact and then in terms of the building itself - its energy usage, structure and aesthetics. The speed of the approval process depends on the region, the size of the project and its purpose but the whole process normally takes six to eight months. Sophisticated buildings such as hotels, condominiums, sports centres or fire stations may take longer. There is no appeal. There are laws on requirements for building structures and facility standards which must be rigidly adhered to. There are Korean Standards (KS) for building materials such as bricks, glass, steel and aggregates.

CONSTRUCTION COST DATA

Cost of labour

The figures below are typical of labour costs in South Korea as at the first quarter 1993. The wage rate is the basis of an employee's income, while the cost of labour indicates the cost to a contractor of employing that employee. The difference between the two covers a variety of mandatory and voluntary contributions - a list of items which could be included is given in section 2.

	Wage rate (daily=12 hrs) Won	Cost of labour (daily=12hr) Won	Number of hours worked per year
Site operatives			
Mason/bricklayer	70,800	77,800	3,720
Carpenter	71,300	78,400	3,720
Plumber	51,800	57,000	3,720
Electrician	50,700	55,700	3,720
Structural steel erector	58,600	64,400	3,720
HVAC installer	52,600	57,900	3,720
Semi-skilled worker	49,500	54,500	3,720
Unskilled labourer	34,800	38,300	3,720
Equipment operator	58,400	64,200	3,720
Watchman/security	42,900	47,200	3,720
Site supervision			
General foreman	74,600	71,100	3,720
Trades foreman	50,800	55,900	3,720
Clerk of works	41,300	45,400	3,720
Contractors' personnel	*(per month)*	*(per month)*	
Site manager	1,980,000	2,376,000	3,190
Resident engineer	1,100,000	1,320,000	3,190
Resident surveyor	1,100,000	1,320,000	3,190
Junior engineer	1,430,000	1,720,000	3,190
Junior surveyor	1,430,000	1,720,000	3,190
Planner	1,430,000	1,720,000	3,190
Consultants' personnel			
Senior architect	1,820,000	2,180,000	3,190
Senior engineer	1,820,000	2,180,000	3,190
Senior surveyor	1,820,000	2,180,000	3,190
Qualified architect	2,150,000	2,570,000	3,190
Qualified engineer	2,200,000	2,640,000	3,190
Qualified surveyor	2,200,000	2,640,000	3,190

Cost of materials

The figures that follow are the costs of main construction materials, delivered to site in the Seoul area, as incurred by contractors in the first quarter 1993.   These assume that the materials would be in quantities as required for a medium sized construction project and that the location of the works would be neither constrained nor remote.   All the costs in this section exclude value added tax (VAT - see below).

	Unit	Cost Won
Cement and aggregate		
Ordinary portland cement in 40kg bags	40 kg	2,090
Coarse aggregates for concrete	m³	9,460
Fine aggregates for concrete	m³	9,460
Ready mixed concrete (40-135-8)	m³	39,500
Ready mixed concrete (25-210-12)	m³	47,500
Precast concrete pile D350 x 65 x 10m	nr	132,000
Steel		
Mild steel reinforcement (over D16)	tonne	284,000
High tensile steel reinforcement (over D16)	tonne	579,000
Structural steel sections (rolled H Beam)	tonne	374,000
Bricks and blocks		
Common bricks (190 x 90 x 57mm)	1,000	49,500
Good quality facing bricks (190 x 90 x 57mm)	1,000	209,000
Hollow concrete blocks (150 x 190 x 390mm)	each	572
Autoclaved lightweight concrete blocks (100 x 400 x 600mm)	each	2,750
Precast concrete cladding units with plain surface finish	m²	19,800
Timber and insulation		
Softwood sections for carpentry	m³	21,500
Softwood for joinery	m³	594,000
Hardwood for joinery	m³	363,000
Exterior quality plywood (15mm)	m²	5,830
Plywood for interior joinery (12mm)	m²	7,430
Softwood strip flooring (22 x 129 x 3700mm)	m²	74,100
Chipboard sheet flooring (18 x 1210 x 2420mm)	m²	3,140
100mm thick quilt insulation	m²	12,800
100mm thick rigid slab insulation (expanded polystyrene)	m²	6,270
Softwood internal door complete with frames and ironmongery	each	165,000
Glass and ceramics		
Float glass (3mm)	m²	2,970
Sealed double glazing units	m²	15,700
Plaster and paint		
Good quality ceramic wall tiles (150 x 150mm)	m²	6,600
Plaster in 25kg bags	bag	1,430

	Unit	Cost Won
Plasterboard (9mm thick)	m²	2,150
Emulsion paint in 5 litre tins	litre	2,090
Gloss oil paint in 5 litre tins	litre	2,150

Tiles and paviors

	Unit	Cost Won
Clay floor tiles (200 x 200 x 10mm)	m²	20,900
Vinyl floor tiles (300 x 300 x 3mm)	m²	3,630
Precast concrete paving slabs (300 x 300 x 60mm)	m²	6,050
Clay roof tiles (300 x 360 x 21mm)	1,000	880,000
Precast concrete roof tiles (400 x 750 x 12mm)	1,000	605,000
Granite 20-24mm thick polished finish medium quality	m²	55,000
Granite 20-24mm thick polished finish high quality	m²	82,500

Drainage

	Unit	Cost Won
WC suite complete	each	132,000
Lavatory basin complete	each	88,000
100mm diameter PVC drain pipes	m	19,800
150mm diameter cast iron drain pipes	m	13,600

Unit rates

The descriptions below are generally shortened versions of standard descriptions listed in full in section 4. Where an item has a two digit reference number (e.g. 05 or 33), this relates to the full description against that number in section 4. Where an item has an alphabetic suffix (e.g. 12A or 34B) this indicates that the standard description has been modified. Where a modification is major the complete modified description is included here and the standard description should be ignored; where a modification is minor (e.g. the insertion of a named hardwood) the shortened description has been modified here but, in general, the full description in section 4 prevails.

The unit rates below are for main work items on a typical construction project in the Seoul area in the first quarter 1993. The rates include all necessary labour, materials and equipment. Allowances of 10% to cover preliminary and general items and 12% to cover contractors' overheads and profit should be added to the rates. All the rates in this section exclude value added tax (VAT - see below).

		Unit	Rate Won
Excavation			
01	Mechanical excavation of foundation trenches	m³	660
02	Hardcore filling making up levels	m²	1,980
03	Earthwork support	m²	1,320
Concrete work			
04	Plain insitu concrete in strip foundations in trenches	m³	61,600
05	Reinforced insitu concrete in beds	m³	52,800
06	Reinforced insitu concrete in walls	m³	63,800

		Unit	Rate Won
07	Reinforced insitu concrete in suspended floor or roof slabs	m³	63,800
08	Reinforced insitu concrete in columns	m³	63,800
09	Reinforced insitu concrete in isolated beams	m³	63,800
10	Precast concrete slab	m²	39,600

Formwork

11	Softwood formwork to concrete walls	m²	11,000
12	Softwood or metal formwork to concrete columns	m²	13,200
13	Softwood or metal formwork to horizontal soffits of slabs	m²	10,450

Reinforcement

14	Reinforcement in concrete walls	tonne	418,000
15	Reinforcement in suspended concrete slabs	tonne	418,000
16	Fabric reinforcement in concrete beds	m²	770

Steelwork

17	Fabricate, supply and erect steel framed structure	tonne	616,000

Brickwork and blockwork

18	Precast lightweight aggregate hollow concrete block walls	m²	13,200
19	Solid (perforated) concrete blocks	m²	11,220
21	Facing bricks	m²	28,000

Roofing

22	Concrete interlocking roof tiles 430 x 380mm	m²	4,400
23	Plain clay roof tiles 260 x 160mm	m²	6,050
24	Fibre cement roof slates 600 x 300mm	m²	15,400
25	Sawn softwood roof boarding	m²	9,350
26	Particle board roof coverings	m²	13,200
27	3 layers glass-fibre based bitumen felt roof covering	m²	16,500
28	Bitumen based mastic asphalt roof covering	m²	16,500
29	Glass-fibre mat roof insulation 100mm thick	m²	19,250
30	Rigid sheet loadbearing roof insulation 75mm thick	m²	17,050
31	Troughed galvanized steel roof cladding	m²	7,150

Woodwork and metalwork

32	Preservative treated sawn softwood 50 x 100mm	m	2,640
33	Preservative treated sawn softwood 50 x 150mm	m	3,960
34A	Single glazed casement window in Lanan hardwood, size 650 x 900mm	each	49,500
35A	Two panel glazed door in Lanan hardwood, size 850 x 2000mm	each	352,000
36A	Solid core half hour fire resisting aluminium internal flush doors, size 800 x 2000mm	each	198,000
37A	Aluminium double glazed window, size 1200 x 1200mm	each	110,000
38A	Aluminium double glazed door, size 850 x 2100mm	each	154,000
39A	Hardwood skirtings (Lanan)	m	2,200
40	Framed structural steelwork in universal joist sections	tonne	660,000

	Unit	Rate Won
41 Structural steelwork lattice roof trusses	tonne	660,000

Plumbing

	Unit	Rate Won
42 UPVC half round eaves gutter	m	8,250
43 UPVC rainwater pipes	m	6,600
44 Light gauge copper cold water tubing	m	4,400
45 High pressure plastic pipes for cold water supply	m	3,740
46 Low pressure plastic pipes for cold water distribution	m	4,180
47 UPVC soil and vent pipes	m	13,200
48 White vitreous china WC suite	each	88,000
49 White vitreous china lavatory basin	each	66,000
50 Glazed fireclay shower tray	each	132,000
51 Stainless steel single bowl sink and double drainer	each	88,000

Electrical work

	Unit	Rate Won
52 PVC insulated and copper sheathed cable	m	3,410
53 13 amp unswitched socket outlet	each	38,700
54 Flush mounted 20 amp, 1 way light switch	each	45,700

Finishings

	Unit	Rate Won
55 2 coats gypsum based plaster on brick walls	m^2	8,580
56 White glazed tiles on plaster walls	m^2	20,400
57 Red clay quarry tiles on concrete floor	m^2	13,200
XX Granite veneer 20mm thick for walls, fixed with cement mortar	m^2	82,500
58 Cement and sand screed to concrete floors	m^2	4,950
59 Thermoplastic floor tiles on screed	m^2	6,820
60 Mineral fibre tiles on concealed suspension system	m^2	16,500

Glazing

	Unit	Rate Won
61 Glazing to wood	m^2	6,820

Painting

	Unit	Rate Won
62 Emulsion on plaster walls	m^2	1,650
63 Oil paint on timber	m^2	2,090

Approximate estimating

The building costs per unit area given below are averages incurred by building clients for typical buildings in the Seoul area as at the first quarter 1993.   They are based upon the total floor area of all storeys, measured between external walls and without deduction for internal walls.

Approximate estimating costs generally include mechanical and electrical installations but exclude furniture, loose or special equipment, and external works; they also exclude fees for professional services.   The costs shown are for specifications and standards appropriate to South Korea and this should be borne in mind when attempting comparisons with similarly described building types in other countries. A discussion of this issue is included in section 2. Comparative data for countries covered in this publication, including construction cost data, is presented in Part Three.

Approximate estimating costs must be treated with caution; they cannot provide more than a rough guide to the probable cost of building. All the rates in this section exclude value added tax (VAT - see below).

	Cost m² Won	Cost ft² Won
Industrial buildings		
Factories for letting	499,000	46,400
Factories for owner occupation (light industrial use)	532,000	49,500
Factories for owner occupation (heavy industrial use)	566,000	52,600
Factory/office (high-tech) for letting (shell and core only)	732,000	68,000
Factory/office (high-tech) for letting (ground floor shell, first floor offices)	699,000	64,900
Factory/office (high tech) for owner occupation (controlled environment, fully finished)	832,000	77,300
High tech laboratory workshop centres (air conditioned)	1,500,000	139,000
Warehouses, low bay (6 to 8m high) for letting (no heating)	299,000	27,800
Warehouses, low bay for owner occupation (including heating)	333,000	30,900
Warehouses, high bay for owner occupation (including heating)	399,000	37,100
Cold stores/refrigerated stores	1,160,000	108,000
Administrative and commercial buildings		
Civic offices, non air conditioned	532,000	49,500
Civic offices, fully air conditioned	333,000	30,900
Offices for letting, 5 to 10 storeys, non air conditioned	732,000	68,000
Offices for letting, 5 to 10 storeys, air conditioned	799,000	74,200
Offices for letting, high rise, air conditioned	765,000	71,100
Offices for owner occupation 5 to 10 storeys, non air conditioned	832,000	77,300
Offices for owner occupation 5 to 10 storeys, air conditioned	932,000	86,600
Offices for owner occupation high rise, air conditioned	865,000	80,400
Prestige/headquarters office, 5 to 10 storeys, air conditioned	732,000	68,000
Prestige/headquarters office, high rise, air conditioned	932,000	86,600

	Cost m² Won	Cost ft² Won
Health and education buildings		
General hospitals (100 beds)	1,160,000	108,000
Teaching hospitals (100 beds)	998,000	92,700
Private hospitals (100 beds)	665,000	61,800
Health centres	832,000	77,300
Nursery schools	665,000	61,800
Primary/junior schools	599,000	55,600
Secondary/middle schools	599,000	55,600
University (arts) buildings	665,000	61,800
University (science) buildings	765,000	71,100
Management training centres	665,000	61,800
Recreation and arts buildings		
Theatres (over 500 seats) including seating and stage equipment	1,330,000	124,000
Theatres (less than 500 seats) including seating and stage equipment	1,660,000	155,000
Concert halls including seating and stage equipment	1,830,000	170,000
Sports halls including changing and social facilities	1,160,000	108,000
Swimming pools (international standard) including changing and social facilities	998,000	92,700
Swimming pools (schools standard) including changing facilities	832,000	77,300
National museums including full air conditioning and standby generator	832,000	77,300
Local museums including air conditioning	665,000	61,800
City centre/central libraries	832,000	77,300
Branch/local libraries	665,000	61,800
Residential buildings		
Social/economic single family housing (multiple units)	732,000	68,000
Private/mass market single family housing 2 storey detached/semidetached (multiple units)	599,000	55,600
Purpose designed single family housing 2 storey detached (single unit)	665,000	61,800
Social/economic apartment housing, low rise (no lifts)	433,000	40,200
Social/economic apartment housing, high rise (with lifts)	466,000	43,300
Private sector apartment building (standard specification)	532,000	49,500
Private sector apartment buildings (luxury)	832,000	77,300
Student/nurses halls of residence	433,000	40,200
Homes for the elderly (shared accommodation)	433,000	40,200
Homes for the elderly (self contained with shared communal facilities)	466,000	43,300
Hotel, 5 star, city centre	1,160,000	108,000
Hotel, 3 star, city/provincial	998,000	92,700
Motel	832,000	77,300

Regional variations

The approximate estimating costs are based on projects in Seoul and other big cities. For other parts of country, add 5% to these costs.

Value added tax (VAT)

The standard rate of value added tax (VAT) is currently 10%, chargeable on general building work.

EXCHANGE RATES AND INFLATION

The combined effect of exchange rates and inflation on prices within a country and price comparisons between countries is discussed in section 2.

Exchange rates

The graph below plots the movement of the Korean won against sterling, the US dollar and the Japanese yen since 1980. The figures used for the graph are quarterly and the method of calculating these and other related issues are discussed in section 2. The exchange rate at the first quarter 1993 was Won 1,176 to the pound sterling, Won 794 to the US dollar and Won 6.46 to the Japanese yen.

THE SOUTH KOREAN WON AGAINST STERLING, THE US DOLLAR
AND THE JAPANESE YEN

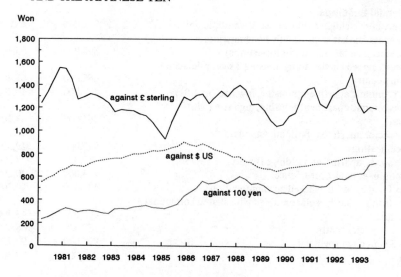

Price inflation

The table below presents retail prices and building price inflation in South Korea since 1980.

RETAIL PRICE AND BUILDING PRICE INFLATION

| | Retail price index | | Building price index | |
| | average | average | average | average |
Year	index	change %	index	change %
1980	100		100	
1981	121	21.0	105	5.0
1982	130	7.4	115	9.5
1983	134	3.1	117	1.7
1984	138	3.0	119	1.7
1985	141	2.2	124	4.2
1986	145	2.8	125	0.8
1987	149	2.8	126	0.8
1988	160	7.4	135	7.1
1989	169	5.6	155	14.8
1990	183	8.3	173	11.6
1991	201	9.8	182	5.2

USEFUL ADDRESSES

Public Organizations

Korea Development Corporation
    Central POB 218
    Seoul
    Tel: 02 713 7272
    Fax: 02 718 3570
    Telex: POLEMAN K26467

Ministry of Construction
    1 Jungang-Dong
    Kwachun-Shi
    Kyonggi-Do
    Republic of Korea
    Tel: 010 822 503 7171
    Fax: 010 822 503 7409

Public Information Officer
    Tel: 010 822 503 7312

The National Statistical Office
90 Kyungwoon-Dong
Jongro-Ku
Seoul
Korea
Tel: 010 822 222 1901/5
Fax: 010 822 736 4298

Economic Planning Board
1 Jung Aug-Dong
Kwachon
Kyonggi-Do
Tel: 010 822 503 1717
Fax: 010 822 503 9033

Korean Standards Association
13-31 Youido-Dong
Youngdeungpo-Ku
Seoul
South Korea
Tel: 010 822 369 8114
Fax: 010 822 369 8109

Korea Research Institue of Standards and Science
966-5 Daechi-Dong
Kangnam-Ku
Seoul
South Korea
Tel: 010 822 569 7818
Fax: 010 822 569 7819

Korea Land Development Corporation
71-1 Nonhyun-Dong
Kangnam-Ku
Seoul
South Korea
Tel: 010 822 513 8114
Fax: 010 822 544 1944

Korea National Housing Corporation
254 Nonkyun-Dong
Kangnam Ku
Seoul
Korea
Tel: 010 822 513 3114
Fax: 010 822 545 1854

Korea Institute of Construction Technology
    142 Umyon-Dong, Socho-Ku
    Seoul
    Korea
    Tel: 010 822 577 5006
    Fax: 010 822 572 8998
    Telex Kictex k28878

Trade and Professional Organisations

Korean Institute of Architects (section Coreenne de L'UIA)
    1-117 Dongsung-Dong
    Chongro-Ku
    Seoul
    Korea
    Tel: 010 822 744 8050/744 3725
    Fax: 010 822 743 5363

Korea Institute of Registered Architecture
    1603-55 Seocho-Dong
    Seocho-Ku
    Seoul
    Korea
    Tel: 010 822 581 5711
    Fax: 010 822 586 8823

Korea Construction Engineers Association
    705-14 Yeaksam-Dong
    Kang Nam-Ku
    Seoul
    Korea
    Tel: 010 822 567 5571
    Fax: 010 822 558 3936/569 0619

Korea Engineering Services Association
    61-5 Nonhyun-Dong
    Kangnam-Ku
    Seoul
    Korea
    Tel: 010 822 541 1736
    Fax: 010 822 543 5074

The Architectural Institute of Korea
    635-4 Yeoksam-Dong
    Kang Nam-Ku
    Seoul
    Korea
    Tel: 010 822 553 4715/6
    Fax: 010 822 562 2584

The Korean Professional Engineers Association
    635-4 Yeoksam-Dong
    Kang Nam-Ku
    Seoul
    Korea
    Tel: 010 822 557 1352
    Fax: 010 822 557 7408

Construction Association of Korea
    71-2, Nonhyon-Dong
    Kangnam-Ku
    Seoul
    Korea
    Tel: 010 822 547 6101
    Fax: 010 822 545 1761

Korea Housing Builders Association
    25-5 Yoido-Dong
    Youngdeungpo-Ku
    Seoul
    Korea
    Tel: 010 822 782 2966/7
    Fax: 010 822 782 7149

Other

Housing Association of Korea
    71-2, Nonhyon-Dong
    Kangnam-Ku
    Seoul
    Tel: 010 822 547 1835/546 4902
    Fax: 010 822 545 1761

Korea Housing Bank
    36/3 Yoido-Dong
    Youngdeungpo-Ku
    Seoul 150-010
    Republic of Korea
    Tel: 010 822 769 7114 or 769 8114
    Fax: 010 822 769 8789 or 784 3403

Korea Development Bank
    10-2 Kwanchui-Dong
    Chongro-Ku
    Seoul
    South Korea
    Tel: 010 822 398 6114
    Fax: 010 822 733 2994

Frank Lloyd Wright and Japan

The role of traditional Japanese art and architecture in the work of Frank Lloyd Wright

K H Nute, Architect, Cambridge, UK

A unique combination of text and graphics to illustrate the influence of Japan on Wright's work

Supported by The Japan Foundation

Frank Lloyd Wright's admiration for traditional Japanese art is well known, as is his insistence that neither the art nor the architecture had any direct *formal* influence on his own work. This book examines the evidence that, quite apart from their philosophical lessons, certain forms of Japanese art and architecture did in fact have a significant formal impact on Wright's formal vocabulary, and one which may cast light on his general approach to design.

The book also explains Wright's particular perception of tradtional Japanese art and architecture in terms of his own "organic" design principles, and by illustrating how he brought together disparate forms and ideas in new creative syntheses it attempts to clarify the nature of his artistic originality.

Contents: Acknowledgements. Forewords. Introduction. 'Japanism' and the Boston orientalists. Japanese homes: the Japanese house dissected. The Ho-O-den: the temple and the villa married in south Chicago. Fenollosa and the "organic" nature of Japanese art. Composition: the picture, the plan, and the pattern, as aesthetic line-ideas. The wookblock print and the geometric abstraction of natural, man-made and social forms. Okakura and the social and aesthetic *Ideals of the East.* Jaean itself: giving and receiving in "Yedo". Japan as inspiration: analogies with Japanese built-forms. Japan as confirmation: the universal manifested in the particular. Appendices: summary of events; biographical sketches; Kakuzo Okakura's catalogue of the Ho-o-den; Ernest Fenollosa's essay on "The Nature of Fine Art"; Frederick Gookin's reviews of Kakuzo Okakura's books; glossary. Bibliography. Illustration acknowledgements. Index.

September 1993: 297x210: 256pp, 133 line illus, 92 halftone illus, 11colour illus
Hardback: 0-412-57420-9

Chapman & Hall

For further information and to order, please contact: The Promotion Dept., Chapman & Hall, 2-6 Boundary Row, LONDON SE1 8HN
Tel 071 865 0066 Fax 071 522 9623

In Thailand:

DAVIS LANGDON & SEAH (THAILAND) LTD
LECE (THAILAND) LTD

The strategic and integrated management of cost, time and quality - the client "risk" areas of a contract - are essential functions, which are necessary to ensure the satisfactory planning, procurement, execution and operation of construction projects.

We specialise in the financial management of construction projects and their risk areas, from project inception to completion and we concentrate on:

* being positive and creative in our advice, rather than simply reactive;

* providing value for money via efficient management, rather than on superficial cost monitoring;

* giving advice that is matched to the Client's requirements, rather than imposing standard or traditional solutions;

* paying attention to the life-cycle costs of constructing and occupying a building, rather than to the initial capital cost only.

Our aim is to provide our clients with risk assurance, cost control and value for money, via effective advice, cost planning and management.

DAVIS LANGDON & SEAH (THAILAND) LTD
8th Floor, Kian Gwan Building
140 Wireless Road
Bangkok 10330, Thailand
Tel : (010 662) 253 7390
Fax : (010 662) 253 4977

DAVIS LANGDON & SEAH INTERNATIONAL

MANAGE AND LIMIT CLIENT RISK - ADDING VALUE

Thailand

KEY DATA

Population
Population	60m
Urban population	23%
Population under 15	34%
Population over 65	3%
Average annual growth rate (1980 to 1990)	1.8%

Geography
Land area	513,000 km²
Agricultural area	41%
Capital city	Bangkok
	(population 8m)

Economy
Monetary unit	Thai baht (Bt)
Exchange rate (average first quarter 1993) to:	
the pound sterling	Bt 37.77
the US dollar	Bt 25.48
the yen x 100	Bt 20.73
Average annual inflation (1980 to 1990)	3.3%
Inflation rate (1991)	6%
Gross Domestic Product (GDP)	Bt 2,051.2bn
GDP per capita	Bt 36,032
Real GDP growth (1980 to 1990)	7.6%
Private consumption as a proportion of GDP	57%
Public consumption as a proportion of GDP	10%
Investment as a proportion of GDP	37%
Central government expenditure as a proportion of Gross National Product	15%

Construction
Gross value of construction output (1991)	Bt 390bn
Net value of construction output	Bt 146.8bn
Net value of construction output per capita	Bt 2,622
Net value of construction output as a proportion of GDP	7.1%

Note: All data relate to 1990 unless otherwise indicated.

THE CONSTRUCTION INDUSTRY

Construction output

The net value of construction output excluding building materials in 1990 was about 147 billion baht equivalent to US$5.6 billion or 7.1% of GDP. After a recession for most of the 1980s there had been a rapid increase in investment towards the end of the decade. Indeed in the late 1980s construction output grew sometimes by over 10% a year transforming the large cities and tourist resorts with multi-storey buildings. At the same time the economy as a whole was expanding at record rates and in 1990 the growth rate was estimated at 9.5%. There has been a substantial increase in overseas investment in factories, offices and housing. Housing demand has been stimulated by the high level of growth. Public sector expenditure on infrastructure has also increased to meet the increased needs due to the expanding level of activity. Transport facilities, including new roads, electricity supply and water supplies are critical. In Bangkok, for example, a major expressway development programme has been initiated.

Most industrial activities are concentrated in and around Bangkok and its five surrounding provinces although the government has for many years emphasized its policy of decentralization and this is now producing results in the form of new factories opening further afield in the lower Northeast and Central Plains and on the Eastern Seaboard. The government is also now formulating plans for the development of a Southern Seaboard region similar to the Eastern Seaboard to facilitate trade between the Middle East, Europe and the Pacific countries through the use of a land bridge linking the Andaman Sea and the Gulf of Thailand. There will also be accompanying industrial development.

Very recently, the political crisis has reduced activity. Many housing projects have recently been cancelled. There has been a sharp drop in tourism and many private developments such as condominiums, golf courses and resorts aimed particularly at Japanese tourists may not be built. This may, however, give the opportunity for government to accelerate investment plans without fear of boosting inflation.

Characteristics and structure of the industry

The number of contracting companies has increased significantly over the last few years and it is estimated that there are now over 4,500 construction firms. Most of these are small Thai firms and most of the top ten contracting firms are of foreign origin, often joint ventures. Competition from foreign contractors has been increasing in recent years, notably those from South Korea and Taiwan.

Clients and finance

The three main categories of clients of the industry are:

- the government consisting of various government departments that are financed by the Treasury;
- state enterprises: that is government and private sector, joint venture organizations financed by the Treasury and from foreign loans;
- the private sector comprising private property developers, insurance companies, and other financial institutions financed by banks or the developer's own resources.

Selection of design consultants

The government has in-house design teams to undertake its own projects. However, if it is felt that the nature, scope etc. of a proposed project cannot be adequately undertaken by an in-house design team, then outside consultants are invited to bid. There is a process of pre-qualification based on reputation, past experience, staff capacity etc. When tenders are invited, a brief is given together with all the predetermined rules and regulations. The level of professional fee is also predetermined. The selection committee seeks the best overall design to satisfy the brief. Design competitions are frequently held to appoint consultants.

In the case of a state enterprise, tenders may be invited. The level of fee quoted is one of the factors taken into consideration when awarding a contract whereas, in the private sector, the design concept and fees are the major considerations in awarding work to consultants. In-house design organizations usually function as project co-ordinators. Depending on the terms of engagement of consultants, in-house design organizations may have an important role.

The method used for selecting consultants is the same for housing, building works and civil engineering.

Contractual arrangements

Construction contract documents may be prepared either in Thai or English. Government works use several versions of the standard form of contract while no standard form of contract exists for the private sector. However, a commonly used form is a simplified version of a contract produced by the Joint Contracts Tribunal in the UK.

Liability and insurance

Contractors may be liable for injury to persons and property caused during the carrying out of the works. Professionals may also be held liable for negligence.

Contractors are usually required to offer a 6 to 12 month warranty period after project completion during which defects for which the contractors are responsible are to be made good at no cost to the owners. It is usual therefore for a contractor to take out a Contractor's All Risks Insurance Policy.

Consultants do not usually, however, offer the owners any design warranty, but foreign investors normally ask for a 12 month warranty period. Insurance is not compulsory for professionals.

It is usual for claims to be settled out of court. Some designers limit claims by clients to an amount not exceeding their fees.

Development control and standards

Land use planning is based on zoning for various types of development. For the application of planning permission, the consultants must submit a set of submission drawings to the city hall. In the case of a factory, an environmental study must also be provided. The submission drawings will be forwarded to the land use department within the city hall to check for compliance with land use requirements. If approved, these drawings are then passed on to the structural, architectural and the mechanical and electrical departments for checking against compliance with by-laws. If the drawings satisfy all these requirements they are endorsed with the signature of either the governor or deputy governor of the city hall for the granting of planning permission.

The whole process of obtaining planning permission takes 45 days and the chances of approval are high. If an application is turned down, an appeal may be made in writing to the city hall. It is to be noted that the city hall might approve a minor departure from the land use requirements if it can be shown that such departure actually benefits the general public.

There is a set of building regulations applicable to the whole country. A building of more then 10,000m² needs an occupancy permit. The city hall officers will inspect the completed building against the approved planning submission. Depending on the type of development, officers from relevant departments will inspect the building. For example, the health authority will inspect a hospital, and the health and fire authority will inspect a hotel.

The national standard for building materials/products is the TIS (Thai Industrial Standard). However, many foreign equivalents (e.g. BS, ASTM, DIN, JIS, etc.) are also acceptable.

CONSTRUCTION COST DATA

Cost of labour

The figures below are typical of labour costs in the Bangkok area as at
November 1992.

	Cost of labour (per hour) Bt
Site operatives	
Unskilled labourer	25
Semi-skilled labourer	30
Skilled labourer	39

Cost of materials

The figures that follow are the costs of main construction materials,
delivered to site in the Bangkok area, as incurred by contractors in the
first quarter 1993.   These assume that the materials would be in
quantities as required for a medium sized construction project and that
the location of the works would be neither constrained nor remote.   All
the rates in this section exclude value added tax (VAT - see below).

	Units	Cost Bt
Cement and aggregate		
Ordinary portland cement in 50kg bags	tonne	1,600
Coarse aggregates for concrete	m^3	320
Fine aggregates for concrete	m^3	230
Ready mixed concrete (mix Grade 20)	m^3	1,200
Ready mixed concrete (mix Grade 24)	m^3	1,250
Steel		
Mild steel reinforcement	tonne	11,500
High tensile steel reinforcement	tonne	11,500
Structural steel sections	tonne	15,000
Bricks and blocks		
Common bricks (160 x 35 x 70mm)	1,000	450
Good quality facing bricks (220 x 65 x 105mm)	1,000	4,000
Hollow concrete blocks (390 x 105 x 65mm)	1,000	1,100
Precast concrete cladding units with exposed aggregate finish	m^2	1,400
Timber and insulation		
Softwood for carpentry	m^3	7,000

	Units	Cost Bt
Softwood for joinery	m³	10,000
Hardwood for joinery	m³	12,000
Exterior quality plywood (20mm)	m²	500
Plywood for interior joinery (4mm)	m²	50
Plywood for interior joinery (20mm)	m²	400
Softwood strip flooring (19mm)	m²	700
Chipboard sheet flooring (25mm)	m²	210
100mm thick quilt insulation	m²	150
100mm thick rigid slab insulation	m²	1,250
Softwood internal door complete with frames and ironmongery	each	1,500

Glass and ceramics

Float glass (6mm)	m²	450

Plaster and paint

Good quality ceramic wall tiles (200 x 200mm)	m²	600
Plaster in 50kg bags	tonne	1,500
Plasterboard (12mm thick)	m²	80
Emulsion paint in tins	gallon	250
Gloss oil paint in tins	gallon	500

Tiles and paviors

Clay floor tiles (100 x 100mm)	m²	250
Vinyl floor tiles (230 x 230 x 2.0mm)	m²	160
Precast concrete paving slabs (500 x 500 x 25mm)	m²	50
Clay roof tiles (255 x 140mm)	1,000	6,000
Precast concrete roof tiles (420 x 330mm)	1,000	10,000

Drainage

WC suite complete (medium quality)	each	3,000
Lavatory basin complete (medium quality)	each	1,500
100mm diameter clay drain pipes	m	600
150mm diameter cast iron drain pipes	m	1,200

Unit rates

The descriptions below are generally shortened versions of standard descriptions listed in full in section 4. Where an item has a two digit reference number (e.g. 05 or 33), this relates to the full description against that number in section 4. Where an item has an alphabetic suffix (e.g. 12A or 34B) this indicates that the standard description has been modified. Where a modification is major the complete modified description is included here and the standard description should be ignored; where a modification is minor (e.g. the insertion of a named hardwood) the shortened description has been modified here but, in general, the full description in section 4 prevails.

The unit rates below are for main work items on a typical construction project in the Bangkok area in the first quarter 1993. The rates include all necessary labour, materials and equipment. An allowance of 8% has been included in the rates to cover preliminary and general items, a further 15% should be added to cover contractors' overheads and profit. All the rates in this section exclude value added tax (VAT - see below).

	Unit	Rate Bt
Excavation		
01A Mechanical excavation of foundation trenches including earthwork support	m^3	120
02A Hardcore filling making up levels	m^3	400
Concrete work		
04　Plain insitu concrete in strip foundations in trenches	m^3	1,820
05　Reinforced insitu concrete in beds	m^3	1,820
06　Reinforced insitu concrete in walls	m^3	1,820
07　Reinforced insitu concrete in suspended floor or roof slabs	m^3	1,820
08　Reinforced insitu concrete in columns	m^3	1,820
09　Reinforced insitu concrete in isolated beams	m^3	1,820
10　Precast concrete slab	m^2	425
Formwork		
11　Softwood formwork to concrete walls	m^2	300
12　Softwood formwork to concrete columns	m^2	300
13　Softwood formwork to horizontal soffits of slabs	m^2	300
Reinforcement		
14　Reinforcement in concrete walls	tonne	15,000
15　Reinforcement in suspended concrete slabs	tonne	15,000
16　Fabric reinforcement in concrete beds	m^2	73
Steelwork		
17　Fabricate, supply and erect steel framed structure	tonne	28,000
Brickwork and blockwork		
19　Solid (perforated) concrete blocks	m^2	240
21　Facing bricks	m^2	545
Roofing		
22A Concrete interlocking roof tiles 400 x 330mm	m^2	485
23A Plain clay roof tiles 255 x 140mm	m^2	1,090
25　Sawn softwood roof boarding	m^2	665
30A Glass-fibre mat roof insulation 160mm thick	m^2	120
31A Troughed galvanized steel roof cladding	m^2	605

	Unit	Rate Bt

Woodwork and metalwork

		Unit	Rate Bt
32	Preservative treated sawn softwood 50 x 100mm	m	120
33	Preservative treated sawn softwood 50 x 150mm	m	182
34A	Single glazed casement window in hardwood, size 650 x 900mm	each	1,820
35A	Two panel glazed door in hardwood, size 850 x 2,000mm	each	6,050
36	Solid core half hour fire resisting hardwood internal flush doors, size 800 x 2,000mm	each	18,200
39	Hardwood skirtings	m	60
40	Framed structural steelwork in universal joist sections	tonne	28,000
41	Structural steelwork lattice roof trusses	tonne	30,300

Plumbing

		Unit	Rate Bt
42A	Light gauge galvanized sheet box gutter 150 x 100mm	m	242
43A	PVC rainwater pipes	m	545
44	Light gauge copper cold water tubing	m	218
45A	High pressure polybutylene pipes for cold water supply	m	109
46A	Low pressure polybutylene pipes for cold water distribution	m	182
47	UPVC soil and vent pipes	m	725
48	White vitreous china WC suite	each	4,240
49	White vitreous china lavatory basin	each	2,420
50	Glazed fireclay shower tray	each	5,450
51	Stainless steel single bowl sink and double drainer	each	3,030

Electrical work

		Unit	Rate Bt
52	PVC insulated and copper sheathed cable	m	48
53A	10 amp unswitched socket outlet	each	725
54	Flush mounted 20 amp, 1 way light switch	each	605

Finishings

		Unit	Rate Bt
55	2 coats gypsum based plaster on brick walls	m^2	120
56	White glazed tiles on plaster walls	m^2	545
58	Cement and sand screed to concrete floors	m^2	150
60	Mineral fibre tiles on concealed suspension system	m^2	665

Glazing

		Unit	Rate Bt
61	Glazing to wood	m^2	484

Painting

		Unit	Rate Bt
62	Emulsion on plaster walls	m^2	55
63	Oil paint on timber	m^2	65

Approximate estimating

The building costs per unit area given below are averages incurred by building clients for typical buildings in the Bangkok area as at the first quarter 1993. They are based upon the total floor area of all storeys, measured between external walls and without deduction for internal walls.

Approximate estimating costs generally include mechanical and electrical installations but exclude furniture, loose or special equipment, and external works; they also exclude fees for professional services. The costs shown are for specifications and standards appropriate to Thailand and this should be borne in mind when attempting comparisons with similarly described building types in other countries. A discussion of this issue is included in section 2. Comparative data for countries covered in this publication, including construction cost data, is presented in Part Three.

Approximate estimating costs must be treated with caution; they cannot provide more than a rough guide to the probable cost of building. All the rates in this section exclude value added tax (VAT - see below).

	Cost m² Bt	Cost ft² Bt
Industrial		
Light duty flatted factories, 150 lb loading	7,500	695
Single storey conventional factory of structural		
steelwork	7,000	650
Office/commercial		
Average standard offices, high rise	13,500	1,250
Prestige offices, high rise	19,500	1,810
Domestic		
Detached houses and bungalows	12,500	1,160
Average standard apartments, high rise	12,500	1,160
Luxury apartments, high rise	15,000	1,390
Hotels		
3 star budget hotel inclusive of fixtures and fittings	22,000	2,040
5 star luxury hotels inclusive of fixtures and fittings	30,000	2,790
Others		
Car parks, above ground	6,500	605
Retail/department stores (without finishes)	12,500	1,160

Value added tax (VAT)

The standard rate of value added tax (VAT) is currently 7%.

Regional variations

The approximate estimating costs are based on projects in the Bangkok area. For other parts of Thailand, adjust these costs by the following factors:

North	Chiangmai	+10%
South	Phuket/Samui	+12%
South Coast	Pattaya/Cha-Am	+5%

EXCHANGE RATES

The graph below plots the movement of the Thai baht against sterling, the US dollar and the Japanese yen since 1980. The figures used for the graph are quarterly and the method of calculating these and other related issues are discussed in section 2. The exchange rate at the first quarter 1993 was Bt37.8 to the pound sterling, Bt25.5 to the US dollar and Bt20.7 to 100 Japanese yen.

THE THAI BAHT AGAINST STERLING, THE US DOLLAR
AND THE JAPANESE YEN

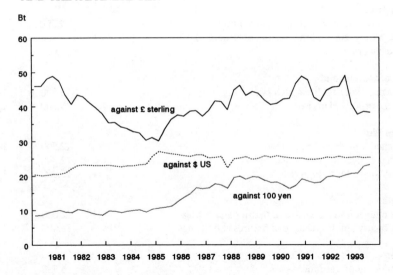

USEFUL ADDRESSES

Public Organizations

Public Works Department
   Ministry of Interior
   218/1 Rama 6 Road
   Bangkok 10400
   Tel: 272 0061, 273 0878, 273 0860
   Fax: 273 0878 Ext 115

Department of Town and Country Planning
  Ministry of Interior
  224 Rama 9 Road, Huay Kwang
  Bangkok 10310
  Tel: 245 1420
  Fax: 246 0180

Office of Board for the Control of the
Engineering and Architectural Profession
  Visuthkasart Road
  Bangkok 10200
  Tel: 281 1421, 282 2861

Thai Industrial Standard Institution
  Ministry of Industry, Rama 6 Road, Rajthavi
  Bangkok 10400
  Tel: 246 1170
  Fax: 246 4085

The Engineering Institute of Thailand
  Faculty of Engineering
  Chulalongkorn University, Anglee Dunan Road
  Bangkok 10330
  Tel: 252 6051

The National Statistical Office
  Larn Luang Road, Pomp Prarp
  Bangkok 10100
  Tel: 282 1535

Department of Commercial Registration
  Ministry of Commerce
  Maharaj Road, Pra Rajawang
  Pra Nakorn
  Bangkok 10200
  Tel: 222 6918, 222 9851, 222 2870

Thailand Institute of Scientific and Technological Research
  196 Paholyothin Road, Jat Tu Jak
  Bangkok 10900
  Tel: 579 1121/30 Ext. 2112
  Fax: 561 4771, 579 4940

Trade and Professional Associations

Thai Contractor Association
    110 Wireless Road, Pathumwan
    Bangkok 10330
    Tel: 251 0697, 252 2953
    Fax: 255 3990

The Association of Siamese Architects
    under Royal Patronage
    248/1 Soi Japanese School
    Rama 9 Road, Huay Kwang
    Bangkok 10310
    Tel: 319 4124, 319 6555
    Fax: 319 6419

The Consulting Engineer Association of Thailand
    37/1 Soi Petchburi 15, Petchburi Road
    Bangkok 10400
    Tel: 251 0092
    Fax: 253 4283

Journal of
Property
Research

VOLUME NINE
NUMBER TWO
SUMMER 1992

formerly
Land Development
Studies

Journal of Property Research

Formerly Land Development Studies.

Editors: **Bryan D MacGregor,** University of Aberdeen, UK, **David Hartzell** and **Mike Miles,** University of North Carolina, USA

The Journal of Property Research is the only international journal covering all aspects of real estate investment and development. Formerly Land Development Studies, the Journal's title has been changed to reflect the enormous expansion of research, particularly applied research, into property investment and development.

The Journal of Property Research publishes theoretical and empirical papers, case studies and critical literature surveys, concentrating on two main areas: Property Investment Portfolios - including such areas as the role of property as an investment class, forecasting of markets and property portfolio construction. Much of this research will be an application to property of techniques developed in other investment markets. Land Development - covering a wide range of issues surrounding the development and redevelopment of property. The focus may be financial, economic, environmental, urban, rural, public or private sector. In addition to research and review papers, the Journal publishes regular editorials, book reviews and market briefings.

A Selection of Papers

Development constraints, market processes and the supply of industrial land. **C D Adams, L Russell and C S Taylor (UK).** An analysis of the relative importance of security of income as a determinant of the capitalization rate for CBD office investment property in Sydney. **D R R Parker (Australia).** Economic diversification in European real estate portfolios. **D Hartzell, P Eichholtz and A Slender (USA and The Netherlands).** Valuation accuracy: developing the economic issues. **G R Brown (New Zealand).** Marxian concepts, capital accumulation and offices. **L Luithlen (UK).** Singapore high technology cluster: origin and present situation. **B Yuen (Australia).**

Subscription Information

ISSN: 0959-9916
Published three times per year
Volume 10 will be published in 1993
European Community: £105
USA/Canada: $194
Rest of World: £115

Individual rates
European Community: £45
USA/Canada: $83
Rest of World: £45

For a free sample copy, or to subscribe, please contact:
Journals Promotion Dept., Chapman & Hall,
2-6 Boundary Row, London SE1 8HN, UK
Tel: +44 (71) 865 0066 Fax: +44 (71) 522 9623 email: journal@chall.mhs.compuserve.com
or
Journals Promotion Dept., Chapman & Hall,
29 West 35th Street, New York, NY 10001-2299, USA
Tel: +1 (212) 244 3336 Fax: +1 (212) 563 2269 email: 71201.1651.@compuserve.com

In the United Kingdom:

DAVIS LANGDON & EVEREST
DAVIS LANGDON CONSULTANCY
DAVIS LANGDON MANAGEMENT

The strategic and integrated management of cost, time and quality - the client "risk" areas of a contract - are essential functions, which are necessary to ensure the satisfactory planning, procurement, execution and operation of construction projects.

We specialise in the financial management of construction projects and their risk areas, from project inception to completion and we concentrate on:

*   being positive and creative in our advice, rather than simply reactive;

*   providing value for money via efficient management, rather than on superficial cost monitoring;

*   giving advice that is matched to the Client's requirements, rather than imposing standard or traditional solutions;

*   paying attention to the life-cycle costs of constructing and occupying a building, rather than to the initial capital cost only.

Our aim is to provide our clients with risk assurance, cost control and value for money, via effective advice, cost planning and management.

London, Bristol, Cambridge, Cardiff, Chester, Edinburgh, Gateshead, Glasgow, Ipswich, Leeds, Liverpool, Manchester, Milton Keynes, Newport, Norwich, Oxford, Plymouth, Portsmouth, Southampton

DAVIS LANGDON & SEAH INTERNATIONAL

MANAGE AND LIMIT CLIENT RISK - ADDING VALUE

United Kingdom

KEY DATA

Population

Population	57.4m
Urban population	89%
Population under 15	19%
Population over 65	16%
Average annual growth rate (1980 to 1990)	0.2%

Geography

Land area	244,000 km²
Agricultural area	77%
Capital city	London (population 6.7m)

Economy

Monetary unit	Pound sterling (£)
Exchange rate (average first quarter 1993) to:	
the US dollar	£0.67
the yen x 100	£0.55
Average annual inflation (1980 to 1990)	5.8%
Inflation rate (1991)	4.1%
Gross Domestic Product (GDP)	£497.0bn
GDP per capita	£8,659
Real GDP growth (1980 to 1990)	3.1%
Private consumption as a proportion of GDP	63%
Public consumption as a proportion of GDP	20%
Investment as a proportion of GDP	19%
Central government expenditure as a proportion of Gross National Product	34.8%

Construction

Gross value of construction output (1991)	£43.7bn
Net value of construction output (1991)	£33.7bn
Net value of construction output per capita (1991)	£587
Net value of construction output as a proportion of GDP (1991)	6.8%

Note: All data relate to 1990 unless otherwise indicated.

THE CONSTRUCTION INDUSTRY

Construction output

In 1991 the value of the gross output of the UK construction industry was
£43.7 billion, equivalent to US$77.3 billion. This represents under 9% of
GDP - low by comparison with other European countries. Output has
decreased substantially from 1990 and 1989 levels.

The breakdown of output by type of work is shown below.

OUTPUT BY TYPE OF WORK IN GREAT BRITAIN, 1991

Type of work	£bn	% of total
New housing		
Public	0.8	1.8
Private	4.8	11.0
Other new work		
Public	5.8	13.3
Private industrial	5.3	12.1
Private commercial	8.2	18.8
All new work	25.0	57.2
Repair and maintenance	18.7	42.8
Total work	43.7	100.0

Source: DoE Housing and Construction Statistics.

Commercial buildings and particularly offices have accounted for a
very high percentage of UK output; even in 1991, 33% of new construction
output was for the building of offices, shops and other commercial
buildings. In 1990 the percentage was 37%. The commercial boom ended in
1989 and construction output is expected to fall in 1992 and decline
further in 1993.

It is noteworthy that residential repair and maintenance is greater
than new residential construction. In part this is because new house
construction is low compared to previous years. However, total
maintenance expenditure is much higher than is indicated by the table
above. Expenditure on DIY (do-it-yourself) materials (£4.7 billion in
1989) by the residential sector and substantial expenditure on maintenance
(undertaken by private direct labour organizations and therefore
unrecorded) by the non-residential sector may increase actual maintenance
expenditure by as much as 40%. In addition there is thought to be
uncounted expenditure for work done by those avoiding tax and insurance
obligations.

One of the most marked features of construction activity over recent years has been the shift in activity by region. Historically, construction work throughout the country has been closely related to population. The table below lists percentages showing the 1985 population for the standard economic regions plus construction new orders for 1979, 1986 and 1991.

REGIONAL POPULATION AND NEW ORDERS 1979 to 1991

Region	Population 1985 (%)	New Orders 1979 (%)	1986 (%)	1991 (%)
North	5.6	5.5	3.8	4.8
Yorks and Humberside	8.9	9.2	7.2	7.9
East Midlands	7.1	5.8	6.3	7.0
East Anglia	3.6	4.6	4.8	4.1
South East	31.2	32.3	42.5	33.3
South West	8.2	7.7	8.5	9.0
West Midlands	9.4	8.1	6.8	8.8
North West	11.6	10.9	8.4	9.4
Wales	5.1	4.7	4.3	5.8
Scotland	9.3	11.2	7.5	10.0
Total	100.0	100.0	100.0	100.0

Sources: DoE Housing and Construction Statistics and CSO Regional Trends

In 1979 four regions had construction new orders 10% above or below their share of population. The East and West Midlands each had less than their shares; Scotland and East Anglia had substantially more than their shares. In 1986 only East Anglia, the South East, and the South West had more than their share. All other regions had significantly less than their share by population. However, by 1991 there was a distinct movement back to the 1979 relationships. The three regions in the South still have a higher share than their 1985 population but only marginally so. Scotland and Wales are also doing better than their population share but other regions are doing less well.

In 1991 British contractors obtained orders abroad totalling £2,205 million as shown in the table overleaf, a slight fall on 1990 levels at current prices. Hong Kong accounted for 24% of the Far East contracts compared with 30% in 1986 but was nevertheless a very significant market. The Far East and North America between them account for over 60% of the total markets. In 1981/82 by comparison, the Middle East alone accounted for 37% of the total market.

UK CONSTRUCTION WORK OVERSEAS
(£ million - current prices)

Areas of world	1986	%	1991	%
EC	79	4.6	83	3.8
Rest of Europe	21	1.2	22	1.0
Middle East	261	15.3	245	11.1
Far East	172	10.1	575	26.1
Africa	174	10.2	234	10.6
North America	789	46.3	781	35.4
Rest of America	55	3.2	65	2.9
Oceania	153	9.0	200	9.1
Total	1,704	100.0	2,205	100.0

Source: *DoE Housing and Construction Statistics.*

Characteristics and structure of the industry

The bulk of building work is carried out by general contractors who traditionally employed their own labour force but now increasingly use labour-only subcontractors. Specialist subcontractors may be nominated by the client's consultant team or employed by the general contractor.

Traditionally, building work in the UK has been administered by professional consultants appointed by the building client. The consultants are responsible for the design and specification of the work, the contractual arrangements and the supervision of the contract. However, over the last 20 years, design-and-build contractors offering a single point of responsibility have also established a sizeable share of the market as have other, less traditional, arrangements (see 'Contractual arrangements').

The construction industry in the UK consists of a large number of small firms and several very large firms. In 1991 there were estimated to be 207,000 firms of which 39 employed over 1,200 persons and 234 employed over 300. However, figures do not truly indicate the importance of large firms because of the prevalence of labour-only subcontractors. A better indication is that in *Building* magazine's 'Top 300 European Contractors' there are 79 UK companies and 23 in the top 100 - more than any other country. The *Engineering News Record*'s 'Top International Contractors' lists 6 UK contractors in the top 100 in 1991 (13 in 1988). In both the *Building* and *Engineering News Record* lists, some contractors are very specialized, for example in engineering or housing development, rather than building and civil engineering. However, the comparison between countries is relevant.

The principal UK contractors with some of their characteristics are shown in the table on the next page.

MAJOR UK CONTRACTORS

Major contractors	Place in Building's 'Top 500 European Contractors' 1991	Place in ENR's 'Top 225 International Contractors' 1991	Main work/types
BICC	3	49*	Largest because conglomerate in cables etc. Balfour Beatty is construction arm
Tarmac	6	131	Materials, property, construction
Trafalgar House	7	41	Shipping, other businesses, construction
AMEC	11	-	Nearly all construction but includes development. Construction for offshore.
Kier	15+	101	Mainly construction, property and materials, formerly Beazer
Wimpey	17	-	Property, construction
John Laing	20	144	Mainly construction, property and plant and mechanical and electrical engineering
Bovis	21@	14	Construction subsidiary of P&O
Taylor Woodrow	24	102	Mainly construction, property, offshore and mechanical and electrical engineering
Mowlem	26	94	Mainly construction and scaffolding
Costain	27	72	Property, construction and some mining
Alfred McAlpine	51	-	Mainly construction

Sources: Building; Engineering News Record
* Balfour Beatty
+ Beazer
@ P&0

For consistency, contractors are listed in the order quoted in *Building* magazine's list which is based on total turnover. This does not, however, really represent their construction size nor their contracting size. Other businesses in which they operate are shown on the table.

One feature of British contractors is the extent of diversification beyond general contracting into property development, speculative housebuilding, material production and other businesses such as mining or airports. This was thought to have enabled the larger contractors to weather the fluctuations in construction demand and, in many cases, gives a better return on capital employed. However, in the present recession, some of the non-construction businesses have been the cause of financial failure amongst medium size contractors and the larger firms have found it necessary to divest themselves of such subsidiary businesses.

Construction design work is undertaken mainly by architects and engineers. In April 1992 there were about 29,200 architects in the UK, about 510 per million inhabitants. Of these only 72% are working full time. About 80% of architects are members of the Royal Institute of British Architects (RIBA). In 1989, 61% of architects were working in private practice - two thirds as principals and one third salaried. About 70% of practices have fewer than six architects, but some practices employ over 100. The remaining architects are employed by local authorities or government, in education or in other private employment.

Civil engineers are normally members of the Institution of Civil Engineers with a membership approaching 50,000. Structural engineers are members of the Institution of Structural Engineers, with a membership of about 11,000. Building services engineers are members of the Chartered Institution of Building Service Engineers having a membership of over 7,000. The title of Chartered Engineer is registered and protected, either by the professional institution or by the Engineering Council. Most construction design work in the UK is undertaken by private practices. The amount of in-house work has shrunk considerably in the last ten years and contractors' design departments are relatively small being mostly concerned with building rather than civil engineering work. Civil and structural engineers are most important numerically in private practice. In 1989, nine engineering consultancy firms had over 1,000 staff and of these, seven had more than 1,000 civil and structural staff. There is a long tradition of British consulting engineers working abroad.

The surveying profession is very important in the UK. The Royal Institution of Chartered Surveyors is an umbrella organization for quantity surveyors and building surveyors as well as a number of other surveyor disciplines more concerned with property than the construction industry. In 1991 there were about 24,000 quantity surveyors and about 6,000 building surveyors. The quantity surveyor plays a key role in the UK construction industry and countries influenced by UK practices. Originally his role was to prepare a bill of quantities and measure work on site. The profession has, however, developed consultancy services for clients and has a full professional status equivalent to that of designers. In 1990 over 54% of quantity surveyors worked in private practice, 19% with contractors, 16% in public service, 9% in commercial organizations and 2% in education. Most quantity surveying practices are small but there are a number of very large firms employing several hundred staff. The top 10 firms account for about 10% of QS division membership.

Clients and finance

Historically, the UK construction industry maintained a fairly even split between orders in the public and private sectors. However, since 1979 there has been a marked decline in public sector investment. In 1979, 41% of new construction output was for public sector clients; by 1985 this had reduced to 32%; and by 1991 to 26%. Although this decline has been for all types of public construction it has been most dramatic in the public housing sector. In 1991 public sector housing starts were only 13.5% of their 1981 levels, whereas private sector housing starts in 1991 were 110% of their 1981 level. However, housing associations are increasing in importance and their 1991 starts were 156% of 1981 levels. They are to some extent replacing local authorities in housing and now account for 12% of all starts. A large part of the purchase of housing, both existing and new, is financed by mortgages. In 1991 mortgage finance was provided as follows:

SOURCES OF MORTGAGE FINANCE

Source	%
Building societies	70
Banks	29
Insurance companies	1
Local authorities	negligible
Total	100

Other buildings in the private sector may be financed in a number of ways:

- they may be built and owned by owner occupiers
- they may be built by developers/investors and let.

It is estimated, for example, that owner occupiers account for up to 80% of new construction of industrial buildings. However, the amount of other private buildings built and owned by the occupiers is much less. Such statistics as are available suggest that the majority of non-industrial building and non-housing building is financed by the banking, pension and insurance sectors or by property developers' own funds.

Selection of design consultants

The selection of design consultants is not regulated by law in the UK, even in the public sector. The public sector client, where there is no in-house department, selects the designer - normally an architect for building work and civil engineering consultant for civil work - from a list of designers considered capable of undertaking the work. Interviews may be conducted with a short-list of designers who will present their credentials, including relevant experience, and may discuss their ideas for the design. Fees are negotiable and have, in recent years, become an element in the selection process. Indeed some form of competition is becoming increasingly common especially for public contracts. The general move towards privatization in the UK means that many in-house teams are

being disbanded. The Property Services Agency (PSA), which was in charge
of government buildings, has been split and privatized.

In the private sector, the procedures are similar to the public
sector, but with more variability; for example, the private client may
appoint a quantity surveyor, even before an architect, if the project is
one where cost is critical.

Contractual arrangements

Probably about two-thirds of contracts are awarded on a lump sum basis as
a result of competitive tenders received from a short list of firms that
have been selected by client's consultants. The National Joint
Consultative Committee, which comprises a group of client and consultant
bodies, publishes codes for selective tendering. Generally, prices are
based on firm bills of quantities though sometimes approximate bills of
quantities or specifications and drawings are used.

The predominant form of contract used in the UK is the Joint Contracts
Tribunal (JCT) 1980 Standard Form of Contract with quantities. This
contract assumes the use of measured bills of quantities that are normally
prepared by the quantity surveyor. The JCT also produce the 1984
Intermediate Form of Building Contract for works of simpler content. The
tender documentation under both these forms of contract might comprise:

- drawings
- specification
- bills of quantities, schedules of works or schedules of rates.

The JCT building contracts are produced in private and local authority
editions. Government buildings and civil engineering contracts are placed
using the General Conditions of Government Contracts for Building and
Civil Engineering Works, otherwise known as Form GC/Works/1.

For civil engineering, local authority and private clients generally
use the Institution of Civil Engineers Conditions of Contract, fifth
edition, but an amended version of GC/Works/1 is also sometimes used.

Contracts of up to 18 months duration or less are generally let on a
fixed price basis. Fluctuations in labour, materials and plant costs on
longer term contracts can be adjusted, where the contract permits. Such
increased costs on private contracts may be paid on the basis of invoices
for materials and plant, and time sheets for labour. Local authority
government contracts and some private contracts generally involve the use
of an adjustment formula based on monthly published indices.

A number of alternative contractual arrangements are available, most
notably management contracting, design-and-build and construction
management. Under management contracting, the client enters into separate
contracts with a designer and a management contractor and the management
contractor enters into subcontracts with works contractors. However,
construction management, in which the client enters into separate
contracts with a designer, a construction manager and works contractors is
increasingly being used in preference to management contracting.

There are separate contract forms for the other types of construction arrangements.   In addition, there are some contracts, notably the Association of Consulting Architects' (ACA) British Property Federation Contract, which has been developed as an alternative to the JCT form, but their use is not significant.

Liability and insurance

Since the mid 1970s there has been a marked increase in litigation on professional liability.   Liability may arise in contract or in tort.   In contract, proof is required of a breach of contract.   However, contracts do not normally define clearly the limits of work or duties of the professional and are in any case often informal, thus giving plenty of opportunity for litigation.   The claims under tort, though increasing in the 1970s, have more recently declined as a result of various legal judgements.

Largely because of the reliance on case law made by the courts, the great problem of the English system is its uncertainty and complexity. There is no certainty on whether liability exists, on the amount involved, the period of liability or the time lag before any liability is determined.

Not all professional practices carry professional indemnity insurance.   However, most larger ones are insured.   The cost of premiums is now very high.

The proposals of the European Commission for a standard liability throughout the Community may substantially alter the UK position and create greater certainty.

Development control and standards

The system for planning and control of development was introduced by the Town and Country Planning Act 1947. Although this has been amended, notably by the Town and Country Planning Act 1971, the principles remain the same.   The main responsibility for planning lies with local authorities: the county councils and metropolitan areas and large towns as well as the district councils.   A development plan for each area must be produced and every development (which is very widely defined) must receive permission from the relevant authority.

In general, applications for development must be made to the relevant district council.   The total volume of applications is about 400,000 a year, of which about 44% are householder applications for very small alterations to dwellings; 12% are for changes of use not involving building works; 40% are minor developments and only 4% are major developments of more than 10 dwellings or 1,000 square metres of floor space.   Most planning applications are therefore simple and go through a process which varies from district to district but is straightforward. Judgement of the local planning officer and ultimately of the elected council members has an important role and therefore there is no certainty that an application will be granted.   Negotiation on changes to the original application which could be acceptable is often possible. About 6% of applications by householders and nearly 20% of those for change of use are refused. On average 10% of all applications are refused.

Decisions on planning applications have to be given within 8 weeks unless extension of the period is arranged. About 60% to 70% of planning applications are dealt with within this period.

All new construction in the UK has to comply with Building Regulations, which are couched in terms of a series of technical requirements. These requirements are backed up by Approved Documents which set out ways in which the requirements can be met. These documents give guidance but are not mandatory. In many areas the Approved Document will refer a designer to an appropriate British Standard on complex issues. At present, approval for construction work is given by local authorities. In the case of private sector housing the National House Builders Council (NHBC) can act as an alternative Approved Inspector. The 1985 Building Act has provision for other persons or bodies to act as Approved Inspectors, but to date this has not happened, primarily because of the problem of liability insurance.

CONSTRUCTION COST DATA

Cost of labour

The figures below are typical of labour costs in the London area as at the first quarter 1993. The wage rate is the basis of an employee's income, while the cost of labour indicates the cost to a contractor of employing that employee. The difference between the two covers a variety of mandatory and voluntary contributions - a list of items which could be included is given in section 2.

	Wage rate (per hour) £	Cost of labour (per hour) £	Number of hours worked per year
Site operatives			
Mason/bricklayer	4.12	5.44	1,802
Carpenter	4.14	5.46	1,802
Plumber	4.83	6.37	1,733
Electrician	7.12	8.93	1,733
Structural steel erector	5.56	6.41	1,771
HVAC installer	6.62	8.57	1,756
Semi-skilled worker	3.69	4.93	1,802
Unskilled labourer	3.51	4.71	1,802
Equipment operator	3.84	5.04	1,802
Watchman/security	3.69	4.93	1,802
Site supervision			
General foreman	4.61	5.76	1,802
Trades foreman	4.40	5.50	1,802

	Wage rate (per year) £	Cost of labour (per year) £
Clerk of works	19,250	-
Contractors' personnel		
Site manager	26,100	33,160
Resident engineer	17,700	22,950
Resident surveyor	21,400	27,480
Junior engineer	15,200	17,690
Junior surveyor	15,500	18,030
Planner	20,000	25,880
Consultants' personnel		
Senior architect	21,500	27,590
Senior engineer	25,650	32,640
Senior surveyor	22,460	28,690
Qualified architect	20,140	26,040
Qualified engineer	21,770	27,900
Qualified surveyor	20,850	26,850

Cost of materials

The figures that follow are the costs of main construction materials, delivered to site in the London area, as incurred by contractors in the first quarter 1993.   These assume that the materials would be in quantities as required for a medium sized construction project and that the location of the works would be neither constrained nor remote.

All the costs in this section exclude value added tax (VAT - see below).

	Unit	Cost £
Cement and aggregate		
Ordinary portland cement in 50kg bags	tonne	63.02
Coarse aggregates for concrete	m^3	6.84
Fine aggregates for concrete	m^3	7.04
Ready mixed concrete (11.50N/mm^2)	m^3	35.15
Ready mixed concrete (26.00N/mm^2)	m^3	40.30
Steel		
Mild steel reinforcement (12mm)	tonne	239.25
High tensile steel reinforcement (12mm)	tonne	260.95
Structural steel sections	tonne	400.00
Bricks and blocks		
Common bricks (215 x 102.5 x 65mm)	1,000	100.00
Good quality facing bricks (215 x 102.5 x 65mm)	1,000	300.00
Hollow concrete blocks (450 x 225 x 140mm)	1,000	500.00

	Unit	Cost £
Solid concrete blocks (450 x 225 x 140mm)	1,000	510.00
Precast concrete cladding units with exposed aggregate finish	m^2	325.00

Timber and insulation

Softwood sections for carpentry	m^3	120.00
Softwood for joinery	m^3	290.00
Hardwood for joinery	m^3	600.00
Exterior quality plywood (18mm)	m^2	10.51
Plywood for interior joinery (6mm)	m^2	2.84
Softwood strip flooring (22mm)	m^2	4.23
Chipboard sheet flooring (18mm)	m^2	2.34
100mm thick quilt insulation	m^2	2.15
100mm thick rigid slab insulation	m^2	4.10
Softwood internal door complete with frames and ironmongery (826 x 2040 x 40mm)	each	37.30

Glass and ceramics

Float glass (6mm)	m^2	29.31
Sealed double glazing units	m^2	40.00
Good quality ceramic wall tiles (198 x 64.5mm)	m^2	18.58

Plaster and paint

Plaster in 50kg bags	tonne	85.86
Plasterboard (6mm thick)	m^2	1.45
Emulsion paint in 5 litre tins	litre	1.82
Gloss oil paint in 5 litre tins	litre	2.20

Tiles and paviors

Clay floor tiles (150 x 150 x 12.5mm)	m^2	8.74
Vinyl floor tiles (250 x 250 x 2.5mm)	m^2	4.62
Precast concrete paving slabs (200 x 100 x 65mm)	m^2	5.00
Clay roof tiles (plain 265 x 165mm)	1,000	248.40
Precast concrete roof tiles (419 x 330mm)	1,000	607.75

Drainage

WC suite complete	each	124.34
Lavatory basin complete	each	72.44
100mm diameter clay drain pipes	m	2.85
150mm diameter cast iron drain pipes	m	32.68

Unit rates

The descriptions below are generally shortened versions of standard descriptions listed in section 4. Where an item has a two digit reference number (e.g. 05 or 33), this relates to the full description against that number in section 4. Where an item has an alphabetic suffix (e.g. 12A or 34B) this indicates that the standard description has been modified.

Where a modification is major the complete modified description is included here and the standard description should be ignored; where a modification is minor (e.g. the insertion of a named hardwood) the shortened description has been modified here but, in general, the full description in section 4 prevails.

The unit rates below are for main work items on a typical construction project in the London area in the first quarter 1993. The rates include all necessary labour, materials and equipment. No allowance to cover preliminary and general items is provided but an allowance of 6.5% to cover contractors' overheads and profit has been included in the rates. All the rates in this section exclude value added tax (VAT - see below).

	Unit	*Rate £*
Excavation		
01 Mechanical excavation of foundation trenches	m³	3.09
02A Hardcore filling making up levels (250mm)	m²	4.54
03 Earthwork support	m²	0.93
Concrete work		
04A Plain insitu concrete in strip foundations in trenches 15N/m²	m³	40.34
05A Reinforced insitu concrete in beds 21N/m²	m³	43.11
06 Reinforced insitu concrete in walls	m³	50.15
07A Reinforced insitu concrete in suspended floor or roof slabs 26N/m²	m³	53.80
08A Reinforced insitu concrete in columns 3N/m²	m³	61.34
09A Reinforced insitu concrete in isolated beams 3N/m²	m³	57.18
10 Precast concrete slab	m²	23.13
Formwork		
11 Softwood formwork to concrete walls	m²	15.46
12 Softwood or metal formwork to concrete columns	m²	18.48
13 Softwood or metal formwork to horizontal soffits of slabs	m²	15.64
Reinforcement		
14A Reinforcement in concrete walls (10mm)	tonne	453.80
15A Reinforcement in suspended concrete slabs (10mm)	tonne	453.80
16 Fabric reinforcement in concrete beds	m²	1.67
Steelwork		
17 Fabricate, supply and erect steel framed structure	tonne	761.77
Brickwork and blockwork		
18A Precast lightweight aggregate hollow concrete block walls (100m thick)	m²	10.09
19 Solid (perforated) concrete blocks (100m thick)	m²	10.58
20A Solid (perforated) sand lime bricks (half brick thick)	m²	18.06
21 Facing bricks	m²	28.95

		Unit	*Rate £*
Roofing			
22	Concrete interlocking roof tiles 430 x 380mm	m²	13.71
23A	Plain clay roof tiles 265 x 165mm	m²	28.27
24	Fibre cement roof slates 600 x 300mm	m²	12.98
25	Sawn softwood roof boarding	m²	14.28
27A	3 layers glass-fibre based bitumen felt roof covering incl. chippings	m²	13.08
28	Bitumen based mastic asphalt roof covering	m²	9.63
29A	Glass-fibre mat roof insulation 60mm thick	m²	4.48
30	Rigid sheet loadbearing roof insulation 75mm thick	m²	13.83
31	Troughed galvanized steel roof cladding	m²	13.02
Woodwork and metalwork			
32	Preservative treated sawn softwood 50 x 100mm	m	2.32
33	Preservative treated sawn softwood 50 x 150mm	m	3.07
34A	Single glazed casement window in Meranti hardwood, size 630 x 900mm	each	66.51
35A	Two panel glazed door in W African Mahogany hardwood, size 838 x 1981mm	each	241.79
36A	Solid core half hour fire resisting hardwood internal flush doors, size 838 x 1981mm	each	90.99
37A	Aluminium double glazed window, size 1200 x 1200mm	each	194.79
38A	Aluminium double glazed door, size 850 x 2100mm	each	735.00
39A	Hardwood skirtings (W African Mahogany) 25 x 100mm	m	6.02
40	Framed structural steelwork in universal joist sections	tonne	760.00
41	Structural steelwork lattice roof trusses	tonne	1,035.00
Plumbing			
42A	UPVC half round eaves gutter (112mm)	m	4.24
43A	UPVC rainwater pipes (110mm)	m	6.08
44A	Light gauge copper cold water tubing (15mm)	m	2.97
45A	High pressure plastic pipes for cold water supply (20mm)	m	1.31
46	Low pressure plastic pipes for cold water distribution	m	2.96
47	UPVC soil and vent pipes	m	7.92
48	White vitreous china WC suite	each	141.93
49	White vitreous china lavatory basin	each	55.69
50A	White glazed fireclay shower tray	each	114.05
51	Stainless steel single bowl sink and double drainer	each	126.78
Electrical work			
52A	PVC insulated and PVC sheathed copper cable core and earth	m	1.41
53	13 amp unswitched socket outlet	each	10.01
54A	Flush mounted 5 amp, 1 way light switch	each	11.43
Finishings			
55	2 coats gypsum based plaster on brick walls	m²	4.09

	Unit	Rate £
56 White glazed tiles on plaster walls	m²	18.40
57 Red clay quarry tiles on concrete floor	m²	21.49
58A Cement and sand screed to concrete floors 25mm thick	m²	4.14
59 Thermoplastic floor tiles on screed	m²	6.13
60 Mineral fibre tiles on concealed suspension system	m²	22.82

Glazing

	Unit	Rate £
61A Glazing to wood 6mm	m²	19.34

Painting

	Unit	Rate £
62A Emulsion on plaster walls (1 mist + 2 emulsion)	m²	1.65
63 Oil paint on timber (knot, 1 primer, 2 undercoat and 1 finish)	m²	3.59

Approximate estimating

The building costs per unit area given below are averages incurred by building clients for typical buildings in the United Kingdom as at the first quarter 1993. They are based upon the total floor area of all storeys, measured between external walls and without deduction for internal walls.

Approximate estimating costs generally include mechanical and electrical installations but exclude furniture, loose or special equipment, and external works; they also exclude fees for professional services. The costs shown are for specifications and standards appropriate to the United Kingdom and this should be borne in mind when attempting comparisons with similarly described building types in other countries. A discussion of this issue is included in section 2. Comparative data for countries covered in this publication, including construction cost data, are presented in Part Three.

Approximate estimating costs must be treated with caution; they cannot provide more than a rough guide to the probable cost of building. All the rates in this section exclude value added tax (VAT - see below).

	Cost m² £	Cost ft² £
Industrial buildings		
Factories for letting (incl. lighting, power and heating)	230	21
Factories for owner occupation (light industrial use)	296	28
Factories for owner occupation (heavy industrial use)	489	45
Factory/office (high-tech) for letting (shell and core only)	308	29
Factory/office (high-tech) for letting (ground floor shell, first floor offices)	490	46
Factory/office (high tech) for owner occupation (controlled environment, fully finished)	640	59
High tech laboratory (air conditioned)	1,318	122
Warehouses, low bay (6 to 8m high) for letting (no heating)	161	15

	Cost m² £	Cost ft² £
Warehouses, low bay for owner occupation (including heating)	234	22
Warehouses, high bay for owner occupation (including heating)	312	29
Cold stores/refrigerated stores	345	32

Administrative and commercial buildings

	Cost m² £	Cost ft² £
Civic offices, non air conditioned	610	57
Civic offices, fully air conditioned	740	69
Offices for letting, 5 to 10 storeys, non air conditioned	528	49
Offices for letting, 5 to 10 storeys, air conditioned	662	62
Offices for letting, high rise, air conditioned	838	78
Offices for owner occupation 5 to 10 storeys, non air conditioned	610	57
Offices for owner occupation 5 to 10 storeys, air conditioned	797	74
Offices for owner occupation high rise, air conditioned	1,018	95
Prestige/headquarters office, 5 to 10 storeys, air conditioned	1,018	95
Prestige/headquarters office, high rise, air conditioned	1,318	122

Health and education buildings

	Cost m² £	Cost ft² £
General hospitals	652	61
Teaching hospitals	552	51
Private hospitals	724	67
Health centres	500	46
Nursery schools	603	56
Primary/junior schools	466	43
Secondary/middle schools	425	39
University (arts) buildings	526	49
University (science) buildings	619	58
Management training centres	635	59

Recreation and arts buildings

	Cost m² £	Cost ft² £
Theatres (over 500 seats) including seating and stage equipment	917	85
Theatres (less than 500 seats) including seating and stage equipment	687	64
Concert halls including seating and stage equipment	1,316	122
Sports halls including changing and social facilities	448	42
Swimming pools (international standard) including changing and social facilities	775	72
Swimming pools (schools standard) including changing facilities	552	51
National museums including full air conditioning and standby generator	1,617	150
Local museums including air conditioning	652	61
City centre/central libraries	666	62
Branch/local libraries	535	50

	Cost m² £	Cost ft² £
Residential buildings		
Social/economic single family housing (multiple units)	307	29
Private/mass market single family housing 2 storey detached/semidetached (multiple units)	307	29
Purpose designed single family housing 2 storey detached (single unit)	339	31
Social/economic apartment housing, low rise (no lifts)	376	35
Social/economic apartment housing, high rise (with lifts)	400	37
Private sector apartment building (standard specification)	368	34
Private sector apartment buildings (luxury)	593	55
Student/nurses halls of residence	433	40
Homes for the elderly (shared accommodation)	474	44
Homes for the elderly (self contained with shared communal facilities)	417	39
Hotel, 5 star, city centre	1,078	100
Hotel, 3 star, city/provincial	821	76
Motel	521	48

Regional variations

The approximate estimating costs are based on average UK rates. Adjust these costs by the following factors for regional variations:

Greater London	:+8%	North West	: -1%
South East	: 0%	North	:+2%
South West	: -6%	Scotland	:+6%
Midlands	: -3%	Wales	: -5%
East Anglia	: -3%	Northern Ireland	:-18%
Yorkshire and Humberside	: -2%		

Value added tax (VAT)

The standard rate of value added tax (VAT) is currently 17.5%, chargeable on general building work.

EXCHANGE RATES AND INFLATION

The combined effect of exchange rates and inflation on prices within a country and price comparisons between countries is discussed in section 2.

Exchange rates

The graph below plots the movement of sterling against the US dollar and the Japanese yen since 1980. The figures used for the graph are quarterly and the method of calculating these and other related issues are discussed in section 2. The exchange rates at the first quarter 1993 were 1.48 US dollars and 182 Japanese yen to the pound sterling.

STERLING AGAINST THE US DOLLAR AND THE JAPANESE YEN

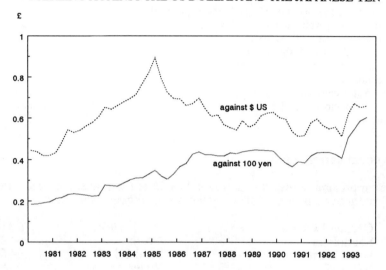

Price inflation

The table on the next page presents retail price, building cost and tender price inflation in the United Kingdom since 1980. The basis of the first column is the official consumer price index. The other two indices have been produced by Davis Langdon & Everest: the building cost index provides an index of price movements in general building costs, and the tender price index indicates movements in general building prices in the Greater London area.

CONSUMER PRICE AND BUILDING COST AND PRICE INDICES

Year	Retail price index average index	average change %	Building cost index average index	average change %	Tender price index average index	average change %
1980	100		100		100	
1981	112	12.0	112	12.0	102	2.0
1982	122	8.9	124	10.7	101	-1.0
1983	127	4.1	131	5.6	105	4.0
1984	133	4.7	139	6.1	111	5.7
1985	142	6.8	146	5.0	115	3.6
1986	146	2.8	154	5.5	121	5.2
1987	152	4.1	162	5.2	136	12.4
1988	160	5.3	172	6.2	163	19.9
1989	172	7.5	185	7.6	179	9.8
1990	189	9.9	198	7.0	163	-8.9
1991	200	5.8	209	5.6	138	-15.3
1992	207	3.5	215	2.9	128	-7.2

USEFUL ADDRESSES

Public Organizations

Department of the Environment
    2 Marsham Street
    London
    SW1P 3EB
    Tel: (071) 212 3000

Building Research Establishment
    Bucknalls Lane, Garston
    Watford
    Herts
    WD2 7JR
    Tel: 0923 674040

Trade and Professional Associations

Construction Industry Research and Information Association
    6 Storeys Gate
    London
    SW1P 3AL

Engineering Council
  Canberra House
  10-16 Maltravers Street
  London
  WC2 3ER

Royal Institute of British Architects (RIBA)
  66 Portland Place
  London
  W1N 4AD
  Tel: (071) 580 5533

Institution of Civil Engineers
  1-7 Great George Street
  London
  SW1P 3AA

The Association of Consulting Engineers (ACE)
  Alliance House
  12 Caxton Street
  London
  SW1H 0QL
  Tel: (071) 222 6557

Royal Institution of Chartered Surveyors (RICS)
  12 Great George Street
  London
  SW1P 3AD
  Tel: (071) 222 7000

British Standards Institution
  2 Park Street
  London
  W1A 2BS
  Tel: (071) 629 9000

Chartered Institute of Building Services (CIBS)
  Delta House
  222 Balham High Road
  London
  SW8 9BS
  Tel: (081) 675 5211

Building Employers Confederation
  82 New Cavendish Street
  London
  W1M 8AD
  Tel: (071) 580 5588

Transport and General Workers Union, Building Crafts Section
    Transport House
    Smith Square
    London
    SW1P 3AJ
    Tel: (071) 828 7788

Union of Construction and Allied Trades and Technicians
    UCATT House
    Abbeville Road
    London
    SW4 9RL
    Tel: (071) 622 2442

Building Advisory Service (BAS)
    18 Mansfield Street
    London
    W1M 9FG
    Tel: (071) 636 2862
    Fax: (071) 631 3872

Building Centre Group (Building Centre)
    26 Store Street
    London
    WC1E 7BT
    Tel: 071 637 1022 (administration)
         (0344) 884999 (information)

Building Cost Information Service (BCIS)
    85/87 Clarence Street
    Kingston-upon-Thames
    Surrey
    KT1 1RB
    Tel: (081) 546 7554
    Fax: (081) 547 1238

British Board of Agrément (BBA)
    PO Box 195
    Bucknalls Lane
    Garston
    Watford
    Herts
    WD2 7NG
    Tel: (0923) 670844
    Fax: (0923) 662133

International Dictionary of Heating, Ventilating and Air Conditioning

2nd Edition

REHVA, Federation of European Heating and Ventilating Associations

The International Dictionary of Heating, Ventilating and Air Conditioning is the result of a collaborative effort by an international panel of professional engineers set up by REHVA. Each member of the panel has considerable experience in this specialist engineering field and is responsible for the terms in his own mother tongue, thus ensuring the accuracy and general acceptability of the terms and translations given.

The dictionary comprises two major divisions. The main sequence of the book consists of some **4,000 terms** (covering heating, ventilation, air conditiong and related mechanical/electrical comonents), given in English, in alphabetical order, with their translations. The remainder of the book consists of alphabetical indexes for the other eleven languages covered:

* Danish, Dutch,
  French, Finnish,
  German,
  Hungarian,
  Italian
  Polish,
  Russian,
  Spanish, and Swedish,

Each alphabetical index is keyed to serial numbers which refer the user to the correct item in the main sequence. The book will be an invaluable reference for all manufacturers, contractors and consulting engineers engaged in heating, ventilating and air conditioning.

September 1993: 234x156: c.792pp
Hardback: 0-419-15390-X

For further information and to order please contact: **The Promotion Dept.**, **E & F N Spon**, 2-6 Boundary Row, London SE1 8HN Tel 071 865 0066 Fax 071 522 9623

United States of America

KEY DATA

Population

Population	248.7m
Urban population	74%
Population under 15	22%
Population over 65	13%
Average annual growth rate (1980 to 1990)	0.9%

Geography

Land area	9,372,614 km²
Agricultural area	47%
Capital city	Washington DC
	(population 3.9m)
Largest city	New York
	(population 18.1m)

Economy

Monetary unit	US dollar ($)
Exchange rate (average first quarter 1993) to:	
the pound sterling	$1.48
the yen x 100	$0.81
Average annual inflation (1980 to 1990)	3.7%
Inflation rate (1991)	3.8%
Gross Domestic Product (GDP) (1991)	$5,677.5bn
GDP per capita (1991)	$22,690
Real GDP growth (1980 to 1990)	3.4%
Private consumption as a proportion of GDP	67%
Public consumption as a proportion of GDP	18%
Investment as a proportion of GDP	16%
Central government expenditure as a proportion of Gross National Product	24%

Construction

Gross value of construction output (1991)	$498bn
Net value of construction output (1991)*	$250bn
Net value of construction output per capita (1991)*	$1,005
Net value of construction output as a proportion of GDP (1991)*	4.4%

Note: All data relate to 1990 unless otherwise indicated.
* estimate

THE CONSTRUCTION INDUSTRY

Construction output

The total value of gross output of the US construction industry in 1991
was at US$498 billion. Of this, the value of new construction in 1991 was
US$401 billion, the remainder being repair and maintenance.   Gross
construction output represents 8.8% of GDP. The table on the next page
shows the detailed breakdown of new work. Construction output in real
terms has fallen every year since 1987 and the fall has affected all
regions of the USA. It can be seen from the table that the public sector
accounts for only 27% of total construction output - though this is a
larger proportion than in the previous few years.

The US residential market is dominated by single family housing and is
drifting more towards this type of development rather than multiple unit
housing. The housing market in 1990 was depressed and is not expected to
recover until about 1994.

With the exception of expenditure on educational facilities, public
highways and sewerage systems, which has increased, the level of
expenditure on public construction has remained fairly static since 1985.

The geographical distribution of work other than housing, compared to
that of population, is fairly even. New York, for example, with 8% of the
population has a 7% share of construction output. The most notable
exception is California, which, with a little over 10% of the population,
has a 14% share of construction output.

Characteristics and structure of the industry

The construction industry has over a million firms employing about 3.5
million persons and has 15 million working partners or self-employed
proprietors. Some states require contractors to be licensed, though this
is rarely strictly administered. It is a way of gaining some revenue from
the licence fee. About 40% of main contractors and trade contractors are
union contractors which use union registered employees and negotiate wages
with the unions. Open-shop contracting has grown significantly over the
last 20 years, especially in housebuilding. This growth has moderated the
behaviour and wage demands of unions. One adverse affect, however, is
that the fall off in union influence has brought about a decline in
training, as the unions traditionally run good education programmes.

There are a large number of specialist trade contractors and they play
an important role. They usually have to provide working drawings, they
are used to organizing and managing the work on site with little direction
from the main contractor, and they often supply major items of plant and
equipment. Labour-only subcontracting is very little used.

BREAKDOWN OF NEW CONSTRUCTION OUTPUT, USA, 1991

Type of construction		Billion US$	%
Residential			
Private	housing and redevelopment	157.8	39.4
Public	housing and redevelopment	3.5	0.9
Total residential building		161.3	40.2
Non-residential building			
Private	Industrial	22.3	5.6
	Commercial	25.5	6.4
	Offices	23.0	5.7
	Hotels	6.3	1.6
	Education	3.9	1.0
	Health	9.2	2.3
	Miscellaneous	10.3	2.6
	Total private	100.5	25.1
Public	Industrial	1.8	0.4
	Education	23.8	5.9
	Hospitals	2.7	0.7
	Miscellaneous	18.7	4.7
	Total public	47.0	11.7
Total non-residential building		147.5	36.8
Civil engineering			
Private	Telecommunications	8.8	2.2
	Railways)		
	Electricity)	20.4	5.1
	Gas)		
	Petroleum pipelines)		
	Other	3.2	0.8
	Total private	32.4	8.1
Public	Highways and streets	29.9	7.5
	Sewerage and water supply	15.0	3.7
	Miscellaneous	14.9	3.7
	Total public	59.8	14.9
Total civil engineering		92.2	23.0
TOTAL ALL WORK		401.0	100
of which			
Private		290.7	72.5
Public		110.2	27.5

Source: US Department of Commerce
Note: items do not always sum exactly due to rounding.

Measured in terms of the value of contracts won, the USA was the base for seven of the world's top ten contractors in 1991. The table overleaf shows the leading US contractors in 1991 from the *Engineering News*

Record's (ENR's) 'Top 225 International Contractors'. The USA accounted for over 45% of the work of these top international contractors in the world.

LEADING US INTERNATIONAL CONTRACTORS 1991
(by contracts won in US$ millions)

Company	Total US$ millions	% of work in USA	Ranking in ENR
Fluor-Daniel	21,376	23.3	8
Bechtel	18,334	63.4	1
M W Kellogg	13,127	74.5	3
Parsons Corporation	13,100	38.2	7
Foster Wheeler	12,459	90.3	2
Brown and Root	12,051	65.6	5
Morrison Knudsen	9,796	8.8	42
CRSS Inc.	7,860	42.1	12
Jacobs Engineering Group	7,521	9.0	51
ABB Lummus Crest	6,840	75.1	6

Source: McGraw-Hill Inc.; Engineering News Record

The title of architect is protected in the USA and the regulations for registration vary from state to state. However, the National Council of Architectural Registration Boards grants a certificate to a qualified architect which is usually recognized in all states. There are about 60,000 architects (1987 data, 250 per million inhabitants), mostly in very small practices. The architect in the USA tends not to get involved in site operations and much detailed design is done by contractors. There are very few quantity surveyors in the USA as the architect is more concerned with cost than in the UK. However, there are construction cost consultants who may originally have been architects or engineers but are increasingly being augmented by quantity surveyors. The contractors are often prepared to give cost advice to the architect. There are many more building engineers than architects: 341,000, or 1,427 per million inhabitants. Engineers have to be registered, which generally requires a recognized engineering degree and 4 years work experience. There are a number of substantial multi-disciplinary practices in the USA.

Client and finance

Over 70% of new construction is commissioned by the private sector and for housing the figure is 98%. Fifty-five per cent of all housing units were owner occupied in 1950 but this rose to 64% by 1987. Private rented property accounts for the bulk of the remainder. Publicly provided housing known as 'project housing' is relatively unimportant. Most mortgages are now variable interest. The average house price rose 40% from 1985 to 1990.

Selection of design consultants

In 1972 Congress established as federal law a policy to select architects
and engineers on the basis of the highest qualification for each project
and at a fair and reasonable price. For large public projects, invitations
are published for interested architects and engineers (usually only in the
state where the project is located) to indicate their interest and to
submit detailed, specific information on their qualifications. A panel of
private sector architects and engineers, who are not paid, recommends five
firms. These five make presentations, attend interviews, and so on, and
three are chosen. The most favoured of these enters into negotiations
with the client. If these break down, the second negotiates, and so on.
The process is costly to firms entering for a project.

Several states have followed the federal example and the American
Institute of Architects (AIA) recommends the procedure for private
clients. It is often followed by the large corporations, though sometimes
in a form which gives earlier prominence to estimated construction prices
and fees.

Contractual arrangements

The most usual methods of selecting a general contractor are by
competitive bidding, by negotiation or by a combination of the two. There
are two types of competitive bidding, 'open' and 'closed'. Open is the
predominant type, where all contractors use the same proposal form. In
the closed type, the competing contractors are required to submit their
qualifications along with their bids and are encouraged to suggest cost
saving proposals. There are numerous forms of negotiated contract, but
most are of the cost-plus-fee type. Negotiated contracts are normally
limited to privately financed work since competitive bidding is a legal
requirement for most public projects.

Fixed price contracts are the most common. Tenders for buildings are
customarily prepared on a lump sum basis, whereas engineering projects are
generally bid as a series of unit prices. It is standard practice for
contractors to prepare their own quantities which do not form part of the
contract. With few exceptions, bids are accompanied by a bid bond
guaranteeing that the contractor will enter into a contract if declared
successful.

Standard contract conditions have been developed by various bodies,
including the American Institute of Architects, the National Society of
Professional Engineers, the Associated General Contractors of America and
various federal, state and municipal governments. Where a contract
provides for arbitration, most stipulate that it shall be conducted under
the auspices of the Construction Industry Arbitration Association.

There has been an increasing use for large projects of management fee
or construction management arrangements, but often still retaining a
guaranteed maximum price. However, the tendency is now less apparent.
Design and build projects are also becoming more popular though there are
often other provisions for the contractor to offer advice at the design
stage.

Specialist trade contractors are usually invited to bid, often from a list selected or approved by the architect. Eight to ten bidders are usual. Nomination is virtually unknown.

The lien laws in the USA provide a large degree of protection to the contractors and subcontractors working on a project. Under their provisions a contractor can place a lien on the real property if he has not received payment for goods and services provided. This lien is registered on the title deed of the property and if not resolved can be a major impediment for subsequent sale or mortgage financing on the property. The owner is therefore obligated to ensure all payments are properly effected to each supplier of goods or services. In the event that the employer has made a payment to the general contractor, but the general contractor has not paid his subcontractors, then the subcontractors are entitled to place a lien on the property. In this case the employer may have to pay for the works twice to radiate (remove) the lien unless he has a labour and material payment bond in force in which case he can recover the double payment from the bond company. Standard bond forms are available and in common use throughout the USA. Employers and their agents need to monitor payments carefully on projects to avoid lien actions.

Development control and standards

The planning process in the USA is known as planning control and zoning control. It is very fragmented and every town has its own system. There may be 50 separate zoning authorities in one state. There is normally a Zoning Commission Board, a Zoning Board of Appeal and often a Planning Commission or Board in each town. The ease with which development zones of a town can be changed varies according to the attitude of the town or the state.

There is no single national building code for the whole of the USA. Approximately 19,000 municipalities are involved and many have their separate codes. Nevertheless, various national codes have been prepared. The most widely used is the International Conference of Building Officials (ICBO) Uniform Building Code. Others are the Building Officials and Code Administrators International (BOCA), and the Southern Building Code Congress International (SBCC). There are also specialist codes for fire safety, etc. The codes are basically performance codes rather than specifications for the form of construction. Several organizations are working on harmonization of codes, notably the National Institute of Building Sciences (NIBS), a non-governmental institution set up with representation from all parts of the building community.

The specific arrangements for obtaining planning permission and the statutory period for approval varies from state to state. Once the plans have been passed and construction has commenced, field inspection takes place. This is generally regarded as very important and the number of visits are often specified in the codes.

Standards are continually referred to in the building codes. They may be mandatory or discretionary. There are some 150 organizations which develop standards of which perhaps a dozen or so are important. These include the American Society for Testing and Materials (ASTM), the American National Standards Institute (ANSI) and the American Insurance Association (AIA).

Liability and insurance

The contractor is liable for damages caused by his own acts or omissions. He must therefore obtain comprehensive liability insurance to protect himself and his subcontractors.

The liability of designers and contractors varies with the contract used and from state to state. In the USA the architect or engineer has a contractual obligation to check the shop drawings of specialist trade contractors and this affects the liability. Normally, professional liability extends three to four years, but in some circumstances it can extend up to ten years.

Professional indemnity insurance covers the liability of parties involved in design, except that trade contractors may not be covered or, if they are, may be insufficiently so. Professional indemnity insurance is, in any case, very expensive in the USA. A survey of 1986 found that liability insurance was the major concern of the industry. Many companies in 1989 were paying double the insurance premiums of 1984, often with a reduced coverage.

CONSTRUCTION COST DATA

Cost of labour

The figures below are typical of labour costs in the Washington DC area as at the first quarter 1993. The wage rate is the basis of an employee's income, while the cost of labour indicates the cost to a contractor of employing that employee. The difference between the two covers a variety of mandatory and voluntary contributions - a list of items which could be included is given in section 2.

	Wage rate (per hour) US$	Cost of labour (per hour) US$	Number of hours worked per year
Site operatives			
Mason/bricklayer	23.40	35.75	2,000
Carpenter	22.85	35.55	2,000
Plumber	26.45	39.90	2,000
Electrician	26.10	38.95	2,000
Structural steel erector	25.15	44.80	2,000
HVAC installer	25.75	39.70	2,000

	Wage rate (per hour) US$	Cost of labour (per hour) US$	Number of hours worked per year
Semi-skilled worker	18.00	28.00	2,000
Unskilled labourer	17.55	27.20	2,000
Equipment operator	23.25	35.20	2,000
Site supervision			
General foreman	23.90	37.25	2,000
Trades foreman	25.40	39.60	2,000
	(per week)	*(per week)*	
Clerk of works	605	940	2,000
Contractors' personnel	225	350	2,000
Site manager	1,040	1,620	2,000
Resident engineer	695	1 080	2,000
Resident surveyor	695	1 080	2,000
Junior engineer	520	810	2,000
Junior surveyor	520	810	2,000

Cost of materials

The figures that follow are the US national average costs for main construction materials, delivered to site in the Washington DC area, as incurred by contractors in the first quarter 1993. These assume that the materials would be in quantities as required for a medium sized construction project and that the location of the works would be neither constrained nor remote.

	Units	Cost US$
Cement and aggregate		
Ordinary portland cement in 50kg bags	bag	6.70
Coarse aggregates for concrete	ton	9.85
Fine aggregates for concrete	ton	10.88
Ready mixed concrete (mix 2,500 psi)	yd^3	50.95
Ready mixed concrete (mix 3,000 psi)	yd^3	52.30
Steel		
Mild steel reinforcement	ton	555.00
High tensile steel reinforcement	ton	605.00
Bricks and blocks		
Common bricks (8" x 2.67" x 4")	1,000	250.00
Good quality facing bricks (8" x 2.67" x 4")	1,000	385.00
Hollow concrete blocks (8" x 8" x 16") 4,000 psi	each	1.14
Solid concrete blocks (4" x 8" x 16") 4,000 psi	each	0.94

	Units	Cost US$
Precast concrete cladding units with exposed aggregate finish	ft²	11.95

Timber and insulation

	Units	Cost US$
Softwood sections for carpentry	mbf	375.00
Exterior quality plywood	msf	360.00
Plywood for interior joinery	ft²	1.55
Softwood strip flooring	ft²	1.88
Chipboard sheet flooring	ft²	0.33
75mm thick quilt insulation	ft²	0.21
50mm thick rigid slab insulation	ft²	0.88
Softwood internal door complete with frames and ironmongery	each	175.00

Glass and ceramics

	Units	Cost US$
Float glass (0.25" thick)	ft²	2.00
Sealed double glazing units (0.625")	ft²	6.65

Plaster and paint

	Units	Cost US$
Good quality ceramic wall tiles (4.5" x 4.5")	ft²	1.95
Plaster in 50kg bags	bag	15.85
Plasterboard (0.5" thick)	yd²	3.54
Gloss oil paint in one gallon tins	gallon	20.05

Tiles and paviors

	Units	Cost US$
Clay floor tiles (4" x 4" x 0.5")	ft²	2.98
Vinyl floor tiles (12" x 12" x 0.125")	ft²	1.75
Clay roof tiles (158 pcs per 100 sq ft)	100ft²	275.00
Precast concrete roof tiles (158 pcs per 100 sq ft)	100ft²	54.00

Drainage

	Units	Cost US$
WC suite complete	each	365.00
Lavatory basin complete	each	287.00
100mm diameter clay drain pipes	ft	2.95
150mm diameter cast iron drain pipes	ft	6.12

Unit rates

The descriptions below are generally shortened versions of standard descriptions listed in section 4. Where an item has a two digit reference number (e.g. 05 or 33), this relates to the full description against that number in section 4. Where an item has an alphabetic suffix (e.g. 12A or 34B) this indicates that the standard description has been modified. Where a modification is major the complete modified description is included here and the standard description should be ignored; where a modification is minor (e.g. the insertion of a named hardwood) the shortened description has been modified here but, in general, the full description in section 4 prevails.

The unit rates below are US national average rates for main work items on a typical construction project as at the first quarter 1993. The rates include all necessary labour, materials, equipment and allowances to cover preliminary and general items and contractors' overheads and profit.

		Units	Rate US$
Excavation			
01	Mechanical excavation of foundation trenches	yd^3	6.97
02	Hardcore filling making up levels	yd^2	3.36
03	Earthwork support	ft^2	1.39
Concrete work			
04	Plain insitu concrete in strip foundations in trenches	yd^3	12.35
05	Reinforced insitu concrete in beds	yd^3	27.00
06	Reinforced insitu concrete in walls	yd^3	16.50
07	Reinforced insitu concrete in suspended floor or roof slabs	yd^3	23.00
08	Reinforced insitu concrete in columns	yd^3	43.00
09	Reinforced insitu concrete in isolated beams	yd^3	43.00
10	Precast concrete slab	ft^2	4.39
Formwork			
11	Softwood formwork to concrete walls	ft^2	2.81
12	Softwood or metal formwork to concrete columns	ft	22.00
13	Softwood or metal formwork to horizontal soffits of slabs	ft^2	3.33
Reinforcement			
14	Reinforcement in concrete walls	ton	1,075.00
15	Reinforcement in suspended concrete slabs	ton	1,100.00
16	Fabric reinforcement in concrete beds	100ft^2	46.00
Brickwork and blockwork			
18	Precast lightweight aggregate hollow concrete block walls	ft^2	4.11
19	Solid (perforated) concrete blocks US$275 per m^2 delivered	1,000	1,175.00
20	Sand lime bricks US$265 per m^2 delivered	1,000	1,100.00
21	Facing bricks US$280 per m^2 delivered	1,000	1,175.00
Roofing			
22	Concrete interlocking roof tiles 430 x 380mm	100 ft^2	265.00
23	Plain clay roof tiles 260 x 160mm	100 ft^2	475.00
27	3 layers glass-fibre based bitumen felt roof covering	100 ft^2	135.00
28	Bitumen based mastic asphalt roof covering	100 ft^2	125.00
29	Glass-fibre mat roof insulation 160mm thick	ft^2	0.64
30	Rigid sheet loadbearing roof insulation 75mm thick	ft^2	1.46
31	Troughed galvanized steel roof cladding	ft^2	1.73

	Units	Rate US$
Woodwork and metalwork		
32A Preservative treated sawn softwood 50mm x 100mm (7 feet high)	ft	8.05
33A Preservative treated sawn softwood 50 x 150mm (1000 board feet)	mbf	955.00
34 Single glazed casement window in hardwood, size 650 x 900mm	each	170.00
36 Solid core half hour fire resisting hardwood internal flush doors, size 800 x 2000mm	each	306.48
41 Structural steelwork lattice roof trusses	ton	1,525.00
Plumbing		
42 UPVC half round eaves gutter	ft	3.28
43 UPVC rainwater pipes	ft	2.36
44 Light gauge copper cold water tubing	ft	4.95
45 High pressure plastic pipes for cold water supply	ft	6.60
46 Low pressure plastic pipes for cold water distribution	ft	7.00
47 UPVC soil and vent pipes	ft	15.55
48 White vitreous china WC suite	each	615.00
49 White vitreous china lavatory basin	each	313.00
50 Glazed fireclay shower tray	each	610.00
51 Stainless steel single bowl sink and double drainer	each	379.00
Electrical work		
52 PVC insulated and copper sheathed cable	100 ft	345.00
53 13 amp unswitched socket outlet	each	66.41
54 Flush mounted 20 amp, 1 way light switch	each	63.00
Finishings		
55 2 coats gypsum based plaster on brick walls	yd^2	15.85
56 White glazed tiles on plaster walls	ft^2	4.67
57 Red clay quarry tiles on concrete floor	ft^2	7.30
60 Mineral fibre tiles on concealed suspension system	ft^2	1.97
Glazing		
61 Glazing to wood	ft^2	6.45
Painting		
62 Emulsion on plaster walls	ft^2	1.75
63 Oil paint on timber	ft^2	0.95

Approximate estimating

The building costs per unit area given below are US national averages incurred by building clients for typical buildings as at the first quarter 1993. They are based upon the total floor area of all storeys, measured between external walls and without deduction for internal walls.

Approximate estimating costs generally include mechanical and electrical installations but exclude furniture, loose or special equipment, and external works; they also exclude fees for professional services. The costs shown are for specifications and standards appropriate to the United States and this should be borne in mind when attempting comparisons with similarly described building types in other countries. A discussion of this issue is included in section 2. Comparative data for countries covered in this publication, including construction cost data, are presented in Part Three.

Approximate estimating costs must be treated with reserve; they cannot provide more than a rough guide to the probable cost of building.

	Cost m² US$	Cost ft² US$
Industrial buildings		
Factories for letting	290	26.80
Factories for owner occupation (light industrial use)	415	38.50
Factories for owner occupation (heavy industrial use)	685	63.75
Warehouses, low bay (6 to 8m high) for letting (no heating)	230	21.30
Warehouses, low bay for owner occupation (including heating)	320	29.60
Warehouses, high bay for owner occupation (including heating)	490	45.65
Administrative and commercial buildings		
Offices for letting, 5 to 10 storeys, non air conditioned	585	54.50
Offices for letting, 5 to 10 storeys, air conditioned	660	61.20
Offices for letting, high rise, air conditioned	695	64.50
Offices for owner occupation, high rise, air conditioned	885	82.30
Prestige/headquarters office, 5 to 10 storeys, air conditioned	1,085	101.00
Health and education buildings		
General hospitals	1,110	103.00
Teaching hospitals	1,335	124.00
Private hospitals	1,840	171.00
Health centres	845	78.50
Primary/junior schools	720	67.10
Secondary/middle schools	725	67.35
Recreation and arts buildings		
Theatres (over 500 seats) including seating and stage equipment	680	63.15
Theatres (less than 500 seats) including seating and stage equipment	1,030	95.50
Sports halls including changing and social facilities	570	52.90
Swimming pools (international standard) including changing and social facilities	1,160	108.00

	Cost m^2 US$	Cost ft^2 US$
Swimming pools (schools standard) including changing facilities	820	76.30
City centre/central libraries	1,090	101.00
Branch/local libraries	870	81.00

Residential buildings

Private/mass market single family housing 2 storey detached/semidetached (multiple units)	455	42.40
Purpose designed single family housing 2 storey detached (single unit)	615	57.10
Social/economic apartment housing, low rise (no lifts)	390	36.10
Social/economic apartment housing, high rise (with lifts)	590	54.65
Private sector apartment building (standard specification)	615	57.00
Private sector apartment buildings (luxury)	760	70.65
Student/nurses halls of residence	955	88.85
Hotel, 5 star, city centre	935	87.00
Hotel, 3 star, city/provincial	790	73.20
Motel	605	56.35

Regional variations

The approximate estimating costs are based on US national average costs. Adjust these costs by the following factors for regional variations:

Los Angeles, CA.	:+13.3%	Providence, R.I.	:	-0.8%
Hartford, CONN.	: -3.5%	Fort Worth, Texas	:	-12.8%
Miami, FLA.	: -12.8%	Columbia, S Carolina	:	-21%
New York, N.Y.	:+31.1%	Seattle, Washington	:	+2%
Philadelphia, PENN.	: +9.5%	Dallas, Texas	:	-13.6%

EXCHANGE RATES AND INFLATION

The combined effect of exchange rates and inflation on prices within a country and price comparisons between countries is discussed in section 2.

Exchange rates

The graph on the next page plots the movement of the American dollar against sterling and the Japanese yen since 1980. The figures used for the graph are quarterly and the method of calculating these and other related issues are discussed in section 2. The exchange rate at the first quarter 1993 was US$1.48 to the pound sterling and US$0.81 to 100 Japanese yen.

THE US DOLLAR AGAINST THE £ STERLING AND THE JAPANESE YEN

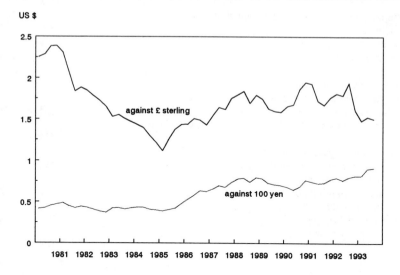

Price inflation

The table below presents consumer price, construction cost and building cost inflation in the USA since 1980.

CONSUMER PRICE, CONSTRUCTION COST AND BUILDING COST INFLATION

Year	Consumer price inflation average index	average change %	Construction cost index average index	average change %	Building cost index average index	average change %
1980	100		100		100	
1981	104	4.0	109	9.0	108	8.0
1982	117	12.5	118	8.3	115	6.5
1983	121	3.4	126	6.8	123	7.0
1984	126	4.1	128	1.6	125	1.6
1985	131	4.0	130	1.6	125	0.0
1986	133	1.5	133	2.3	128	2.4
1987	138	3.8	136	2.3	131	2.3
1988	143	3.6	140	2.9	134	2.3
1989	150	4.9	143	2.1	136	1.5
1990	159	6.0	146	2.1	139	2.2
1991	165	3.8	149	2.1	142	2.2

The above indices are compiled by Engineering News Record

USEFUL ADDRESSES

Public Organizations

General Service Administration (GSA)
    Central Office
    18th & F Streets, NW
    Washington DC

For Regional Government Construction Ministries:
    Regional GSA Office in each state

Department of Housing and Urban Development Headquarters (HUD)
    451 7th Street, SW
    Washington DC

Department of Transportation
    400 7th Street, SW
    Washington DC

Department of Commerce, Office of Research and Environmental Information
    14th Street between E Street and Constitution Avenue, NW
    Washington DC

Army Corps of Engineers
    20 Massachusetts Avenue, NW
    Washington DC 20314-1000

Small Business Administration
    1441 L Street, NW
    Washington DC

National Statistics Organization
    Department of Commerce
    14th Street between E Street and Constitution Avenue, NW
    Washington DC

National Institute of Standards and Technology
    Gaithersburg
    Maryland

National Academy of Science
    Building Research Advisory Board
    Army Corp of Engineers Research Laboratory

Trade and Professional Associations

Associations of General Contractors (AGC - union)
    1957 E Street, NW
    Washington DC 20006

Associations of Building Contractors of America (ABC - non-union)
    729 15th Street, NW
    Washington DC 20005

For Constractors Registration Board
    Respective county/city Chamber of Commerce

American Institute of Architects (AIA)
    1735 New York Avenue, NW
    Washington DC

National Society of Professional Engineers (NSPE)
    1420 King Street
    Alexandria, Virginia

American Association of Cost Engineer (AACE)
    Morgantown, West Virginia

AFL-CIO
    810 16th Street, NW
    Washington DC

4. Amplified descriptions of construction items

The Multilingual Dictionary of Real Estate

A guide for the property professional in the Single European Market

L van Breugel, Gooch and Wagstaff, UK,
B Wood, and
R H Williams, both of University of Newcastle upon Tyne, UK

* Dutch *

* English *

* French *

* German *

* Italian *

* Spanish *

The Multilingual Dictionary of Real Estate is *more than* merely a word-for-word dictionary of specialist and technical terminology; it offers explanations of terms which cannot be translated exactly or are liable to cause confusion. A supplementary section of the dictionary provides detailed notes as well as translations of particularly tricky terms. There are also invaluable sections outlining the real estate and planning hierarchies and real estate associations throughout Europe.

March 1993: 234x170: 414pp
Hardback: 0-419-18020-6

Here's what is included in *The Multilingual Dictionary of Real Estate* in all 6 languages
* how to use this dictionary * objectives * word index * translations * explanations * key questions * government and planning hierarchies

For further information on this and other property related titles, please contact:
The Promotion Dept., E & F N Spon,
2-6 Boundary Row, London SE1 8HN
Tel 071 865 0066 Fax 071 522 9623

Excavation
(Assume excavation in firm soil)

1. Mechanical excavation of foundation trenches. Starting from ground level (including removal of excavation material from site). Over 0.30m wide, not exceeding 2.00m deep.

2. Hardcore filling in making up levels. Hard brick, broken stone (or sand where appropriate). Crushed to pass a 100mm ring 150mm deep.

3. Earthwork support. Sides of trench excavation. Distance between opposing faces not exceeding 2.00m. Maximum depth 2.00m.

Concrete work
(Formwork and reinforcement measured separately)

4. Plain insitu concrete in strip foundations in trenches $20N/mm^2$. Ordinary Portland Cement, 20mm coarse aggregate. Size 500mm wide x 300mm thick.

5. Reinforced insitu concrete in beds $20N/mm^2$. Ordinary Portland Cement, 20mm coarse aggregate. 200mm thick.

6. Reinforced insitu concrete in walls $20N/mm^2$. Ordinary Portland Cement, 20mm coarse aggregate. 200mm thick.

7. Reinforced insitu concrete in suspended floor or roof slabs $20N/mm^2$. Ordinary Portland Cement, 20mm coarse aggregate. 150mm thick.

8. Reinforced insitu concrete in columns $20N/mm^2$. Ordinary Portland Cement, 20mm coarse aggregate. Size 400 x 400mm.

9. Reinforced insitu concrete in isolated beams $20N/mm^2$. Ordinary Portland Cement, 20mm coarse aggregate. Size 400 x 600mm deep.

10. Precast concrete slab (including reinforcement as necessary). Contractor designed for total loading of $3N/mm^2$. 5.00m span.

Formwork
(Assume a simple repetitive design which allows 3 uses of formwork)

11. Softwood or metal formwork to concrete walls. Basic finish. (One side only.)

12. Softwood or metal formwork to concrete columns. Basic finish. Columns 1600m girth.

13. Softwood or metal formwork to horizontal soffits of slabs. Basic finish. Slab 150mm thick, not exceeding 3.50m high.

Reinforcement

14. Reinforcement in concrete walls.   Hot rolled high tensile bars cut, bent and laid, 16mm diameter.

15. Reinforcement in suspended concrete slabs.   Hot rolled high tensile bars cut, bent and laid, 25mm diameter.

16. Fabric (mat) reinforcement in concrete beds (measured separately). Weight approximately 3.0 kg/m². Laid in position with 150mm side and end laps.

Steelwork

17. Fabricate, supply and erect steel framed structure. Including painting all steel with one coat primer.

Brickwork and blockwork
(Assume a notional thickness of 100mm for bricks and blocks. Rates should be for the nearest standard size to 100mm)

18. Precast lightweight aggregate hollow concrete block walls.   Gauged mortar. 100mm thick.

19. Solid (perforated) clay or concrete common bricks (priced at .... per m² delivered to site). Gauged mortar. 100mm thick walls.

20. Solid (perforated) sand lime bricks (priced at .... per m² delivered to site). Gauged mortar. 100mm thick walls.

21. Facing bricks (priced at .... per m² delivered to site). Gauged mortar, flush pointed as work proceeds. Half brick thick walls.

Roofing

22. Concrete interlocking roof tiles 430 x 380mm (or nearest equivalent). On and including battens and underfelt. Laid to 355mm gauge with 75mm laps (excluding eaves fittings or ridge tiles).

23. Plain clay roof tiles 260 x 160mm (or nearest equivalent).   On and including battens and underfelt. Laid to 100mm lap (excluding eaves fittings or ridge tiles).

24. Fibre cement roof slates 600 x 300mm (or nearest equivalent).   On and including battens and underfelt.   Laid flat or to fall as coverings for roofs.

25. Sawn softwood roof boarding, preservative treated 25mm thick.   Laid flat or to fall.

26. Particle board roof coverings with tongued and grooved joints 25mm thick. Laid flat or to fall.

27. 3 layers glass-fibre based bitumen felt roof covering. Finished with limestone chippings in hot bitumen. To flat roofs.

28. Bitumen based mastic asphalt roof covering in 2 layers. On and including sheathing felt underlay, with white chippings finish. To flat roofs.

29. Glass-fibre mat roof insulation 160mm thick. Laid flat between ceiling joists.

30. Rigid sheet resin-bonded loadbearing glass-fibre roof insulation 75mm thick. Laid on flat roofs.

31. 0.8mm troughed galvanized steel roof cladding in single spans of 3.00m with loading of 0.75 KN/m². Fixed to steel roof trusses with bolts. To pitched roofs.

Woodwork and metalwork
(Hardwood should be assumed to be of reasonable exterior quality)

32. Preservative treated sawn softwood. Size 50 x 100mm. Framed in partitions.

33. Preservative treated sawn softwood. Size 50 x 150mm. Pitched roof members.

34. Single glazed casement window in (.............) hardwood including hardwood frame and sill. Including steel butts and anodized aluminium espagnolette bolt. Size approx. 650 x 900mm with 38 x 100mm frame and 75 x 125mm sill.

35. Two panel door with panels open for glass in (............) hardwood including hardwood frame and sill. Including glazing with 6mm wired polished plate security glass fixed with hardwood beads and including steel butts, anodized handles and push plates and security locks. Size approximately 850 x 2000mm with 38 x 100mm frame and 38 x 150mm sill.

36. Solid core half hour fire resisting hardwood internal flush door lipped on all edges. Unpainted, including steel butts, anodized handles and push plates and mortice lock. Size approximately 800 x 2000mm.

37. Aluminium double glazed window and hardwood sub-frame. Standard anodized horizontally sliding double glazed in (.............) hardwood sub-frame and sill. Including double glazing with 4mm glass, including all ironmongery. Size approximately 1200 x 1200mm with 38 x 100mm sub-frame and 75 x 125mm sill.

38. Aluminium double glazed door set and hardwood sub-frame. Standard anodized aluminium, double glazed in (...............) hardwood sub-frame and sill. Including double glazing with 4mm glass, including all ironmongery. Size approximately 850 x 2100mm with 38 x 100mm sub-frame and 75 x 125mm sill.

39. Hardwood skirtings. Wrought (...............) hardwood. Fixed on softwood grounds. Size 20 x 100mm.

40. Framed structural steelwork in universal joist sections. Bolted or welded connections, including erecting on site and painting one coat at works.

41. Structural steelwork lattice roof trusses. Bolted or welded connections, including erecting on site and painting one coat at works.

Plumbing
(Sizes of sanitary installations and pipes are indicative)

42. UPVC half round eaves gutter. Screwed to softwood at 1.00m centres. 110mm external diameter (excluding bends, outlets etc.).

43. UPVC rainwater pipes with pushfit joints. Screwed to brickwork at 1.50m centres. 100mm external diameter (excluding bends, outlets etc.).

44. Light gauge copper cold water tubing with compression or capillary fittings. Screwed to brickwork horizontally at 1.00m centres. 15mm external diameter.

45. High pressure polypropylene, polythene or UPVC (as appropriate) pipes for cold water supply. Fixed horizontally to brick walls at 1.00m centres. 15mm external diameter, complete with fittings.

46. Low pressure polypropylene, polythene or UPVC (as appropriate) pipes for cold water distribution. With plastic compression fittings 20mm external diameter, laid in trenches.

47. UPVC soil and vent pipes with solvent welded or ring seal joints. Fixed vertically to brickwork with brackets at 1.50m centres. 100mm external diameter.

48. White vitreous china WC suite with black plastic seat and cover and plastic low level cistern, 9 litre capacity. Complete with ball valve and float and flush pipe to WC suite. Fixed to concrete.

49. White vitreous china lavatory basin with 2 No. chrome plated taps (or medium quality chrome plated mixer taps). Including plug, overflow and waste connections (excluding trap). Size approximately 560 x 400mm, fixed to brickwork with concealed brackets.

50. Glazed fireclay shower tray. Including overflow and waste (excluding trap). Size approximately 750 x 750 x 175mm, fixed to concrete.

51. Stainless steel single bowl sink and double drainer (excluding taps). Including plug, overflow and connections (excluding trap). Size approximately 1500 x 600mm, fixed to softwood sink unit (excluding sink base).

Electrical work

52. PVC insulated and copper sheathed cable, 450/750 volt grade, twin core and ECC 6mm² cross section area. Fixed to timber with clips.

53. 13 amp, 2 gang flush mounted white, unswitched socket outlet. Including 6.0m of 2.5mm² concealed PVC insulated copper cable (excluding conduit). Flush mounted to brickwork including all fittings and fixing as necessary.

54. Flush mounted 20 amp, 2 gang, 1 way white light switch. Including 6.0m of 1.5mm² concealed mineral insulated copper cable (excluding conduit). Flush mounted to brickwork including all fittings and fixings as necessary.

Finishings

55. 2 coats gypsum based plaster on brick walls 13mm thick. Floated finish.

56. White glazed tiles on plaster walls size 100 x 100 x 4mm. Fixed with adhesive and grouted between tiles.

57. Red clay quarry tiles on concrete floors size 150 x 150 x 16mm. Bedded and jointed in mortar.

58. Floor screed. Cement and sand screed to concrete floors 1:3 mix. 50mm thick. Floated finish.

59. Thermoplastic floor tiles on screed 2.5mm thick. Fixed with adhesive.

60. Suspended ceiling system. Fissured mineral fibre tiles size 300 x 300 x 15mm. On galvanized steel concealed suspension system. Fixed to concrete soffits with 500mm drop (excluding lamp fittings).

Glazing

61. Glazing to wood. Ordinary quality 4mm glass. Softwood beads.

Painting

62. Emulsion on plaster walls. One coat diluted sealer coat and 2 coats full vinyl emulsion paint.

63. Oil paint on timber. One coat primer and 2 coats oil based paint.

PART THREE
COMPARATIVE DATA

Spon's European Construction Costs Handbook

Edited by **Davis Langdon & Everest**, Chartered Quantity Surveyors, UK

A unique source of information on the world's largest construction market.
27 countries arranged in alphabetical order, each have their own chapter containing the following information.

* key data on the main economic and construction industries

* an outline of the national construction industry, covering structure, tendering and contract procedures, regulations and standards

* labour and material costs data

* measured rates (in local currency) for up to 63 construction operations

* costs per unit area for a range of building types from housing to offices and factories

* regional variations percentages, tax details, cost and price indices, exchange rates with £ sterling and $US

* addresses of authorities, professional institutions, trade associations etc.

* multilingual glossary with fully detailed specifications, in 5 languages for the operations priced as measured rates

Countries covered in detail: Austria * Belgium * Cyprus * Denmark * Finland * France * Germany * Greece * Hungary * Ireland * Italy * Japan * Luxembourg * Malta * Netherlands * Norway * Poland * Portugal * Spain * Sweden * Switzerland * Turkey * UK * USA * USSR(CIS) * Yugoslavia * Japan and the USA are included for the purpose of comparison

March 1992: 234x156: 544pp
Hardback: 0-419-17480-X

For further information and to order please contact: **The Promotion Dept.**, **E & F N Spon**, 2-6 Boundary Row, London SE1 8HN Tel 071 865 0066 Fax 071 522 9623

5. Introductory notes

Part Three brings together data from a variety of sources but mainly Part Two, and presents them in the form of tables to allow rapid comparison among the countries included in the book. This also helps place countries, their main statistical indicators and their construction costs in an international context.

There are twenty five tables derived from Part Two arranged in three sections:

Key national indicators
· Population
· Geography
· The economy

Construction output indicators
· Construction output
· Construction output per capita

Construction cost data
· Mason/bricklayer and unskilled labour costs
· Site manager and qualified architect labour costs
· Material costs - Cement and concrete aggregates
· Material costs - Ready mixed concrete and reinforcing steel
· Material costs - Common bricks and hollow concrete blocks
· Material costs - Softwood for joinery and quilt insulation
· Material costs - Sheet glass and plasterboard
· Material costs - Emulsion paint and vinyl floor tiles
· Approximate estimating - Factories and warehouses
· Approximate estimating - Offices
· Approximate estimating - Housing
· Approximate estimating - Hospitals and schools
· Approximate estimating - Theatres and sports halls
· Approximate estimating - Hotels

The first five tables are based on the Key data sheets at the beginning of each country section, the remainder are drawn from the Construction cost data in each country section. Each table is prefaced by explanatory notes. There are inherent dangers in attempting to compare international data, particularly where two sets of data are used (e.g.: construction output and population) and, even more so, when exchange rates are used. While these tables can provide useful initial comparisons between countries they should, nevertheless, be used with caution.

6. Key national indicators

POPULATION

The table below summarizes population statistics for all fifteen countries included in this book. The table highlights not only the differences in total population among the countries but also variations in the distribution of population between age groups within countries, in population growth rates and in the proportion of the population living in urban areas.

The table includes the most populous country in the world (China) and three others from the top ten most populous countries (the United States, Indonesia and Japan). The developed countries generally have high rates of urbanization though so also do the two city states of Hong Kong and Singapore. The developed countries also have relatively low proportions of population under 15 and relatively high populations over 65. Interestingly the population of working age (between 15 and 65) does not vary by so much; it is between 57% (Philippines) and 70% (Hong Kong) with the figures for Australia and China being identical.

Population growth rates vary from less than 1% per annum in the UK, the US, New Zealand and Japan to over 2% in Singapore, Philippines, Malaysia and Brunei. At 0.7% annual compound growth, population doubles in 100 years; at 2.5% compound, it doubles in less than 30 years.

| | Population | | | | |
Country	Total (m)	Urban %	Under 15 %	Over 65 %	Growth % pa
Australia	17.1	86	22	11	1.5
Brunei	0.3	n.a.	n.a.	n.a.	3.5
Canada	26.5	77	17	22	1.0
China	1,158.2	26	27	6	1.4
Hong Kong	5.9	94	21	9	1.0
Indonesia	183.0	31	35	3	1.8
Japan	123.5	77	18	12	0.6
Malaysia	17.6	38	38	4	2.6
New Zealand	3.4	76	23	12	0.8
Philippines	64.6	44	40	3	2.4
Singapore	2.8	100	23	6	2.2
South Korea	42.8	72	25	6	1.1
Thailand	60.0	23	34	3	1.8
United Kingdom	57.4	89	19	16	0.2
United States	248.7	74	22	13	0.9

THE ECONOMY

This table summarizes economic data for the countries included in this book. In the country sections Gross Domestic Product (GDP) figures are given in national currencies; here they have been converted to US dollars using the average exchange rate for the appropriate year - usually 1991. The table contains the two wealthiest nations in the world - the US and Japan - and some of the poorest. As with population density, GDP per capita is a more helpful measure of national wealth than total GDP. Again, the US and Japan have amongst the highest GDPs per capita in the world. Brunei has one of the highest GDP per capita in the world while total GDP is less than a tenth of neighbouring Malaysia.

The GDP growth rates are perhaps more interesting indicators of potential wealth.   The growth rates are real, that is the effects of inflation are excluded. South Korea, China, Thailand and Hong Kong have all doubled or more than doubled their GDP in the past decade. With the exception of New Zealand and the Philippines, average annual inflation 1980-1990 in all countries is below 10%, often well below.

| | 1991 | | 1980 – 1990 | |
| | GDP | GDP per capita | GDP growth | Inflation |
Country	US$ bn	US$	(real) % pa	average % pa
Australia	331	19,300	3.4	7.4
Brunei *	3.6	13,900	n.a.	n.a.
Canada	575	21,700	3.4	4.4
China +	373	300	9.5	5.8
Hong Kong ¯	96	16,200	7.1	7.2
Indonesia *	108	600	5.5	8.4
Japan	3,158	25,600	4.1	1.5
Malaysia	47	2,700	5.2	4.4
New Zealand ˣ	43	12,600	1.1 ˣ	10.5
Philippines *	46	700	0.9	14.9
Singapore	40	14,300	6.4	3.5
South Korea	284	6,600	9.7	5.1
Thailand *	81	1,400	7.6	3.3
United Kingdom *	883	15,400	3.1	5.8
United States	5,678	22,800	3.4	3.7

* 1990

+ China 1991 GNP

¯ Hong Kong 1992 estimate

ˣ New Zealand 1982 – 1992

GEOGRAPHY

The table below summarizes geographical statistics for the countries included in this book.   As with population the table highlights the differences between countries.   It includes three out of the four largest countries in the world (Canada, China and the US) - only Russia is bigger; it also includes two of the smallest (Hong Kong and Singapore).

The figures for population density and the percentage of national population in the largest city are perhaps more helpful indicators of land use than total area.   As might be expected the table shows that the country with the second largest area in the world (Canada) has almost the lowest population density, while Hong Kong with over 5,000 persons per km² has one of the highest population densities in the world.   The percentage of national population in the largest city gives an indication of the relative importance of that city - usually the capital.

| | Land area | | Population | Largest city | |
Country	Total 000 km²	Agricultural area %	per km²	000's	% of total
Australia	7,687	63	2.2	3,700	21.6
Brunei	5.77	2	45	58	22.3
Canada	9,976	8	2.7	2,200	8.3
China	9,600	42	121	10,800	0.9
Hong Kong	1.08	8	5,483	n.a.	n.a.
Indonesia	1,919	18	95	9,500	5.2
Japan	378	14	327	11,900	9.6
Malaysia	330	13	53	1,100	6.3
New Zealand	269	53	13	900	26.5
Philippines	300	31	215	8,400	13.0
Singapore	0.64	2	4,375	n.a.	n.a.
South Korea	99	23	432	9,600	22.4
Thailand	513	41	117	8,000	13.3
United Kingdom	244	77	235	6,700	11.7
United States	9,373	47	27	18,100	7.3

7. Construction output indicators

CONSTRUCTION OUTPUT

The table below summarizes construction output statistics from the country key data sheets. On the key data sheet for each country an output figure is given in national currency and the year to which it relates noted. For some countries more up-to-date figures are available in the main text of the country section.

In this summary table, figures in national currency are listed and, in addition, in order to facilitate (crude) comparisons, US dollar, pound sterling and yen equivalents are presented for each figure. The currency conversions have been carried out using appropriate exchange rates. As noted earlier, construction statistics, including those for construction output, are notoriously unreliable and, in addition, national definitions of construction output vary widely. It would, therefore, be unwise to draw too many conclusions from this table.

Country	National unit of currency	Construction output National currency	UK £	US $	billions Yen
Australia	A$	24.6	8.04	21.49	2,896
Brunei *	B$	0.28	0.09	0.16	22
Canada	C$	56.0	27.63	48.93	6,592
China *	Rmb	114	13.59	24.27	3,496
Hong Kong	HK$	34.0	2.47	4.37	589
Indonesia	Rp	12,856	3.72	6.58	887
Japan	¥	43,000	180.28	319.01	43,000
Malaysia	M$	4.9	1.01	1.78	240
New Zealand	NZ$	3.1	1.02	1.80	242
Philippines *	P	50	1.21	2.17	311
Singapore	S$	4.7	1.53	2.72	366
South Korea	Won	32,056	24.77	43.84	5,903
Thailand *	Bt	147	3.26	5.82	840
United Kingdom	£	33.7	33.70	59.49	8,018
United States	$	250	141.21	250.00	33,676

* 1990

CONSTRUCTION OUTPUT PER CAPITA

This table is based on the previous one, but has each figure for construction output divided by the population of that country. Despite the uncertainty of both construction and population data and the limitations of exchange rates, the table reveals some useful indicators of construction activity. Japan has the highest by far construction output per capita - more than 150 times greater than the lowest in the table (China), though it is reckoned that Chinese output is seriously undervalued. Like China, Indonesia and the Philippines have output per capita of less than $100. The remainder of the Asia Pacific countries are spread over the range from Thailand ($104) to South Korea ($1,024). The UK and the US are similar to South Korea; Australia and Canada are higher.

Country	National unit of currency	Construction output per capita			
		National currency	UK £	US $	Yen
Australia	A$	1,438	469.92	1,256.36	169,267
Brunei *	B$	1,079	336.16	598.60	86,477
Canada	C$	2,113	1,042.58	1,846.10	248,721
China *	Rmb	100	11.90	21.25	3,062
Hong Kong	HK$	5,763	418.73	741.35	99,865
Indonesia	Rp	70,251	20.33	35.98	4,846
Japan	¥	348,000	1,458.99	2,581.73	348,000
Malaysia	M$	277	56.94	100.76	13,574
New Zealand	NZ$	911	298.63	528.29	71,145
Philippines *	P	776	18.69	33.54	4,814
Singapore	S$	1,679	548.07	970.06	130,743
South Korea	Won	748,972	578.66	1,024.30	137,929
Thailand *	Bt	2,622	58.29	104.01	15,002
United Kingdom	£	587	587.00	1,036.25	139,655
United States	$	1,005	567.68	1,005.00	135,378

* 1990

8. Construction cost data

MASON/BRICKLAYER AND UNSKILLED LABOUR COSTS

This table summarizes hourly labour costs for a mason/bricklayer and for unskilled labour in each country as at first quarter 1993. The figures in national currency are taken from each country's construction cost data and have been converted into pound sterling, US dollar and yen equivalents using first quarter 1993 exchange rates. As indicated earlier, the cost of labour is the cost to a contractor of employing that employee; it is based on the employee's income but also includes allowances for a range of mandatory and voluntary contributions which vary from country to country.

It is probable that the definitions of skilled and unskilled and what is included in labour costs varies between countries, thus these figures should not be taken as strictly comparable. The ranking and relative level of labour costs are broadly similar to the GDP per capita figures though there are interesting detailed differences in ranking.

Country	Mason/bricklayer			hour	Unskilled labour			hour
	National currency	*UK £*	*US $*	*Yen*	*National currency*	*UK £*	*US $*	*Yen*
Australia	20.00	9.21	13.66	1,678	18.00	8.29	12.29	1,510
Brunei	n.a.				n.a.			
Canada	32.44	17.30	25.65	3,152	25.77	13.74	20.37	2,504
China	4.60	0.54	0.79	98	2.30	0.27	0.40	49
Hong Kong	75.00	6.53	9.68	1,190	51.63	4.50	6.67	819
Indonesia	862.5	0.28	0.42	51	562.5	0.18	0.27	33
Japan	n.a.				n.a.			
Malaysia	n.a.				n.a.			
New Zealand	n.a.				n.a.			
Philippines	170.0	4.64	6.87	845	135.0	3.68	5.46	671
Singapore	7.15	2.92	4.33	532	5.59	2.28	3.38	416
South Korea	9,725	8.27	12.26	1,506	4,788	4.07	6.03	741
Thailand	n.a.				n.a.			
United Kingdom	5.44	5.44	8.06	991	4.71	4.71	6.98	858
United States	35.75	24.12	35.75	4,393	27.20	18.35	27.20	3,343

SITE MANAGER AND QUALIFIED ARCHITECT LABOUR RATES

This table is from the same source as the previous and is presented in the same way. Site managers and qualified architects are representative of staff rather than site labour.

Country	Site manager National currency	UK£	US $	hour Yen	Qualified architect National currency	UK£	US $	hour Yen
Australia	60.00	27.64	40.97	5,035	65.00	29.94	44.38	5,454
Brunei	34.48	14.09	20.88	2,566	31.61	12.91	19.14	2,352
Canada	35.92	19.16	28.40	3,490	30.17	16.09	23.85	2,931
China	n.a.				n.a.			
Hong Kong	137.9				206.9			
Indonesia	n.a.				n.a.			
Japan	n.a.				n.a.			
Malaysia	n.a.				n.a.			
New Zealand	n.a.				n.a.			
Philippines	520.0	14.19	21.03	2,584	390.0	10.64	15.77	1,938
Singapore	33.48	13.68	20.27	2,491	32.21	13.16	19.51	2,397
South Korea	13,655	11.61	17.21	2,115	14,770	12.56	18.61	2,287
Thailand	n.a.				n.a.			
United Kingdom	15.88	15.88	23.54	2,893	12.47	12.47	18.49	2,272
United States	40.50	27.32	40.50	4,977	n.a.			

MATERIALS COSTS - CEMENT AND CONCRETE AGGREGATES

The table below summarizes costs per tonne for cement and costs per m³ for concrete aggregates as at first quarter 1993. The figures in national currency are taken from each country's construction cost data and converted into US dollar, pound sterling and yen equivalents using first quarter 1993 exchange rates. Converted figures have been rounded to the nearest whole number.

Costs are as delivered to site in a major - usually the capital - city. They assume that the materials are in quantities as required for a medium sized construction project and that the location of the works would be neither constrained or remote. Material costs generally exclude value added or similar taxes.

Despite the fact that there are internationally recognized standards of quality for cement and that it is one of the few internationally traded construction materials, the variation in cost between countries is remarkably large (from $63 to $140 per tonne). This may well be a result of controlled prices or of import protection or of undervalued or overvalued currencies. The variation in aggregate costs is less surprising; quality and availability can be expected to vary widely within, let alone between, countries and a large proportion of aggregate costs can be in their transportation.

Country	Cement National currency	UK £	US $	tonne Yen	Aggregates for concrete National currency	UK £	US $	m³ Yen
Australia	185.0	85.21	126.32	15,523	22.50	10.36	15.36	1,888
Brunei	180.0	73.53	109.00	13,395	38.00	15.52	23.01	2,828
Canada	121.5	64.80	96.06	11,804	15.30	8.16	12.10	1,486
China	550.0	64.06	94.96	11,670	90.00	10.48	15.54	1,910
Hong Kong	525.0	45.73	67.79	8,331	81.00	7.06	10.46	1,285
Indonesia	135,000	44.03	65.26	8,020	25,000	8.15	12.09	1,485
Japan	16,000	87.83	130.20	16,000	4,600	25.25	37.43	4,600
Malaysia	184.0	47.43	70.31	8,640	43.50	11.21	16.62	2,043
New Zealand	270.0	94.13	139.53	17,148	67.60	23.57	34.94	4,293
Philippines	2,650	72.29	107.16	13,169	445.0	12.14	17.99	2,211
Singapore	155.0	63.32	93.86	11,535	18.00	7.35	10.90	1,339
South Korea	52,250	44.42	65.85	8,092	9,460	8.04	11.92	1,465
Thailand	1,600	42.36	62.79	7,717	320.0	8.47	12.56	1,543
United Kingdom	63.02	63.02	93.42	11,480	6.84	6.84	10.14	1,246
United States	134.0	90.40	134.00	16,468	16.74	11.30	16.74	2,058

MATERIALS COSTS - READY MIXED CONCRETE
AND REINFORCING STEEL

The table below summarizes costs per m³ for ready mixed concrete and costs per tonne for reinforcing steel as at first quarter 1993. The figures in national currency are taken from each country's construction cost data and converted into US dollar, pound sterling and yen equivalents using first quarter 1993 exchange rates.

Costs are as delivered to site in a major - usually the capital - city. They assume that the materials are in quantities as required for a medium sized construction project and that the location of the works would be neither constrained or remote. Material costs generally exclude value added or similar taxes.

The range of costs for reinforcing steel is rather less than that for cement or for ready mixed concrete; from a low of $355 per tonne in the United Kingdom to a high of $639 per tonne in China.

| Country | Ready mixed concrete | | | m³ | Mild steel reinforcement | | | tonne |
	National currency	UK £	US $	Yen	National currency	UK £	US $	Yen
Australia	95.00	43.76	64.86	7,971	880.0	405.3	600.9	73,840
Brunei	175.0	71.49	105.97	13,023	680.0	277.8	411.8	50,603
Canada	85.51	45.61	67.60	8,308	600.0	320.0	474.3	58,293
China	n.a.				3,700	431.0	638.8	78,508
Hong Kong	380.0	33.10	49.07	6,030	3,166	275.8	408.8	50,241
Indonesia	120,000	39.13	58.01	7,129	807,000	263.2	390.1	47,943
Japan	11,700	64.23	95.21	11,700	51,000	280.0	415.0	51,000
Malaysia	128.0	33.00	48.91	6,011	1,200	309.3	458.5	56,350
New Zealand	142.0	49.51	73.38	9,018	1,200	418.4	620.2	76,212
Philippines	2,750	75.02	111.20	13,666	11,900	324.6	481.2	59,135
Singapore	97.00	39.63	58.74	7,218	660.0	269.6	399.7	49,115
South Korea	39,500	33.58	49.78	6,117	284,000	241.4	357.9	43,984
Thailand	1,200	31.77	47.10	5,788	11,500	304.5	451.3	55,465
United Kingdom	35.15	35.15	52.10	6,403	239.3	239.3	354.6	43,583
United States	66.64	44.96	66.64	8,190	611.8	412.7	611.8	75,182

MATERIALS COSTS - COMMON BRICKS
AND HOLLOW CONCRETE BLOCKS

The table below summarizes costs per 1,000 for bricks and blocks as at first quarter 1993. The figures in national currency are taken from each country's construction cost data and converted to US dollar, pound sterling and yen equivalents using first quarter 1993 exchange rates.

Costs are as delivered to site in a major - usually the capital - city. They assume that the materials are in quantities as required for a medium sized construction project and that the location of the works would be neither constrained or remote. Material costs generally exclude value added or similar taxes.

The costs of bricks and blocks vary by the availability of raw materials and the national practices in walling construction. Where brick-making clays are not readily available, for example, the cost of bricks may be relatively high. It is probably reasonable to assume that brick dimensions are broadly similar; the dimensions of concrete blocks, however, can and do vary widely.

Country	Common bricks			1,000	Hollow concrete blocks			1,000
	National currency	UK £	US $	Yen	National currency	UK £	US $	Yen
Australia	335.0	154.31	228.73	28,110	1,280	590	874	107,404
Brunei	170.0	69.45	102.94	12,651	450.0	184	272	33,487
Canada	125.0	66.67	98.82	12,144	1,500	800	1,186	145,733
China	300.0	34.94	51.80	6,366	150.0	17.47	25.90	3,183
Hong Kong	671.0	58.45	86.65	10,648	1,114	97.04	144	17,678
Indonesia	70,000	22.83	33.84	4,159	350,000	114	169	20,793
Japan	80,000	439.16	650.98	80,000	213,000	1,169	1,733	213,000
Malaysia	250.0	64.44	95.53	11,740	1,300	335	497	61,045
New Zealand	850.0	296.34	439.27	53,983	2,050	715	1,059	130,195
Philippines	4,250	115.94	171.85	21,120	7,200	196	291	35,779
Singapore	250.0	102.13	151.39	18,604	750.0	306	454	55,812
South Korea	49,500	42.08	62.38	7,666	572,000	486	721	88,587
Thailand	450.0	11.91	17.66	2,170	1,100	29.12	43.17	5,305
United Kingdom	100.0	100.00	148.23	18,217	500.0	500	741	91,083
United States	250.0	168.65	250.00	30,723	1,140	769	1,140	140,097

MATERIALS COSTS - SOFTWOOD FOR JOINERY AND QUILT INSULATION

The table below summarizes costs per m³ for softwood for joinery and costs per m² for 100mm thick quilt insulation as at first quarter 1993. The figures in national currency are taken from each country's construction cost data and converted to US dollar, pound sterling and yen equivalents using first quarter 1993 exchange rates.

Costs are as delivered to site in a major - usually the capital - city. They assume that the materials are in quantities as required for a medium sized construction project and that the location of the works would be neither constrained or remote. Material costs generally exclude value added or similar taxes.

Country	Softwood for joinery National currency	UK£	US $	m³ Yen	Quilt insulation 100mm National currency	UK£	US $	m² Yen
Australia	763.0	351	521	64,023	9.00	4.15	6.15	755
Brunei	2,275	929	1,378	169,298	6.00	2.45	3.63	446
Canada	910.0	485	719	88,412	2.65	1.41	2.10	257
China	1,500	175	259	31,828	150.0	17.47	25.90	3,183
Hong Kong	1,640	143	212	26,025	40.00	3.48	5.17	635
Indonesia	600,000	196	290	35,645	18,000	5.87	8.70	1,069
Japan	127,000	697	1,033	127,000	n.a.			
Malaysia	450.0	116	172	21,131	9.00	2.32	3.44	423
New Zealand	500.0	174	258	31,755	12.00	4.18	6.20	762
Philippines	10,100	276	408	50,190	1,010	27.55	40.84	5,019
Singapore	n.a.				5.60	2.29	3.39	417
South Korea	594,000	505	749	91,994	12,800	10.88	16.13	1,982
Thailand	10,000	265	392	48,231	150.0	3.97	5.89	723
United Kingdom	290.00	290	430	52,828	2.15	2.15	3.19	392
United States	n.a.				3.01	2.03	3.01	370

MATERIALS COSTS - SHEET GLASS AND PLASTERBOARD

The table below summarizes costs per m² for sheet or float glass and for plasterboard as at first quarter 1993. The figures in national currency are taken from each country's construction cost data and converted to US dollar, pound sterling and yen equivalents using first quarter 1993 exchange rates.

Costs are as delivered to site in a major - usually the capital - city. They assume that the materials are in quantities as required for a medium sized construction project and that the location of the works would be neither constrained or remote. Material costs generally exclude value added or similar taxes.

Country	*Sheet/float glass* National currency	UK£	US $	*m²* Yen	*Plasterboard 10mm* National currency	UK£	US $	*m²* Yen
Australia	90.00	41.46	61.45	7,552	12.00	5.53	8.19	1,007
Brunei	30.00	12.26	18.17	2,232	6.75	2.76	4.09	502
Canada	45.00	24.00	35.58	4,372	2.00	1.07	1.58	194
China	40.00	4.66	6.91	849	13.00	1.51	2.24	276
Hong Kong	58.00	5.05	7.49	920	100.0	8.71	12.91	1,587
Indonesia	42,000	13.70	20.30	2,495	14,900	4.86	7.20	885
Japan	4,030	22.12	32.79	4,030	170.0	0.93	1.38	170
Malaysia	41.00	10.57	15.67	1,925	9.00	2.32	3.44	423
New Zealand	98.00	34.17	50.65	6,224	16.00	5.58	8.27	1,016
Philippines	n.a.				630.0	17.19	25.47	3,131
Singapore	86.00	35.13	52.08	6,400	4.00	1.63	2.42	298
South Korea	2,970	2.52	3.74	460	2,150	1.83	2.71	333
Thailand	450.0	11.91	17.66	2,170	80.00	2.12	3.14	386
United Kingdom	29.31	29.31	43.45	5,339	1.45	1.45	2.15	264
United States	21.53	14.52	21.53	2,646	4.23	2.86	4.23	520

MATERIALS COSTS - EMULSION PAINT
AND VINYL FLOOR TILES

The table below summarizes costs per litre for emulsion paint and costs per m² for vinyl tiles as at first quarter 1993. The figures in national currency are taken from each country's construction cost data and converted to US dollar, pound sterling and yen equivalents using first quarter 1993 exchange rates.

Costs are as delivered to site in a major - usually the capital - city. They assume that the materials are in quantities as required for a medium sized construction project and that the location of the works would be neither constrained or remote. Material costs generally exclude value added or similar taxes.

Country	Emulsion paint			litre	Vinyl floor tiles			m²
	National currency	UK£	US$	Yen	National currency	UK£	US $	Yen
Australia	9.00	4.15	6.15	755	20.00	9.21	13.66	1,678
Brunei	8.00	3.27	4.84	595	15.00	6.13	9.08	1,116
Canada	8.00	4.27	6.32	777	5.00	2.67	3.95	486
China	5.00	0.58	0.86	106	20.00	2.33	3.45	424
Hong Kong	20.00	1.74	2.58	317	50.00	4.36	6.46	793
Indonesia	7,000	2.28	3.38	416	10,000	3.26	4.83	594
Japan	350.0	1.92	2.85	350	10,930	60.00	88.94	10,930
Malaysia	9.85	2.54	3.76	463	26.00	6.70	9.93	1,221
New Zealand	6.80	2.37	3.51	432	22.00	7.67	11.37	1,397
Philippines	50.66	1.38	2.05	252	380.0	10.37	15.37	1,888
Singapore	3.50	1.43	2.12	260	6.00	2.45	3.63	446
South Korea	2,090	1.78	2.63	324	3,630	3.09	4.57	562
Thailand	55.07	1.46	2.16	266	160.0	4.24	6.28	772
United Kingdom	1.82	1.82	2.70	332	4.62	4.62	6.85	842
United States	n.a.				18.84	12.71	18.84	2,315

APPROXIMATE ESTIMATING - FACTORIES AND WAREHOUSES

This table summarizes approximate estimating costs per square metre for factories and warehouses. Approximate estimating costs are averages as incurred by building clients for typical buildings in major - usually capital - cities in the first quarter of 1993. They are based upon the total floor area of all storeys, measured between external walls and without deduction for internal walls. Approximate estimating costs generally include mechanical and electrical installations but exclude furniture, loose or special equipment, and external works; they also exclude fees for professional services. Where a range of costs has been given, the mid point is shown. The figures in national currency are taken from each country's construction cost data and converted to US dollar, pound sterling and yen equivalents using first quarter 1993 exchange rates.

It must be borne in mind that even where costs are given under the same description in one or more countries, this is not to say that they are identical, or even physically similar. Approximate estimating costs for a particular country are for the normal standards prevailing in that country. Quality and technical standards vary widely and there are differences between countries in what is, and is not, included. The table, therefore, should be used with care.

Country	Factories for owner occupation (light industrial use) National currency	UK £	US $	Yen m^2	Warehouses, low bay (6 to 8m high) for letting (no heating) National currency	UK £	US $	Yen m^2
Australia	435	200	297	36,500	350	161	239	29,368
Brunei	685	280	415	50,975	650	266	394	48,371
Canada	336	179	266	32,685	231	123	182	22,395
China	n.a.				n.a.			
Hong Kong	3,800	331	491	60,302	4,800	418	620	76,171
Indonesia	579,204	189	280	34,410	517,146	169	250	30,723
Japan	n.a.				200,000	1,098	1,627	200,000
Malaysia	650	168	248	30,523	430	111	164	20,192
New Zealand	400	139	207	25,404	400	139	207	25,404
Philippines	10,400	284	421	51,681	6,500	177	263	32,301
Singapore	950	388	575	70,696	750	306	454	55,812
South Korea	532,000	452	670	82,392	299,000	254	377	46,307
Thailand	7,000	185	275	33,761	n.a.			
United Kingdom	296	296	439	53,921	161	161	239	29,329
United States	415	280	415	51,000	230	155	230	28,265

APPROXIMATE ESTIMATING - OFFICES

This table summarizes approximate estimating costs per square metre for two different types of office buildings. Approximate estimating costs are averages as incurred by building clients for typical buildings in major - usually capital - cities in the first quarter of 1993. They are based upon the total floor area of all storeys, measured between external walls and without deduction for internal walls. Approximate estimating costs generally include mechanical and electrical installations but exclude furniture, loose or special equipment, and external works; they also exclude fees for professional services. Where a range of costs has been given, the mid point is shown. The figures in national currency are taken from each country's construction cost data and converted to US dollar, pound sterling and yen equivalents using first quarter 1993 exchange rates.

It must be borne in mind that even where costs are given under the same description in one or more countries, this is not to say that they are identical, or even physically similar. Approximate estimating costs for a particular country are for the normal standards prevailing in that country. Quality and technical standards vary widely and there are differences between countries in what is, and is not, included. The table, therefore, should be used with care.

	Offices for letting, 5 to 10 storeys air conditioned			m^2	Prestige/headquarters office, high rise, air conditioned			m^2
Country	National currency	UK £	US $	Yen	National currency	UK £	US $	Yen
Australia	1,200	553	819	100,691	2,000	921	1,366	167,818
Brunei	1,100	449	666	81,858	n.a.			
Canada	625	333	494	60,701	921	491	728	89,495
China	n.a.				6,950	810	1,200	147,470
Hong Kong	6,900	601	891	109,496	9,200	801	1,188	145,995
Indonesia	1,137,722	371	550	67,591	1,706,583	557	825	101,386
Japan	n.a.				450,000	2,470	3,662	450,000
Malaysia	1,130	291	432	53,063	2,040	526	780	95,794
New Zealand	1,750	610	904	111,142	2,300	802	1,189	146,072
Philippines	21,600	589	873	107,337	32,400	884	1,310	161,006
Singapore	1,500	613	908	111,625	2,500	1,021	1,514	186,041
South Korea	799,000	679	1,007	123,742	932,000	792	1,175	144,340
Thailand	n.a.				19,500	516	765	94,050
United Kingdom	662	662	981	120,594	1,318	1,318	1,954	240,096
United States	660	445	660	81,109	n.a.			

APPROXIMATE ESTIMATING - HOUSING

This table summarizes approximate estimating costs per square metre for housing. Two types of housing have been taken: private sector, single family houses and medium quality, medium rise apartments. In countries where housing types did not match exactly these descriptions, the nearest equivalent has been taken.

Approximate estimating costs are averages as incurred by building clients for typical buildings in major - usually capital - cities in the first quarter of 1993. They are based upon the total floor area of all storeys, measured between external walls and without deduction for internal walls. Approximate estimating costs generally include mechanical and electrical installations but exclude furniture, loose or special equipment, and external works; they also exclude fees for professional services. Where a range of costs has been given, the mid point is shown. The figures in national currency are taken from each country's construction cost data and converted to US dollar, pound sterling and yen equivalents using first quarter 1993 exchange rates.

It must be borne in mind that even where costs are given under the same description in one or more countries, this is not to say that they are identical, or even physically similar. Approximate estimating costs for a particular country are for the normal standards prevailing in that country. Quality and technical standards vary widely and there are differences between countries in what is, and is not, included. The table, therefore, should be used with care.

Country	Single family housing, private, detached, semidetached			m^2	Private sector apartment building (standard specification)			m^2
	National currency	UK £	US $	Yen	National currency	UK £	US $	Yen
Australia	600	276	410	50,345	1,100	507	751	92,300
Brunei	900	368	545	66,975	1,050	429	636	78,137
Canada	384	205	304	37,354	653	348	516	63,468
China	n.a.				n.a.			
Hong Kong	6,400	558	826	101,562	4,300	375	555	68,237
Indonesia	n.a.				1,241,151	405	600	73,735
Japan	n.a.				n.a.			
Malaysia	590	152	225	27,705	810	209	310	38,036
New Zealand	800	279	413	50,808	1,700	593	879	107,966
Philippines	6,490	177	262	32,251	21,600	589	873	107,337
Singapore	1,400	572	848	104,183	1,200	490	727	89,300
South Korea	599,000	509	755	92,768	532,000	452	670	82,392
Thailand	12,500	331	491	60,288	12,500	331	491	60,288
United Kingdom	307	307	455	55,925	368	368	545	67,037
United States	455	307	455	55,916	615	415	615	75,578

APPROXIMATE ESTIMATING - HOSPITALS AND SCHOOLS

This table summarizes approximate estimating costs per square metre for general hospitals and secondary or middle schools. Approximate estimating costs are averages as incurred by building clients for typical buildings in major - usually capital - cities in the first quarter of 1993. They are based upon the total floor area of all storeys, measured between external walls and without deduction for internal walls. Approximate estimating costs generally include mechanical and electrical installations but exclude furniture, loose or special equipment, and external works; they also exclude fees for professional services. Where a range of costs has been given, the mid point is shown. The figures in national currency are taken from each country's construction cost data and converted to US dollar, pound sterling and yen equivalents using first quarter 1993 exchange rates.

It must be borne in mind that even where costs are given under the same description in one or more countries, this is not to say that they are identical, or even physically similar. Approximate estimating costs for a particular country are for the normal standards prevailing in that country. Quality and technical standards vary widely and there are differences between countries in what is, and is not, included. The table, therefore, should be used with care.

Country	General hospitals (100 beds) National currency	UK £	US $	m² Yen	Secondary / middle schools National currency	UK £	US $	m² Yen
Australia	1,700	783	1,161	142,645	1,000	461	683	83,909
Brunei	1,650	674	999	122,787	1,100	449	666	81,858
Canada	1,298	692	1,026	126,071	614	328	485	59,663
China	n.a.				n.a.			
Hong Kong	9,200	801	1,188	145,995	4,600	401	594	72,998
Indonesia	n.a.				n.a.			
Japan	550,000	3,019	4,475	550,000	n.a.			
Malaysia	n.a.				490	126	187	23,009
New Zealand	2,200	767	1,137	139,721	1,000	349	517	63,510
Philippines	29,300	799	1,185	145,601	13,000	355	526	64,601
Singapore	1,700	694	1,029	126,508	1,100	449	666	81,858
South Korea	1,160,000	986	1,462	179,651	599,000	509	755	92,768
Thailand	n.a.				n.a.			
United Kingdom	652	652	966	118,773	425	425	630	77,421
United States	1,110	749	1,110	136,410	725	489	725	89,097

APPROXIMATE ESTIMATING - THEATRES AND SPORTS HALLS

This table summarizes approximate estimating costs per square metre for theatres and sports halls. Approximate estimating costs are averages as incurred by building clients for typical buildings in major - usually capital - cities in the first quarter of 1993. They are based upon the total floor area of all storeys, measured between external walls and without deduction for internal walls. Approximate estimating costs generally include mechanical and electrical installations but exclude furniture, loose or special equipment, and external works; they also exclude fees for professional services. Where a range of costs has been given, the mid point is shown. The figures in national currency are taken from each country's construction cost data and converted to US dollar, pound sterling and yen equivalents using first quarter 1993 exchange rates.

It must be borne in mind that even where costs are given under the same description in one or more countries, this is not to say that they are identical, or even physically similar. Approximate estimating costs for a particular country are for the normal standards prevailing in that country. Quality and technical standards vary widely and there are differences between countries in what is, and is not, included. The table, therefore, should be used with care.

Country	Theatres including seating and stage equipment, over 500 seats m²				Sports halls including changing and social facilities m²			
	National currency	UK £	US $	Yen	National currency	UK £	US $	Yen
Australia	2,000	921	1,366	167,818	900	415	615	75,518
Brunei	3,350	1,369	2,029	249,295	1,690	690	1,023	125,764
Canada	1,291	688	1,020	125,379	913	487	722	88,717
China	n.a.				n.a.			
Hong Kong	10,300	897	1,330	163,451	n.a.			
Indonesia	n.a.				n.a.			
Japan	610,000	3,349	4,964	610,000	n.a.			
Malaysia	n.a.				910	235	348	42,732
New Zealand	1,500	523	775	95,264	1,300	453	672	82,562
Philippines	24,900	679	1,007	123,736	16,300	445	659	81,000
Singapore	1,800	735	1,090	133,950	1,200	490	727	89,300
South Korea	1,330,000	1,131	1,676	205,979	1,160,000	986	1,462	179,651
Thailand	n.a.				n.a.			
United Kingdom	917	917	1,359	167,047	448	448	664	81,611
United States	680	459	680	83,566	570	385	570	70,048

APPROXIMATE ESTIMATING - HOTELS

This table summarizes approximate estimating costs per square metre for two types of hotels. Approximate estimating costs are averages as incurred by building clients for typical buildings in major - usually capital - cities in the first quarter of 1993. They are based upon the total floor area of all storeys, measured between external walls and without deduction for internal walls. Approximate estimating costs generally include mechanical and electrical installations but exclude furniture, loose or special equipment, and external works; they also exclude fees for professional services. Where a range of costs has been given, the mid point is shown. The figures in national currency are taken from each country's construction cost data and converted to US dollar, pound sterling and yen equivalents using first quarter 1993 exchange rates.

It must be borne in mind that even where costs are given under the same description in one or more countries, this is not to say that they are identical, or even physically similar. Approximate estimating costs for a particular country are for the normal standards prevailing in that country. Quality and technical standards vary widely and there are differences between countries in what is, and is not, included. The table, therefore, should be used with care.

Country	Hotel, 5 star city centre National currency	UK £	US $	m² Yen	Hotel, 3 star city / provincial National currency	UK £	US $	m² Yen
Australia	2,200	1,013	1,502	184,600	1,800	829	1,229	151,036
Brunei	3,260	1,332	1,974	242,598	2,630	1,074	1,593	195,715
Canada	1,059	565	837	102,897	817	436	646	79,378
China	8,688	1,012	1,500	184,338	6,371	742	1,100	135,181
Hong Kong	11,300	984	1,459	179,320	9,300	810	1,201	147,582
Indonesia	2,585,732	843	1,250	153,615	1,861,727	607	900	110,603
Japan	500,000	2,745	4,069	500,000	400,000	2,196	3,255	400,000
Malaysia	3,010	776	1,150	141,344	2,040	526	780	95,794
New Zealand	2,400	837	1,240	152,423	2,000	697	1,034	127,019
Philippines	32,400	884	1,310	161,006	28,100	767	1,136	139,638
Singapore	2,800	1,144	1,696	208,366	2,100	858	1,272	156,275
South Korea	1,160,000	986	1,462	179,651	998,000	848	1,258	154,562
Thailand	30,000	794	1,177	144,692	22,000	582	863	106,107
United Kingdom	1,078	1,078	1,598	196,376	821	821	1,217	149,559
United States	935	631	935	114,904	790	533	790	97,085

Index

Abbreviations *xi*
Addresses, *see* Useful addresses
Aid receipts 5, 6
Approximate estimating 15
    Australia 31–3
    Brunei 44–6
    Canada 60–2
    China 83–4
    factories 299
    Hong Kong 103–4
    hospitals 302
    hotels 304
    housing 301
    Indonesia 119–20
    Japan 138–9
    Malaysia 154–5
    New Zealand 170–2
    offices 300
    Philippines 185–7
    schools 302
    Singapore 201–2
    South Korea 217–19
    sports halls 303
    Thailand 232–3, 234
    theatres 303
    United Kingdom 251–3
    United State of America 269–71
    warehouses 299
Architects
    Australia 24
    Brunei 39
    Canada 52
    Hong Kong 93, 95
    Indonesia 112, 113
    Japan 131
    Malaysia 147
    Philippines 180
    Singapore 194, 195
    United Kingdom 242
    United States of America 262, 263
Area
    abbreviations *xi*
    all countries 4
    conversion factors *xii*
Association of South East Asian Nations
    (ASEAN) 3
Australia
    approximate estimating 31–3
    architects 24
    building approvals 22
    building commencements 22–3
    building cost index 35
    building price index 35
    characteristics and structure of industry
        24–5
    civil engineers 25
    clients 25
    construction key data 21

    construction output 22–4
    contractual arrangements 25–6
    design consultant selection 25
    development control 26
    distribution of work by state 22–4
    economic data 21
    exchange rates 34
    geographical data 21
    insurance and liability 26
    labour costs 27
    large contractors 24
    material costs 28–9
    population 21, 286
    quantity surveyors 25
    standards 26
    unit rates 29–31
    useful addresses 35–6

Blocks
    material costs summary 295
    see also under material costs for individual
        countries
Blockwork
    description 278
    see also under unit rates
Bricks
    material costs summary 295
    see also under material costs for individual
        countries
Brickwork
    description 278
    see also under unit rates
Brunei
    approximate estimating 44–6
    architects 39
    characteristics and structure of industry 39
    civil engineers 39
    clients 39–40
    construction key data 37
    construction output 38–9
    construction workers 39
    economic data 37
    exchange rates 46, 47
    GDP 287
    geographical data 37
    labour costs 40–1
    material costs 41–2
    National Development Plans 39
    population 37, 286
    sponsoring ministry 39
    surveyors 39
    unit rates 42–4
    useful addresses 47–8
Building cost index 17
    Australia 35
    Japan 141
    United Kingdom 255

Building cost inflation
   Canada 65
   Japan 141
   Malaysia 157
   Singapore 204
   United Kingdom 255
Building material prices index 204
Building price index
   Australia 35
   Hong Kong 106
   Malaysia 157
   South Korea 221

Canada
   approximate estimating 60–2
   architects 52
   building cost inflation 65
   characteristics and structure of industry
      51–3
   clients 53
   construction key data 49
   construction output 50–1
   construction price index 65
   consulting engineers 52
   consumer price inflation 63, 64
   contractual arrangements 53–4
   design consultants selection 53
   development controls 55
   economic data 49
   exchange rates 63, 64
   finance 53
   geographical data 49
   insurance and liability 54–5
   labour costs 55–6
   large construction companies 51–2
   material costs 56–8
   population 49
   Project Managers 54
   quantity surveyors 53
   standards 55
   taxation 62
   unit rates 58–60
   useful addresses 65–6
Cement and concrete aggregates
   material costs summary 293
   see also under material costs for individual
      countries
Central government expenditure 17–18
Characteristics and structure of industry
   Australia 24–5
   Brunei 39
   Canada 51–3
   China 70–2
   Hong Kong 92–4
   Indonesia 112–13
   Japan 129–31
   Malaysia 147
   New Zealand 165
   Philippines 179
   Singapore 193–4
   South Korea 211
   Thailand 226
   United Kingdom 240–2
   United States of America 260–2

China
   approximate estimating 83–4
   characteristics and structure of industry 70–2
   clients 73–4
   Consolidated Industrial and Commercial Tax
      84
   construction key data 67
   construction output 8, 68–70
   Construction Unit 72
   consumer price inflation 84, 85
   contractual arrangements 75, 77
   design consultants selection 74–5
   design institute classification 74–5, 76
   Design Unit 72
   development controls 77–8
   Development Unit 72
   economic data 67
   employment 70
   exchange rates 84, 85
   finance 73–4
   geographical data 67
   Gross Domestic Product 287
   Gross National Product 68
   Gross Social Product 68
   joint ventures 72–3, 79–80
   labour costs 78–80
      for joint ventures 79–80
   land use rights 77
   large corporations 72
   material costs 80–1
   Net Material Product 68
   planned economy 8
   population 67, 286
   regional distribution of work 70, 71
   registration of constructors 72
   Special Enterprise Zones 69–70, 92
   taxation 84
   tendering 75
   unit rates 81–3
   Urban Land Regulations 77
   useful addresses 86–9
China State Construction Engineering
      Corporation (CSCEC) 72
Clients
   Australia 25
   Brunei 39–40
   Canada 53
   China 73–4
   Hong Kong 94–5
   Indonesia 113
   Japan 131
   Malaysia 147
   Philippines 179
   Singapore 195
   South Korea 211
   Thailand 226–7
   United Kingdom 242–3
   United State of America 262
Concrete work
   description 277
   see also under unit rates
Construction cost data, *see* Approximate
      estimating; Labour costs; Material
      costs; Unit rates

Construction cost index, New Zealand 173
Construction industry, *see* Characteristics and
    structure of industry; Clients:
    Construction output; Contractual
    arrangements; Design consultant
    selection; Finance; Insurance and
    liability; Standards
Construction Industry Development Board
    (Singapore) 193, 196
Construction Industry Training Authority
    (Hong Kong) 93
Construction key data
  Australia 21
  Brunei 37
  Canada 49
  China 67
  Hong Kong 91
  Indonesia 109
  Japan 127
  Malaysia 145
  New Zealand 163
  Philippines 177
  Singapore 191
  South Korea 209
  Thailand 225
  United Kingdom 237
  United States of America 259
Construction output 18
  all countries 6–8
  Australia 22–4
  Brunei 38–9
  Canada 50–1
  China 8, 68–70
  GDP and 7
  GNP and 7–8
  Hong Kong 92
  housing and dwellings 8, 9
  investment and 7
  Japan 128–9
  Korea 8
  Malaysia 146
  New Zealand 164–5
  per capita 290
  Philippines 178
  Singapore 192–3
  South Korea 210–11
  summary statistics 289–90
  Thailand 226
  United Kingdom 8, 238–40
  United States of America 260
Construction price index, Canada 65
Construction sector organization 8, 10
  size of establishments 9–10
Consumer price inflation
  Australia 34–5
  Canada 63, 64
  China 84, 85
  Hong Kong 105–6
  Japan 141
  Malaysia 157
  New Zealand 173
  Philippines 188–9
  Singapore 203, 204
  South Korea 221

United Kingdom 254, 255
United States of America 273
Contractual arrangements
  Australia 25–6
  Canada 53–4
  China 75, 77
  Hong Kong 96
  Indonesia 114
  Japan 132
  Malaysia 148
  Philippines 179–80
  Singapore 195–6
  South Korea 212
  Thailand 227
  United Kingdom 244–5
  United States of America 263–4
Control of development, *see* Development
    control
Conversion factors *xii–xiv*
Cost data, *see* Approximate estimating; Labour
    costs; Material costs: Unit rates
Cost of labour, *see* Labour costs
Cost of materials, *see* Material costs

Davis Langdon & Seah International *xv–xviii*
Debt, foreign 5, 6
Design consultants selection
  Australia 25
  Canada 53
  China 74–5
  Hong Kong 95–6
  Indonesia 113–14
  Japan 132
  Malaysia 148
  Philippines 179
  Singapore 195
  South Korea 212
  Thailand 227
  United Kingdom 243–4
  United States of America 263
Development
  economic indicators 4
  non-economic indicators 4–5
  without outside help 6
Development control
  Australia 26
  Canada 55
  China 77–8
  Hong Kong 97–8
  Indonesia 114
  Malaysia 148–9
  New Zealand 165
  Philippines 180
  Singapore 196
  South Korea 212
  Thailand 228
  United Kingdom 245–6
  United States of America 264
Dwellings, *see* Housing and dwellings

Earthquake engineering 130
Economic data
  Australia 21

Economic data *contd*
  Brunei 37
  Canada 49
  China 67
  Hong Kong 91
  Indonesia 109
  Japan 127
  Malaysia 145
  New Zealand 163
  Philippines 177
  Singapore 191
  South Korea 209
  summary statistics 287
  Thailand 225
  United Kingdom 237
  United States of America 259
Economic indicators 4
Electrical work
  description 281
  see also under unit rates
Emulsion paint
  material costs summary 298
  see also under material costs for individual
    countries
Engineering News Record list 10
  China contractors 72
  Philippine firms 179
  Singapore contractors 194
  South Korea contractors 211
  UK contractors 240
  US contractors 261–2
  see also International contractors; Large
    contractors
Engineers
  Australia 25
  Brunei 39
  Canada 52
  Indonesia 112, 113
  Malaysia 147
  United Kingdom 242
  United States of America 262
Excavation
  description 277
  see also under unit rates
Exchange rates 15–16, 18
  Australia 34
  Brunei 46, 47
  Canada 63, 64
  China 84, 85
  Hong Kong 104, 105
  importance of 15
  Indonesia 120–1
  Japan 139–40
  Malaysia 156
  New Zealand 172–3
  Philippines 188
  Singapore 203
  South Korea 220
  Thailand 234
  United Kingdom 254
  United States of America 271–2
Expenditure, central government 17–18

Factories

approximate estimating summaries 299
  see also under approximate estimating for
    individual countries
Finance
  Australia 25
  Brunei 40
  Canada 53
  China 73–4
  Hong Kong 94–5
  Indonesia 113
  Japan 131
  Malaysia 147
  Philippines 179
  Singapore 195
  South Korea 211
  Thailand 227
  United Kingdom 243
  United States of America 262
Financial viability 5
Finishings
  description 281
  see also under unit rates
Force
  abbreviations *xi*
  conversion factors *xiv*
Foreign debt 5, 6
Formwork
  description 277
  see also under unit rates

GDP, *see* Gross Domestic Product (GDP)
General Sales Tax
  Canada 62
  New Zealand 172
Geographical data
  Australia 21
  Brunei 37
  Canada 49
  China 67
  Hong Kong 91
  Indonesia 109
  Japan 127
  Malaysia 145
  New Zealand 163
  Philippines 177
  Singapore 191
  South Korea 209
  summary statistics 288
  Thailand 225
  United Kingdom 237
  United States of America 259
Glazing
  description 281
  see also under unit rates
Gross Domestic Product (GDP) 13, 17–18
  all countries 4
  Brunei 287
  China 287
  construction output and 7
  Hong Kong 287
  investment and 7
  Japan 287
  Malaysia 287
  New Zealand 287

Philippines 287
South Korea 287
summary statistics 287
Thailand 287
United States of America 287
Gross National Product (GNP) 17–18
  all countries 4
  China 68
  construction output and 7–8
Gross Social Product (China) 68

Hong Kong
  approximate estimating 103–4
  architects 93, 95
  building price index 106
  characteristics and structure of industry
    92–4
  clients 94–5
  Construction Industry Training Authority
    93
  construction key data 91
  construction output 92
  consumer price inflation 105–6
  contractual arrangements 96
  design consultants selection 95–6
  development control 97–8
  economic data 91
  employment terms 93
  exchange rates 104, 105
  fees 96
  finance 94–5
  GDP 287
  geographical data 91
  Home Ownership Scheme 94–5
  Housing Authority 93, 94
  import of materials 93
  insurance and liability 96–7
  Jockey Club 95
  labour costs 98–9
  material costs 99–100
  population 91, 286
  Port and Airport Strategy Project 92, 93
  professional bodies 94
  quantity surveyors 94
  registration of contractors 92, 93, 96
  Shenzhen Special Enterprise Zone 92
  standards 98
  tender price index 106
  unit rates 100–2
  useful addresses 106–8
Hospitals
  approximate estimating summaries 302
  see also under approximate estimating for
    individual countries
Hotels
  approximate estimating summaries 304
  see also under approximate estimating for
    individual countries
Housing Authority (Hong Kong) 93, 94
Housing and Development Board (Singapore)
    192, 195
Housing and dwellings
  approximate estimating summaries 301

see also under approximate estimating for
    individual countries
Japan 128–9
population per dwelling 8
Housing and Urban Development Corporation
    (Japan) 132–3

Indonesia
  approximate estimating 119–20
  architects 112, 113
  characteristics and structure of industry
    112–13
  clients 113
  construction key data 109
  construction output 110–11
  contractual arrangements 114
  design consultants selection 113–14
  development control 114
  economic data 109
  engineers 112, 113
  exchange rates 120–1
  finance 113
  geographical data 109
  insurance and liability 114
  labour costs 115
  large contractors 112
  material costs 115–16
  population 109, 286
  quantity surveyors 112
  regional output 111
  standards 114
  type of output 110
  unit rates 116–19
  useful addresses 121–5
  VAT 117, 119, 120
Inflation 15, 16
  Australia 34–5
  see also Building cost inflation; Consumer
    price inflation
Insurance and liability
  Australia 26
  Canada 54–5
  Hong Kong 96–7
  Indonesia 114
  Japan 132–3
  Philippines 180
  Singapore 196
  South Korea 212
  Thailand 227–8
  United Kingdom 245
  United States of America 265
International contractors
  South Korea 211
  United Kingdom 240, 241
  United States of America 261–2
Investment 6
  construction output and 7

Japan
  approximate estimating 138–9
  architects 131
  building costs index 141
  building costs inflation 141

Japan *contd*
  characteristics and structure of industry
      129–31
  clients 131
  construction key data 127
  construction methods 133
  construction output 128–9
  consumer price inflation 141
  contractual arrangements 132
  design consultant selection 132
  earthquake engineering 130
  economic data 127
  exchange rates 139–40
  finance 131
  foreign companies in 131
  GDP 287
  geographical data 127
  housing provision 128–9
  Housing and Urban Development
      Corporation 132–3
  insurance and liability 132–3
  labour costs 134
  large companies 129, 130
  licensed contractors 129, 131
  material costs 135–6
  materials 133
  population 127, 286
  Registration Organization for Warranted
      Houses 132–3
  type of work and sector 128
  unit rates 136–8
  useful addresses 141–3
  wholesale price index 141
  zenecon 129
Joint Contracts Tribunal (UK) 227, 244
Joint ventures, China 72–3, 79–80

Key data, *see* Construction key data; Economic
      data; Geographical data; Population
Korea
  construction output 8
  South, *see* South Korea
Korea Housing Bank 211

Labour costs 14
  Australia 27
  Brunei 40–1
  Canada 55–6
  China 78–80
  Hong Kong 98–9
  Indonesia 115
  Japan 134
  Malaysia 149–50
  New Zealand 166
  Philippines 181
  Singapore 197
  South Korea 213
  summary statistics 291–2
  Thailand 229
  United Kingdom 246–7
  United States of America 265–6
Land area, *see* Area
Large contractors 9–10
  Australia 24

  Canada 51–2
  Indonesia 112
  Japan 129, 130
  New Zealand 165
  Philippines 179
  Singapore 194
  South Korea 211
  United Kingdom 240, 241
  United States of America 261–2
Length
  abbreviations *xi*
  conversion factors *xii*
Liability, *see* Insurance and liability

Malaysia
  1998 Commonwealth Games 146
  approximate estimating 154–5
  architects 147
  building price index 157
  building price inflation 157
  characteristics and structure of industry 147
  clients 147
  construction key data 145
  construction output 146
  consumer price inflation 157
  contractual arrangements 148
  design consultant selection 148
  development control 148–9
  economic data 145
  engineers 147
  exchange rates 156
  finance 147
  GDP 287
  geographical data 145
  labour costs 149–50
  material costs 150–1
  population 145
  professional bodies 147
  projects 146
  research 149
  standards 149
  surveyors 147
  unit rates 151–4
  useful addresses 157–62
Mass
  abbreviations *xi*
  conversion factors *xiii–xiv*
Material costs 14
  Australia 28–9
  blocks 295
  bricks 295
  Brunei 41–2
  Canada 56–8
  cement and concrete aggregates 293
  China 80–1
  emulsion paint 298
  Hong Kong 99–100
  Indonesia 115–16
  Japan 135–6
  Malaysia 150–1
  New Zealand 167–8
  Philippines 182–3
  plasterboard 297
  quilt insulation 296

ready mixed concrete 294
reinforcing steel 294
sheet glass 297
Singapore 198–9
softwood for joinery 296
South Korea 214–15
summary statistics 293–8
Thailand 229–30
United Kingdom 247–8
United States of America 266–7
vinyl floor tiles 298
Metalwork
    description 279–80
    see also under unit rates

Net Material Product (China) 68
New Zealand
    approximate estimating 170–2
    Building Industry Authority 165
    Building Industry Commission 165
    characteristics and structure of industry 165
    construction cost index 173
    construction key data 163
    construction output 164–5
    consumer price inflation 173
    development control 165
    economic data 163
    exchange rates 172–3
    GDP 287
    general sales tax 172
    geographical data 163
    house price index 173
    labour costs 166
    large contractors 165
    material costs 167–8
    population 163
    Resource Management Act 165
    standards 165
    taxation 172
    unit rates 168–70
    useful addresses 174–6
Non-economic indicators of development 4–5

Offices
    approximate estimating summaries 300
    *see also under approximate estimating for
        individual countries*
Open tendering 75
Open-shop contracting 260
Organisation of Economic Cooperation and
        Development (OECD) 3
Organizational membership 3

Painting
    description 281
    see also under unit rates
People's Republic of China, *see* China
Philippines
    approximate estimating 185–7
    architects 180
    characteristics and structure of industry 179
    clients 179
    construction key data 177
    construction output 178

consumer price inflation 188–9
contractual arrangements 179–80
design consultants selection 179
development control 180
economic data 177
exchange rates 188
finance 179
GDP 287
geographical data 177
guarantee bond 180
insurance and liability 180
international contractors 179
labour costs 181
large contractors 179
material costs 182–3
population 177, 286
regional distribution of construction 178
standards 180
unit rates 183–5
useful addresses 189–90
VAT 185, 187
Plasterboard
    material costs summary 297
    *see also under material costs for individual
        countries*
Plumbing
    description 280–1
    see also under unit rates
Population
    all countries 4
    Australia 21, 286
    Brunei 37, 286
    Canada 49
    China 67, 286
    Hong Kong 91, 286
    Indonesia 109, 286
    Japan 127, 286
    Malaysia 145
    New Zealand 163
    per dwelling 8
    Philippines 177, 286
    Singapore 191, 286
    South Korea 209
    summary statistics 286
    Thailand 225
    United Kingdom 237
    United States of America 259, 286
Population density 4
Pressure conversion factors *xiv*
Project Managers (Canada) 54
Property Services Agency (United Kingdom)
        244
Public services tax (Canada) 62
Purchasing power parity (PPP) 18

Quantity surveyors
    Australia 25
    Canada 53
    Hong Kong 94
    Indonesia 112
    UK 242
    USA 262
Quilt insulation
    material costs summary 296

Quilt insulation, material costs summary *contd*
    see also under material costs for individual
        countries

Ready mixed concrete
    material costs summary 294
    see also under material costs for individual
        countries
Registration of contractors
    China 72
    Hong Kong 92, 93, 96
    Singapore 193
Registration Organization for Warranted
    Houses (Japan) 132–3
Reinforcement
    description 278
    see also under unit rates
Reinforcing steel
    material costs summary 294
    see also under material costs for individual
        countries
Repair and maintenance, United Kingdom 8,
    238
Research and development
    Malaysia 149
    Singapore 196
Resource Management Act (New Zealand) 165
Roofing
    description 278–9
    see also under unit rates
Royal Hong Kong Jockey Club 95

Schools
    approximate estimating summaries 302
    see also under approximate estimating for
        individual countries
    secondary school enrolment 5
Sheet glass
    material costs summary 297
    see also under material costs for individual
        countries
Singapore
    approximate estimating 201–2
    architects 194, 195
    building costs inflation 204
    building material prices index 204
    Central Provident Fund 195
    characteristics and structure of industry
        193–4
    clients 195
    Construction Industry Development Board
        193, 196
    construction key data 191
    construction output 192–3
    consumer price inflation 203, 204
    contractual arrangements 195–6
    design consultants selection 195
    development control 196
    economic data 191
    exchange rates 203
    finance 195
    geographical data 191
    Housing and Development Board 195
    Housing Development Board 192

    infrastructure projects 193
    insurance and liability 196
    labour costs 197
    large contractors 194
    material costs 198–9
    population 191, 286
    registration of contractors 193
    research and development 196
    standards 196
    surveyors 194
    type of work 192
    unit rates 199–201
    Urban Redevelopment Authority 196
    useful addresses 204–7
Softwood for joinery
    material costs summary 296
    see also under material costs for individual
        countries
South Korea
    approximate estimating 217–19
    building price index 221
    characteristics and structure of industry 211
    clients 211
    construction key data 209
    construction output 210–11
    consumer price inflation 221
    contractual arrangements 212
    design consultants selection 212
    development control 212
    economic data 209
    exchange rates 220
    finance 211
    GDP 287
    geographical data 209
    indicators of activity 210
    insurance and liability 212
    international contractors 211
    Korea Housing Bank 211
    labour costs 213
    large contractors 211
    material costs 214–15
    population 209
    standards 212
    taxation 220
    unit rates 215–17
    useful addresses 221–4
    VAT 220
Special Enterprise Zones (China) 69–70, 92
Sports halls
    approximate estimating summaries 303
    see also under approximate estimating for
        individual countries
Standards
    Australia 26
    Canada 55
    Hong Kong 98
    Indonesia 114
    Malaysia 149
    New Zealand 165
    Philippines 180
    Singapore 196
    South Korea 212
    Thailand 228
    United Kingdom 246

United States of America 265
Steelwork
    description 278
    see also under unit rates
Structure of industry, *see* Characteristics and
        structure of industry
Surveyors
    Brunei 39
    Malaysia 147
    Singapore 194
    United Kingdom 242

Taxation 14
    Canada 62
    China 84
    New Zealand 172
    South Korea 220
    see also Value Added Tax
Telephones 5
Tender price indices 17
    Hong Kong 106
    United Kingdom 255
Tendering
    China 75
    Thailand 227
Thailand
    approximate estimating 232–3, 234
    characteristics and structure of industry 226
    clients 226–7
    construction key data 225
    construction output 226
    contractual arrangements 227
    design competitions 227
    design consultants selection 227
    development control 228
    economic data 225
    exchange rates 234
    expressway development 226
    finance 227
    GDP 287
    geographical data 225
    insurance and liability 227–8
    labour costs 229
    material costs 229–30
    political activity 226
    population 225
    standards 228
    tenders 227
    unit rates 230–2
    useful addresses 234–6
    VAT 233
Theatres
    approximate estimating summaries 303
    *see also under approximate estimating for
        individual countries*
Trade unions 260

UN Development Index 5, 18
UN Development Programme (UNDP) 18
Unit rates 14–15
    Australia 29–31
    Brunei 42–4
    Canada 58–60
    China 81–3

Hong Kong 100–2
Indonesia 116–19
Japan 136–8
Malaysia 151–4
New Zealand 168–70
Philippines 183–5
Singapore 199–201
South Korea 215–17
Thailand 230–2
United Kingdom 248–51
United States of America 267–9
United Kingdom
    approximate estimating 251–3
    architects 242
    building cost inflation 255
    building costs index 255
    characteristics and structure of industry
        240–2
    clients 242–3
    construction key data 237
    construction output 8, 238–40
    consumer price inflation 254, 255
    contractual arrangements 244–5
    design consultants selection 243–4
    development control 245–6
    economic data 237
    engineers 242
    exchange rates 254
    finance 243
    geographical data 237
    insurance and liability 245
    international companies 240, 241
    Joint Contracts Tribunal 227
    Joint Contracts Tribunal contracts 244
    labour costs 246–7
    material costs 247–8
    orders from abroad 239, 240
    population 237
    Property Services Agency 244
    regional output 239
    repair and maintenance 8, 238
    size of companies 240, 241
    standards 246
    surveyors 242
    tender price index 255
    unit rates 248–51
    useful addresses 255–7
    VAT 253
United States of America
    approximate estimating 269–71
    architects 262, 263
    bonds 264
    characteristics and structure of industry
        260–2
    clients 262
    competitive bidding 263
    construction key data 259
    construction output 260
    consumer price inflation 273
    contractual arrangements 263–4
    design consultants selection 263
    development control 264
    economic data 259
    engineers 262